The Psychology of Visual Art

What can art tell us about how the brain works? And what can the brain tell us about how we perceive and create art? Humans have created visual art throughout history and its significance has been an endless source of fascination and debate. Visual art is a product of the human brain, but is art so complex and sophisticated that brain function and evolution are not relevant to our understanding? This book explores the links between visual art and the brain by examining a broad range of issues including: the impact of eye and brain disorders on artistic output; the relevance of Darwinian principles to aesthetics; and the constraints imposed by brain processes on the perception of space, motion and colour in art. Arguments and theories are presented in an accessible manner and general principles are illustrated with specific art examples, helping students to apply their knowledge to new artworks.

George Mather is Professor of Vision Science in the School of Psychology at the University of Lincoln. He has over twenty-five years of experience in teaching courses on human visual perception and the psychology of visual art to undergraduate and postgraduate students and he is the author of *Essentials of Sensation and Perception* (2011), *Foundations of Sensation and Perception* (2009) and *The Motion After-Effect: A Modern Perspective* (1998; co-edited with Stuart Anstis and Frans Verstraten).

D1612124

The Psychology of Visual Art

Eye, Brain and Art

GEORGE MATHER

CAMBRIDGE
UNIVERSITY PRESS

CAMBRIDGE
UNIVERSITY PRESS

University Printing House, Cambridge CB2 8BS, United Kingdom

Cambridge University Press is part of the University of Cambridge.

It furthers the University's mission by disseminating knowledge in the pursuit of education, learning and research at the highest international levels of excellence.

Published in the United States of America by Cambridge University Press, New York

www.cambridge.org
Information on this title: www.cambridge.org/9780521184793

First published 2014

A catalogue record for this publication is available from the British Library

Library of Congress Cataloguing in Publication data
Mather, George.
The psychology of visual art : eye, brain and art / George Mather.
   pages   cm
ISBN 978-1-107-00598-3 (Hardback) – ISBN 978-0-521-18479-3 (Paperback)
1. Art–Psychology.   2. Visual perception.   I. Title.
N71.M285 2013
701′.15–dc23   2013013774

ISBN 978-1-107-00598-3 Hardback
ISBN 978-0-521-18479-3 Paperback

For Anne

Contents

Colour plate section between pages 108 and 109

Illustrations

Figures

Preface

The opportunities for people to engage with visual art are greater now than they have ever been before. In recent years, increasing numbers of people choose to attend major international gallery exhibitions that celebrate visual art both past and present, often at significant cost in terms of time and money. Most houses, shops, restaurants and public buildings display some form of visual art on their walls. It seems that everyone has an opinion about visual art, perhaps a favourite artist, artistic genre or historical era. Where does this universal interest in art spring from? Why have certain visual forms preoccupied artists across generations? What visual qualities underlie our reactions to artworks? Such questions have traditionally been tackled from the perspective of the humanities, especially disciplines such as art history and philosophy.

Psychology is the scientific study of people, the mind and human behaviour. The creation and consumption of visual art is an ancient and universal human activity and, as such, it should also be a prime focus of research in psychology. As a discipline, psychology dates from the mid-nineteenth century, when a small group of European scientists devised new experimental methods for measuring simple human behavioural responses. Over the last 150 years, psychologists have adopted concepts and techniques from a very wide range of scientific disciplines in their quest to understand the human mind and behaviour. Advances in neuroscience have had a crucial impact on psychological theories, providing researchers with fundamental information about the structure and function of the human brain. Mathematics and computer science have supplied deep theoretical principles that help us to understand the information available in visual images and the constraints within which any physical system must operate when trying to make sense of visual information.

Therefore, modern psychology should be ideally placed to make a significant contribution to our understanding of visual art. However, research on the psychology of visual art presently does not occupy a mainstream position in science. Lack of progress in the past is partly a reflection of the fact that research on the psychology of art is undoubtedly more challenging than research on many other aspects of human cognition. As an experimental psychologist interested in visual perception, I usually design experiments with two principles constantly in mind: simplicity and control. The visual images I use as experimental materials are kept as simple as they possibly can be, so that they isolate specific visual features for investigation. Typically they are very basic, precisely defined patterns of dots or bars, which permit inferences about the link between stimulus features and perception to be made with some degree of confidence. Presentation of the images to experimental participants is carefully controlled to minimise the intrusion of extraneous factors in their responses. In the case of research on visual art, on the other hand, the source material is inherently complex and subject to manipulation by the artist rather than the experimenter (mostly not in the interests of simplicity), so inferences are much more difficult to make. However, recent advances in methodology have opened up many new options for studying art from a scientific perspective, which I and many others are taking up with enthusiasm. Sophisticated mathematical techniques now allow us to analyse and describe the detailed physical characteristics of even the most complex artworks. Furthermore, new experimental techniques such as eye movement recording and brain imaging give researchers an unprecedented ability to access the perceptual effects of these images. Consequently, recent progress in our understanding has been rapid.

Another factor has also impeded progress in the developing science of visual art. During the twentieth century, a cultural divide grew between the arts and the sciences, partly driven by educational traditions that steered students towards one or the other but not both, especially at more advanced levels of study. I experienced this directly as a teenager when I was steered away from a childhood preoccupation with art-making towards training in science. Scientific methodology was considered by some to be an inappropriate tool for studying art (and still is in some quarters). In the centuries prior to this modern divide, there was a continuing dialogue between the two cultures. Leonardo da Vinci is now recognised as both a brilliant scientist and a renowned artist, although the term 'scientist' was coined only in the mid-nineteenth century, hundreds of years after his death. Artists have exploited scientific and technological advances for generations. Renaissance artists were well versed in the laws of perspective. Nineteenth-century painters such as Edgar Degas were directly influenced by photographic imagery. Exponents of Op Art in the 1960s were inspired by research in perceptual psychology.

The gap between the two cultures is beginning to close again, partly driven by scientific and technical advances that have become more sophisticated, yet, at the same time, more accessible to non-specialists. Interactive artists such as Daniel Rozin often use complex computer programs to control the interaction with the spectator. Many painters such as David Hockney have embraced the use of digital media in their work. Creativity and originality is increasingly recognised as an essential quality of both great art and great science, closing the perceived gap between the two cultures. On the science side, the fundamental characteristics of the human sensory and perceptual systems are quite well understood now, so I and many other researchers in psychology and neuroscience have begun to apply this knowledge to the search for a deeper scientific understanding of visual art.

This book is an attempt to summarise and evaluate the recent advances that have been made and so encourage others to build on them and forge ahead to make new discoveries. It should appeal both to artists interested in science and to scientists interested in art; indeed, it is aimed at anyone who has an interest in the relationship between visual art and the brain. Little prior knowledge in either sphere is assumed, but an open-minded willingness to take on novel and sometimes controversial issues spanning the two is essential.

The book should find a place in undergraduate and graduate courses across a range of science and art disciplines including psychology, neuroscience, fine art, media and art history. Hopefully it can work well as the course text for a specialist course on the psychology of visual art. I have taught such an interdisciplinary course for a number of years and it is a pleasure to witness the enthusiasm and ingenuity with which students apply concepts and knowledge they have learnt in one domain of study to another domain, whether from science to art or vice versa.

I am grateful to several people for their critical and insightful comments on sections of the manuscript, in particular Al Rees, Stephen Herbert and Anna Franklin, as well as to the editorial team and their reviewers at Cambridge University Press. Any remaining errors are, of course, my own responsibility.

1   Art through history

Introduction

Humans are highly visual creatures. Evolution has honed the human brain into a supremely efficient tool for extracting information from visual images, which far exceeds the capabilities of the most powerful computer vision systems available today. The areas of the brain devoted to our visual sense are much larger than the areas devoted to all of our other faculties. Vision begins with an image cast onto the inside surface of the eyes. Large populations of brain cells analyse this image in terms of several essential visual characteristics, including shape, size, texture, colour and motion. These highly complex brain processes underlie all visual experience but they are largely hidden from conscious awareness. The detailed characteristics of brain function must have a profound role to play in our experience of visual art. The aim of this book is to put forward an approach to understanding visual art that is founded on our knowledge of how the eyes and brain function together to create visual experience.

Before we can embark on this task, it is important to define some fundamental terms of reference. Everyone agrees on what we mean by the brain, namely the 1.4 kg jelly-like mass of nerve cells and fibres cradled inside the human skull. The visual system of the brain includes the eyes, the neural pathways connecting the eyes to the brain and all the neurones in the brain that respond primarily to visual stimulation. On the other hand, it is much more difficult to agree on a definition of art. Philosophers continue to debate the virtues of alternative ways to define art; however, one point is clear: any attempt to define artworks in terms of a single characteristic such as their representational properties or their expressive qualities is bound to fail. Counter-examples to single characteristics such as these can always be found. Maps, for example, are representational because they represent the layout of the land but they are not usually considered to be art; human postures have expressive properties but are not usually considered as art unless adopted during an artistic performance such as ballet. On the other hand, it is difficult to consider the collection of Italian Renaissance paintings in London's National Gallery as anything other than works of art. What about Marcel Duchamp's 'Fountain' (actually a manufactured urinal), or Carl Andre's 'Equivalent VIII' (actually a rectangular arrangement of 120 fire-bricks)? Are these objects works of art?

Some philosophers favour a definition of art in terms of a cluster of features or properties (Dutton, 2009). According to this scheme, no single property is essential for classification as a work of art but some subset of properties may be sufficient. This approach seems to capture the essential characteristics of visual art, at least for the present purposes. An acceptable list might include the following properties.

A work of art should:

1. Have aesthetic merit
2. Express an emotion
3. Present an intellectual challenge
4. Be structurally complex and coherent
5. Offer a novel, individual viewpoint
6. Be original
7. Display skill in its execution
8. Be part of an established historical and cultural art form
9. Be created by an intentional act

We can see that Renaissance paintings tick all the boxes. But what of Duchamp's 'Fountain'? It certainly ticks some boxes in being intellectually challenging, novel and original in conception and intentional. In addition, it played a central role in establishing the conceptual art movement. But it is a manufactured object, normally found in a toilet. It was not created by an act of artistic skill, nor can it be called beautiful. Duchamp also made use of other manufactured objects in his work, which he called 'ready-mades'. His work was a satirical protest at the state of the art world and at conventional judgements of artistic excellence. In a way, Duchamp was deliberately trying to create anti-art, to violate as many of the criteria for art as possible, including a feature that was, to many people, a fundamental property of art – it should be beautiful. In its own way, Duchamp's ready-made art conforms to the defining features of art just as much as do more

Table 1 A timeline of the major art eras over the last thousand years (see list of illustrations)

1000 1100 1200	Romanesque			
1300 1400	Gothic	Cimabue (Figure 1.2)		
1500	Renaissance	van der Weyden (Plate 16) Bellini (Plate 1) Da Messina (Plate 14) Gossaert (Plate 11)	Bermejo (Figure 5.6) Raphael (Plate 1)	Titian (Plate 18)
1600	Mannerism	Beccafumi (Plate 15) Holbein (Figure 5.7) Brueghel (Plate 5)	Pontormo (Plate 17) Beuckelaer (Plate 16)	
1700	Baroque/ Rococo	Rembrandt (Figure 1.3) Claude (Plate 2) Vermeer (Plate 13) Wootton (Figure 6.1)	Velasquez (Plate 5)	
1800 1900	European Academic	Degas (Figure 2.5) Van Gogh (Plate 20)	Canaletto (Figure 4.4) Monet (Plate 3; Plate 9; Plate 10)	
	Modern	Derain (Plate 4) Rothko (Plate 4)		
2000	Postmodern		Riley (Figure 6.7)	

conventional artworks. The 'Fountain' is seen now as a turning point in the history of art. The modern art movement attempted to displace aesthetic beauty from its position at the pinnacle of artistic excellence, a position it had occupied since the Renaissance, and replace it with other elements in the cluster of features defining art, in particular novelty and intentionality. However, aesthetic beauty was pre-eminent for centuries prior to modern art, and it remains, for many non-specialists at least, an essential quality of great art.

This chapter outlines some major milestones in the history of visual art, so as to offer a little contextual background for later discussions about the relationship between visual art and the brain. It sets the broader theoretical and historical scene for the scientific perspective developed in subsequent chapters. As an aid, Table 1 sketches a timeline of the major art eras over the last thousand years, annotated with the artworks used as illustrations in this book. One chapter and table cannot, of course, do justice to such a large and complex subject with such a rich history, so it is necessarily rather selective and sketchy and, no doubt, takes some major liberties with the details and subtleties of the subject, which I hope the reader will forgive.

Prehistory

The archaeological record shows that during the Stone Age when modern humans (Homo sapiens) began to dominate over the preceding Neanderthals, there was a rapid expansion in the creation of apparently artistic artefacts. The oldest known artefacts have been found in Africa. A cave discovered in 1991 on the Southern Cape coast of South Africa has yielded remarkable pieces of engraved ochre, thought to be 77,000 years old (Henshilwood et al., 2002). The slabs are inscribed with lines arranged in regular geometric diamond patterns. The engravings could be an attempt to represent the pattern on snake skin, or perhaps were intended to be purely abstract or symbolic. They may have been decorative, or may have conveyed a message about identity or cultural status. We cannot be sure what the markings meant to the people who created them but, whatever their origin, these patterns represent the earliest known mark-making by humans.

Other finds in Europe reveal early attempts at figurative art. A cave in southern Germany has yielded a 35,000-year-old female figurine with exaggerated sexual characteristics (Conard, 2009). Cave paintings elsewhere in Germany as well as in south-west France and northern Spain include many beautifully rendered images of animals dated at over 30,000 years old (Clottes, 2001; see Figure 1.1). These and many other examples of prehistoric art demonstrate that the impulse to create art clearly emerged very early in the expansion of Homo sapiens, a sign of the visual abilities furnished by their large brain.

Art has occupied a prominent place in all human societies since the dawn of recorded civilisation. It became established as a subject for academic study after the sixteenth century, when the Italian artist and scholar Giorgio Vasari documented the lives of Italian Renaissance painters and their patrons in a book entitled *Lives of the Most Excellent Painters, Sculptors and Architects*. The modern empirically based approach to the study of art history dates from the publication, two hundred years after Vasari's *Lives*, of a monumental work by Johann Joachim Winckelmann in 1764, entitled *History of the Art of Antiquity* (Winckelmann, 1764). Winckelmann surveyed the art of ancient Mediterranean

Figure 1.1 36,000-year-old cave paintings of animals. (Redrawn from Clottes, 2001.)

civilisations in modern-day Egypt, Lebanon, Iran, Greece and Italy. He valued ancient Greek art as superior to all other forms of art and, as such, most worthy of study and imitation. Ancient Greek art is therefore a natural starting point for this brief survey of art through history.

Ancient Greek art

Ancient Greek sculpture is traditionally regarded as the zenith of classical beauty and perfect proportion in figurative art. It defined an artistic 'canon' that had a profound influence on Western art for centuries ('canon' comes from the Greek word *kanon*, meaning a straight rod or ruler, a prototype model). Many ancient Greek statues conform to a precise set of rules governing body proportion, which were described by the Roman architect Vitruvius and illustrated in Leonardo da Vinci's famous drawing of Vitruvian Man (Panofsky, 1955). For example, in a perfectly proportioned human figure, the vertical extent of the head (height from chin to crown) should occupy precisely 1/8 of the total body height. Many ancient Greek statues such as the Riace Warriors (found near the Italian coast in 1972; see Stewart, 1990) conform exactly to the Vitruvian ideal and display a supreme mastery of the art form. These proportions do not necessarily reflect the actual proportions of real human figures (Mather, 2010) but rather idealised proportions. They have guided artistic depictions of the human form for centuries. A possible neuroscientific basis for our preference for certain body proportions will be outlined in Chapter 10.

Ancient Greek philosophers viewed art as a mirror held up to the world, an idealised imitation of nature or of human life. This view represents the earliest theory of art, known as 'mimesis', from the Greek for imitation. Art did not aim simply to imitate nature but to distil the essence of ideal aesthetic beauty in nature and re-present it for the pleasure of the viewer. Accordingly art was judged on its aesthetic merit ('aesthetics' comes from the ancient Greek word *aesthesis*, meaning sensation or perception). Gazing at surviving examples of ancient Greek statues, one can only be impressed by the degree to which the ancient sculptors achieved their aim. Their beauty and fidelity is undeniable. Chapters 8 and 9 will discuss how aesthetic pleasure relates to brain function.

Renaissance art

The Romanesque and Gothic Western art traditions that flourished in the Middle Ages retreated from ancient ideals of mimetic beauty into functionality and a superficial, simplified form of 'naturalness'. There was little attempt, for example, to depict realistic human proportions and facial expressions (Figure 1.2). However, the social, political and intellectual developments that gathered pace in Europe in the fifteenth century were reflected in dramatic changes in visual art. Discoveries about the natural world and the place of humans within it led artists to question the subjugation of individuality that was dominant in the art of the Middle Ages. Newly discovered laws of perspective gave artists tools to emphasise the unique viewpoint of an individual protagonist, who was increasingly rendered in paintings with an unmistakeable personality and emotion. Artists turned to classical antiquity for inspiration. Florentine sculptors such as Ghiberti and Donatello created organic, anatomically realistic human forms, often clad in

Figure 1.2 'The Virgin and Child Enthroned with Two Angels', Cimabue, 1280–1285.

a classical Roman toga. They revived the ancient Greek practice of the *contrapposto* ('placed opposite') stance, in which the upper and lower halves of the body twist in opposite directions to avoid the appearance of unnatural stiffness. Typically, the figure is posed with most of the weight on one leg, while the other leg is relaxed (as in Michelangelo's 'David', or Botticelli's 'Venus').

Vasari coined the term '*Rinascita*' or 'Renaissance' (rebirth) in *Lives* to describe the movement. Renaissance art pursued the ancient tradition of mimesis, striving to capture an idealised depiction of nature in ever greater degrees of faithfulness and aesthetic purity. This pursuit of perfection culminated during the High Renaissance (*c.*1495–1520) in the work of Raphael, Michelangelo and Leonardo da Vinci. Leonardo believed that:

Painting preserves that harmony of corresponding parts which nature, with all its powers, is unable to maintain. It keeps alive the image of a divine beauty whose natural model is soon destroyed by time and death.

Renaissance artists became masters of the technique of chiaroscuro, in which form is modelled by almost imperceptible gradations of light and dark. Look closely, for example, at Raphael's supremely subtle rendering of the skin tones in 'Saint Catherine of Alexandria' (Plate 1; see colour plate section). The art of the High Renaissance was regarded for a long time as the absolute pinnacle of Western art (although that view has been questioned in the modern era). In the three centuries that followed the High Renaissance, art became established in Europe as an institutionalised cultural industry. Academies, galleries, museums and collectors enshrined the artistic values that were developed during the Renaissance, especially in terms of the pre-eminence of the mimetic and aesthetic values encapsulated in the quote by Leonardo. Art academies acquired casts of sculptures from Greek and Roman antiquity and the Renaissance masters. Their students were trained in draughtsmanship, particularly of the human form, and used the casts as reference points for ideal human proportion. Prior to the Renaissance, there had been little attempt to depict individual human features, and landscapes were schematic backdrops lacking in depth and realism. During the period after the Renaissance, the portrait emerged as a legitimate artistic genre in its own right, as did landscape painting (Plate 2). A ranking system developed at art academies, in which paintings were graded according to subject matter (genre). The highest form of art was said to be based on historical, religious or mythical subjects. Portraiture was in the second rank, above landscape and daily life. The lowest rank was assigned to still life. Rankings affected scholarships, prizes and perceived value. Although the pursuit of aesthetic beauty remained pre-eminent, artists moved on from strict adherence to Renaissance ideals. In the Mannerist movement that succeeded the Renaissance, depictions of the human form departed from classical proportion, often as a way of heightening expressiveness. El Greco, for example, frequently rendered human figures with elongated bodies and relatively small heads.

The brain's capacity to interpret visual images has a crucial bearing on the artist's ability to create mimetic art and on the viewer's ability to interpret the mimetic content of art. These aspects of brain function are considered in Chapters 4 and 5. The aesthetic power of mimetic art such as landscapes is analysed in Chapters 8 and 9.

Modernism and abstraction

Towards the end of the nineteenth century there was an increasing desire among artists to move away from the traditional mimetic and aesthetic approach to art as defined by the academies. Artists became increasingly preoccupied with the medium itself, the canvas and paint, rather than with transparent, faithful depictions of nature. A group of French artists advocated painting out-of-doors to catch fleeting impressions of light and colour, rather than in the artificial confines of the studio. They adopted a technique in which paint was applied in distinct, sometimes heavily loaded touches of pure colour, rather than in smoother, blended strokes characteristic of earlier movements (Plate 3). Artists such as Monet, Pissarro, Cezanne, Boudin and Degas became the vanguard of the modern Impressionist movement, which heralded a shift in emphasis in Western art towards significant form in paintings (line, tone, shape, texture and colour) rather than mimetic content. The Fauvist movement that followed on from Impressionism continued the preoccupation with significant form in their use of bold, nonrealistic colours (Plate 4). The leader of Fauvism, Matisse, commented:

I started painting in planes, seeking the quality of the picture by an accord of all the flat colours ... subject matter being unimportant.

The first exhibition by the Fauvist movement took place in Paris, in 1905, and this date is generally regarded as the inception of the Modernist movement in art.

According to the Modernist movement, the quality of art is derived not from its mimetic fidelity but from the involuntary response evoked by its form. In 1890, the Post-Impressionist painter Maurice Denis stated:

Remember that a picture, before it is a picture of a battle horse, a nude woman, or some story, is essentially a flat surface covered in colours arranged in a certain order.

For Denis, aesthetic pleasure was to be found in the painting itself, not in the subject matter. Great art was said to share certain universal formal qualities.

This view led to a critical stance in art known as Formalism, which focused entirely on composition and medium rather than subject matter. Formalism provides a vocabulary for describing and evaluating the aesthetic qualities of artworks: design, composition, texture. Thus, modern art moved away from illusionist painting, mimesis and narrative and, instead, emphasised medium and composition. It advocated certain aesthetic practices such as linearity and geometry. Elements of modernism can be seen in the work of earlier periods and may have inspired modernist painters. Titian, for example, used brushstrokes that manipulated surface texture as a form of expression and explored the purely expressive effects that could be created with colour.

According to the critical techniques of Formalism first described by Wolfflin (1915) in his influential book *Principles of Art History*, any artwork could be evaluated in terms of opposing pairs of descriptors. Wolfflin introduced the descriptors as a way of understanding the contrast between Renaissance art and art from later periods, but they have since been applied more generally to art from all periods.

Wolfflin's 'linear' versus 'painterly' dimension contrasts compositions emphasising outline and contour with those dominated by the tonal effects of light, shade and colour, which blend the borders of objects. He regarded Durer, for example, as primarily a linear artist, while Rembrandt was described as painterly (Figure 1.3). Closely related is the 'clearness' versus 'unclearness' dimension, distinguishing between compositions with a clean, clear expression of form and those clouded with paradox, ambiguity, or shadow. Renaissance paintings tended to display a high degree of clarity in line and form, in which no questions are left unanswered, whereas later works exploit a lack of clarity to convey mood. Tintoretto, for example, used shadows across the face to convey suffering. Wolfflin's 'plane' versus 'recession' distinction refers to the depth relationships in the depicted scene. In some compositions such as Velasquez's 'Venus' (Plate 5), the elements of the scene predominantly lie in a plane parallel to the plane of the picture, while others such as Brueghel the Elder's 'Hunters in the Snow' (also Plate 5) convey a strong sense of receding depth planes. Chapter 5 will discuss some of the techniques artists use to convey depth in paintings.

Cubism followed on soon after Fauvism and represented a further departure from the traditional mimetic approach to art. Cubist art, initiated by Pablo Picasso, attempted to represent different aspects or viewpoints of the same object simultaneously. In the early twentieth century, a growing number of artists began creating work that was not connected in any obvious way with the

Figure 1.3 'Self-Portrait at the Age of 34', Rembrandt Harmenszoon van Rijn, 1640.

appearance of the world. A preoccupation with significant form as exemplified by Wolfflin's principles soon led to the creation of completely abstract paintings containing pure form, devoid of any mimetic content. The shapes and colours they contained had no obvious reference point in reality.

Abstract art forces the viewer to rely entirely on their aesthetic response to the forms, colours and lines. Mark Rothko's abstract paintings, for example (Plate 4), are composed of hazy, deeply saturated rectangles of colour, infused with a glowing meditative quality that reflects his subdued mood at the time. Recent scientific ideas about the source of visual aesthetic pleasure in the brain indicate that there is a much more intimate connection between abstract art and natural images than one might think, as will be discussed in Chapter 9.

Postmodern art

Abstraction may have emerged partly as a response by artists to the introduction of photography. In the early twentieth century, painting had largely been superseded by photography as a vehicle for creating realistic likenesses of nature. This led to the view that art should be evaluated not in terms of its ability to create a likeness of nature but in terms of its emotional power and aesthetic impact. However, modern abstract art was based predominantly on the medium of painting and generally obeyed two fundamental principles (Harrison, 2009). Firstly, it was contained within a traditional picture frame, which leads the viewer to expect engagement with a specific visual experience. Secondly, it created a picture plane, a virtual space, which was in some sense detached from the physical surface of the painting.

In the 1960s and 1970s, artists began to violate these two principles, taking art into a new postmodern phase. Works were no longer confined to a framed area defining the limits of the pictorial experience and often moved off the flat gallery wall into three-dimensional space. Some postmodern artworks took the form of three-dimensional installations, others were defined by a performance rather than some kind of static artefact. Postmodernism challenged the traditional pre-eminence of painting and aesthetic merit in established art. Its eclectic outlook appropriated styles and practices from the past, sometimes for satirical or ironic effect. For example, Jeff Koons' 'Three Balls' and Warhol's soup cans comment on the commodity fetish of late-twentieth-century consumer culture. The movement had actually started over 50 years earlier, with Duchamp's submission of so-called 'ready-made' artefacts such as a urinal for display in a gallery.

Postmodern art moves beyond visual art and visual aesthetics. It communicates ideas and feelings through a physical medium, which need not be a recognisable painting or sculpture, and frequently has little ostensible aesthetic appeal. The conceptual artist Sol LeWitt stated in 1967:

In conceptual art, the idea or concept is the most important aspect of the work... What the work of art looks like isn't too important.

Conceptual art cannot be evaluated by examining its formal and technical qualities alone, because these qualities could be shared with objects that are not works of art. A title, description or commentary may be an essential element of critical assessment. Many postmodern pieces do not even have a specific meaning or a 'correct' interpretation. The viewer is invited to be an active participant in establishing the meaning of the piece. Of course, viewers of art have always been thinkers as well. Artistic engagement with the viewer has its roots in the Renaissance preoccupation with individual perspective viewpoint and emotional expression. But in conceptual art, the formal constraints, the rules of the game, are radically different from those that apply to traditional painting and sculpture. Active participation is undoubtedly part of the appeal of postmodern art for today's patrons and gallery visitors.

A recurring theme in conceptual art is the use of dead animals or bodily fluids such as blood or urine, which aims to shock and perhaps to promote art as entertainment and for profit. Damien Hirst's installations of dead animals and fly-eaten meat, for instance, cannot be considered in terms of aesthetic beauty. Therefore, discussions about visual aesthetics and the brain are less relevant to an understanding of conceptual art, given that it often rejects visual aesthetic considerations entirely. Sol LeWitt summarised this point well in 1967 as follows:

Art that is meant for the sensation of the eye primarily would be called perceptual rather than conceptual. This would include most optical, kinetic, light, and color art.

What matters to a postmodernist is not whether a work of art looks beautiful but whether it exhibits any good ideas and what the intentions of the artist were in creating it. As this book focuses on human visual perception, it is primarily concerned with what LeWitt calls perceptual art rather than conceptual art. However, even in the case of conceptual art, there are legitimate issues to discuss concerning the origin of the urge to create art, whether Postmodern, Modern or Renaissance, and the continuing high esteem in which artists are held. These issues are aired in Chapter 10.

Art in context

Art movements must be placed in the context of the social and cultural climate of their time. As mentioned earlier, Renaissance art emerged at a time of great social and cultural upheaval in Europe, while Modernist movements such as

Impressionism and Futurism (discussed in Chapter 6) were inspired by the scientific and technological innovations of the late nineteenth and early twentieth centuries. Postmodernist art can be seen, at least in part, as a reaction against American socio-economic dominance after World War II, as exemplified by the Modernist abstractionism of Jackson Pollock, Mark Rothko and others. American Modernist abstractionism itself was partly a reaction against the dominance of the old colonial European powers and their art academies (Pook & Newall, 2008). The last decade or so of the twentieth century saw a resurgence in figurative art, perhaps reflecting popular taste and the expanding commercial art market. Some highly regarded artists such as Lucian Freud and David Hockney have continued to work within the painting tradition.

Religious concerns are a significant factor in many early artworks, because they were commissioned by the Church. Aside from religious concerns, many artworks are intended to convey specific ideas and stories. Before the advent of photography, art was the only medium available for preserving a visual record of an idea, event or individual. It was used by the rich and powerful to endorse their prestige, status and ambition. Holbein's portrait of Henry VIII, for example, has come to define the image of this particular monarch.

Theories of art

Art theories, in common with theories in other disciplines, aim to create a principled framework within which to organise a set of empirical observations or artefacts. As such, art theories are vital because they help us to understand and evaluate a hugely complex and universal aspect of human endeavour. They help us to answer questions such as: Why is art valued? What drives an artist's behaviour? Does art serve a function? Different theories emphasise different aspects of art: cultural context, aesthetic qualities, or its institutional basis. These contrasting theories are not mutually exclusive, in that only one can be true to the exclusion of all others. Each may offer a unique, equally valid perspective on the subject.

Historically, discussions of visual art and aesthetics have omitted serious consideration of the role of the brain. However, the expansion in our knowledge of how the brain processes visual information has been so rapid in the modern era that now there are many opportunities to explore the links that can be made between art and the brain, and some deep inroads have been made already (e.g. Zeki, 1999; Chatterjee, 2011). This book is an attempt to strengthen existing links and to forge some new links. It outlines an approach to understanding art based on scientific psychology and neuroscience, which attempts to place visual art in the context of the structure, function and evolution of the human brain as a seeing machine. Certain fundamental aspects of art, and the urge to create it, can be linked directly to how our brains evolved and the way they interact with the world. However, this scientific approach is intended to complement rather than negate the insights achieved by other theories of art and, indeed, can benefit from the broader context offered by other theories and by the historical milieu within which visual art developed.

Summary and prospect

Art is multi-dimensional and cannot be defined in terms of a single property or explained by any one theory alone. Aesthetic beauty was a dominant feature of visual art for centuries and was the driving force behind many art movements from the High Renaissance in the early fifteenth century through Impressionism in the nineteenth century to Abstractionism in the early twentieth century. More recently, postmodern conceptual art does not concern itself with visual aesthetics but focuses instead on intellectual properties and the intentionality of the artist in constructing meaning.

A comprehensive understanding of visual art requires an appreciation of several perspectives, including its historical, cultural and social contexts. This book sets out a neuroscientific approach to visual art, focusing in particular on the role of the human eye and brain, which together constitute the visual system of the brain. The structure and function of the visual system determine the nature of all visual experience and must inevitably make a major impact on visual art and artists. The next two chapters consider how the structure and function of the eye and brain impact on art. Later chapters discuss the relevance of cognitive processes such as memory and attention, as well as the specialised brain processes that mediate our perception of movement, colour and pattern. The last chapter explores the relationship between art and evolution.

2   Art and the eye

Introduction

This chapter concentrates on how the eye works and how this function impacts on art. To set the scene, it will be useful to know a little about the physical properties of the stimulus for vision, light. The precise physical nature of light has perplexed philosophers and scientists for centuries and is not yet completely understood. Light is a form of energy known as electromagnetic energy because it has both electrical and magnetic properties and it is carried in small packets called photons. The electromagnetic field of each photon has a characteristic vibration frequency that can vary from a few thousand vibration cycles per second to many billions of cycles per second. The standard way of measuring vibration frequency is in terms of the distance between adjacent peaks in the vibrating wave, known as its wavelength. Across the full electromagnetic spectrum, wavelength can vary from extremely short wavelengths that are a fraction of the size of atoms (X-rays and gamma rays, the very highest frequencies) to very long wavelengths that can be many kilometres long (the lowest frequencies). The energy that you can see as light spans only a tiny proportion of the electromagnetic spectrum, corresponding to wavelengths between 400 nm and 700 nm (billionths of a metre). Light wavelength is associated with colour experiences, with the longer wavelengths appearing red or orange and the shorter wavelengths appearing blue or violet. Yellow and green sensations are evoked by middle wavelengths. Electromagnetic energy in the visible band-light is well behaved in the sense that it reflects off most surfaces and can be focused by lenses. As the sense organ for vision, the eye takes advantage of this good behaviour.

The structure of the human eye

Seeing begins with an image formed on the inside surface of the eye. In many ways the eye can be compared to a camera. It is an optical instrument that uses a lens system to focus an image onto a light-sensitive surface, as illustrated in Figure 2.1. Light rays emitted or reflected from surfaces in the world enter the eye through a small aperture called the pupil. The rays are brought into focus on the inside surface of the eye by the cornea (the curved transparent surface in front of the pupil) and by a flexible transparent lens positioned behind the pupil. The cornea contributes over 80% of the eye's total focusing power. The lens adds the remaining 20% in a flexible manner, to allow the eye to focus at different distances.

When you focus on a very distant object, light rays entering the eye from the object are almost parallel, and in a relaxed normal eye they come into sharp focus on a sheet of nerve cells that line the inside of the eye, known as the retina (Figure 2.2(a), top). When you focus on a relatively near object, on the other hand, the light rays are diverging as they enter the eye (Figure 2.2(a), middle), so more optical power is needed in the lens system in order to bring the light rays

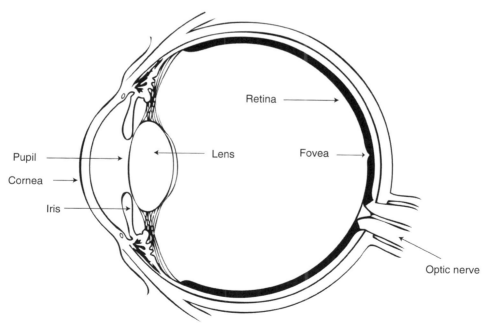

Figure 2.1 The major anatomical components of the human eye, seen in cross-section from above.

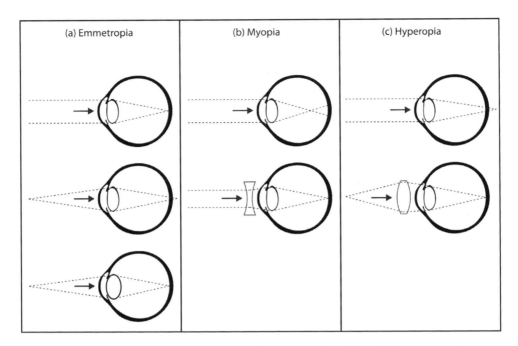

Figure 2.2 Accommodation and accommodative error in vision. (a) In a normal eye (emmetropia) accommodation is used to focus the divergent rays from a nearby object onto the retina. (b) In a short-sighted eye (myopia) rays come into focus in front of the retina, corrected using a diverging lens. (c) In a long-sighted eye (hyperopia) rays come into focus beyond the retina, corrected using a converging lens.

into focus at the retina (Figure 2.2(a), bottom). This increased power is created by a change in the shape and thickness of the lens through the action of muscles inside the eye. The process of adjustment is called accommodation and it ensures that vision remains sharp regardless of the distance of the viewed object. In a camera, the same result is produced by adjusting the distance between the lens and the light-sensitive surface (namely the film or sensor array).

The retina lining the inside of the eye contains a dense matrix of light-sensitive cells called photoreceptors, which each produce a small electrical signal when struck by light. These signals are modified by the network of nerve cells forming the retina before they are sent up the optic nerve at the back of the eye towards the brain, ultimately to create a visual experience. The photoreceptors that function during daylight, known as cone photoreceptors, subdivide into three classes on the basis of the light wavelengths that excite them most. The three classes are usually called 'S-cones' (short-wavelength), 'M-cones' (medium-wavelength) and 'L-cones' (long-wavelength) after the spectral region that is most effective in generating a response (Plate 6; see colour plate section).

A similar tripartite (trichromatic) system is used in modern digital cameras. A typical ten-megapixel compact digital camera contains approximately ten million individual light sensors (pixels) arranged in a regular matrix about 10 mm in diameter. The human eye, on the other hand, contains over 120 million photoreceptors arranged in a matrix over 40 mm in diameter. There are many other significant differences between a digital camera and the eye. A digital camera possesses equal numbers of sensors to detect short-, medium- and long-wavelengths, and the sensors are distributed evenly in triplets across the entire sensor array. In the human eye, there are marked differences in the numbers of S-cones, M-cones and L-cones, and they are distributed very unevenly across the retina. Only one in every twenty cone receptors is an S-cone, while a third are M-cones and nearly two-thirds are L-cones (Hofer et al., 2005). S-cones are so few and far between on the retina that pure blue shapes and patterns appear very indistinct and obscure to us compared to reds and greens. Furthermore, cone photoreceptors are most tightly packed into a central region of the retina called the fovea. When you look directly at a small object, its image falls on the fovea. There are relatively few cone photoreceptors outside this region, which covers an area of the retina only large enough to contain an image of your thumbnail held at arm's length. Outside the fovea the retina is dominated by rod photoreceptors, which mediate vision in dim conditions. Consequently, your ability to resolve fine detail in bright light is restricted to a small region of visual space close to the point of fixation. Try to fixate on a particular word in this text and then direct your attention to the words on either side without moving your eyes. You will find that only one or two words on either side can be seen clearly enough to read. In order to see detail in part of a visual scene we must move our eyes to fixate on it, so our eyes are never still for long but make two or three shifts in fixation position every second of the waking day. These basic anatomical features of the eye have far-reaching consequences on art, both for artists and for viewers. Some of the ways in which ocular structure and function impact on art are covered in this chapter, while others will be covered in Chapters 4 and 5.

Contrast coding in the retina

The network of nerve cells lining the retina processes the signal generated by the photoreceptors before passing information up the optic nerve towards the brain. Retinal processing allows the eye to solve some very challenging problems. The intensity of light arriving at the earth's surface from the sun varies over an enormous range. For instance, the light reflected from a sheet of paper in the midday sun is 200,000 times more intense than light reflected from the same sheet of paper in moonlight (Land & Nilsson, 2002). This range is far too great for any single sensor system to handle, whether in the eye or in a camera. The human eye copes by dividing the range in two: rod photoreceptors cover the lower range of light levels and cones cover the higher light levels. The task of the photoreceptors is made easier by the fact that, in any one visual scene, the variation of intensity from the darkest shadow to the lightest surface varies by a factor of 1:100 at most, and this narrower range is manageable in terms of the available variation in photoreceptor responses. Thus, the most challenging problem for photoreceptors is coping with the variation in illumination across different scenes, such as between daytime and night-time scenes, rather than the variation within any one scene. Hence the eye needs separate cone and rod photoreceptor systems.

The task of the eye and brain is to tell us about the objects present in the visible field of view, in terms of their shapes and surface properties and their positions in the scene. Information about absolute illumination level is not actually very informative in this regard. Variation in illumination across a scene, on the other hand, is highly informative. Objects generally vary intrinsically in the proportion of incident illumination that they reflect. To take a simple example, charcoal always reflects about 5% of the illumination falling on it, while chalk reflects about 75%, regardless of the absolute level of light. The edges of objects in the scene therefore generally correspond to sudden changes in illumination on the retina. Illumination is always higher from chalk than from charcoal, whether we view the two objects in moonlight or in the midday sun. Hence, the retina's neural circuitry has evolved specifically to signal steep changes in illumination in adjacent locations, known as luminance contrast edges. The selective preservation of information about contrast edges has two important consequences for art. Firstly, it means that variation in absolute illumination level does not alter our experience of a visual scene fundamentally. A painting of an outdoor scene on a midsummer's day looks perfectly acceptable, despite the fact that the original scene would probably have been about 1,000 times brighter than the painting, as long as the contrast relationships in the scene are preserved (the darker objects in the original scene are relatively dark in the painting, for example, and the range of luminance levels in natural scenes, from the darkest parts to the brightest parts, is also higher than in paintings; see Graham & Field, 2008b). Secondly, the artist must pay particular attention to edges in the scene but can be relatively relaxed about the areas of even illumination between them because these areas are not represented with great fidelity in the visual system. A contrast edge can be introduced without the need to render an overall change in lightness in the regions extending on either side of the edge.

Plate 7(a) demonstrates a well-known visual illusion known as the Craik-O'Brien illusion (Ratliff, 1972), which demonstrates the visual system's tendency to rely on edge information. The area to the left of the central vertical edge looks darker than the area to the right of the edge, yet the two areas are physically identical. To confirm this for yourself, place a pencil along the edge. The illumination difference is confined to the edge, but subjectively it spreads across the regions on either side. The eye preserves only the edge information and the brain fills in the rest. Artists have exploited this short-cut by the brain since antiquity, as shown by the example in Figure 2.3.

Information about local contrast edges is carried out of the retina along the nerve fibres of cells known as retinal ganglion cells. Some retinal ganglion cells convey information about changes in luminance (a change from bright to dark), while others convey information about changes in colour. Thus, in an abstract sense the neural signals leaving the eye divide into two separate channels. One

Figure 2.3 'Bathers at Asnieres', Georges-Pierre Seurat, 1884.

channel, called the 'chromatic' channel, conveys information about colour contrast to the brain, and the other 'achromatic' channel conveys information about luminance contrast. Coding of colour contrast is based on the three types of cone photoreceptor mentioned earlier (S-, M- and L-cones). The three receptor types respond optimally in different regions of the visible spectrum, as illustrated in Plate 6. Skylight has a preponderance of energy in the blue part of the spectrum and its blue appearance is signalled by the relatively high level of activation in S-cones compared to M-cones and L-cones. The red skin on a tomato reflects light predominantly at the longer wavelengths that excite L-cone photoreceptors the most. Therefore, hue is coded in the visual system by the relative activity levels of the three cone types. Retinal ganglion cells encode these activity ratios by means of two opposing colour pairings. The vast majority of cells (90%) in the central part of the retina code the ratio between L-cone output and M-cone output, known as R-G cells (Callaway, 2005). Only a small minority (less than 10%) of cells code the ratio between S-cones and a combination of M-cones and L-cones, known as B-Y cells (the combination of red and green is described as yellow). The chromatic channel has lower spatial resolution than the achromatic (luminance) channel, so cannot convey as much spatial detail. Morgan and Aiba (1985) found that human spatial acuity is three times worse using patterns defined entirely by colour variations rather than by luminance variations.

The division of retinal coding into achromatic and chromatic channels and the detailed properties of the chromatic channel have several important consequences for visual art. Firstly, spreading of local contrast information also occurs in the chromatic channel. Plate 7(b) demonstrates the watercolour effect (Pinna et al., 2001). The two regions as a whole appear to differ in hue, but the physical hue difference is confined to the edge between the regions. The brain fills in the rest of the hue. Secondly, the internal code based on opposing pairs of colours (red and green, R-G; blue and yellow, B-Y) causes those colours to complement and reinforce each other when present together in a visual scene. Shadows tend to take on the complementary colour to the surround. For instance, a light yellow area induces a hint of blue in adjacent shadows. The blue tint is not physically present but is created inside the visual system (note the blueish shadow in Monet's painting of Rouen cathedral, Plate 9). In 'Barges on the Thames' (Plate 4), Derain exploits red-green contrasts. Thirdly, the lower resolution of the chromatic channel means that paintings that contain colour variation but little lightness variation are prone to appear indistinct and lacking detail, as can be seen in Plate 8. It shows two versions of the same photograph of

Rouen cathedral. The original image is seen in (a), and in (b) the achromatic (luminance) variation has been removed to isolate the chromatic (colour) variation. The result is an apparent lack of definition and detail. Chapter 7 contains a detailed discussion of the use of colour in art.

Optical defects and their consequences for art

The optical properties of the cornea and lens in the eye are crucially important for vision. Defects in either can have potentially profound consequences for vision because they interfere with the very process of image formation on the retina, the first step in vision. Such defects actually affect the majority of the population, the two most common being defective accommodation and cataract. Defects of accommodation limit the ability of the cornea and lens to focus; in other words, to converge light rays onto the surface of the retina rather than in front of or behind it. Cataract reduces the transmission of light through the cornea or lens, thus reducing retinal illumination.

Accommodation

Focusing defects are called errors of accommodation and come in two variants, both of which cause blur in the retinal image. In short-sightedness or myopia, the optical power of the eye is too great, so parallel rays from distant objects come into focus in front of the retina, resulting in a blurred image as depicted at the top of Figure 2.2(b). Near objects can be focused well with little accommodative effort. A short-sighted individual has no problem in resolving detail at distances within 2 m or so, but objects farther away appear blurred and indistinct. Plate 9(b) simulates the view of Rouen cathedral in Plate 8(a) for an individual with short-sightedness.

In long-sightedness or hyperopia, the optical power of the eye is too weak, so parallel rays from distant objects tend to come into focus behind the eye (Figure 2.2(c), top). Accommodative effort can be applied to increase the power of the lens and bring the image into sharp focus at the retina. However, there is insufficient optical power to cope with the diverging rays from nearer objects, which therefore appear blurred. A long-sighted individual has no problem in resolving detail at distances beyond 2 m or so away, but nearer objects appear blurred and indistinct. Older people are prone to long-sightedness because the ocular lens becomes less flexible with age and can no longer change shape to accommodate near viewing distances.

Myopia and hyperopia can be corrected with appropriate spectacles or contact lenses, which subtract or add optical power as required. Short-sighted myopic individuals can wear lenses, which diverge light rays (minus values in your optical prescription) and so allow far objects to be seen clearly (Figure 2.2(b), bottom), while long-sighted hyperopic individuals can wear converging lenses (plus values on your optical prescription), which permit clear vision of near objects (Figure 2.2(c), bottom). Thus, correcting lenses allow even the most short-sighted or long-sighted artists to see both their work and a distant subject with complete clarity. However, corrective lenses became available only during the fourteenth and fifteenth centuries and, in any case, artists were not obliged to wear them.

Myopia may be an advantage to an artist striving for a particular aesthetic effect, because it removes fine details but retains general form, colour and atmosphere. Indeed, several authors have attributed the characteristic lack of detail and blurred appearance of Impressionist paintings to the prevalence of myopia among the Impressionists (Trevor-Roper, 1988; Elliott & Skaff, 1993; Polland, 2004). Was the conscious blurring of vision, or deliberate failure to correct retinal blur, a factor in the realisation of Impressionist artworks? Their paintings often contain no clearly defined edges or textures at all, as for example in Plate 3. Cezanne, Renoir and Pissaro were all reputedly myopic, and allegedly refused to wear optical corrections even when they were available. Cezanne disliked his spectacles and is reported to have said: 'Take those vulgar things away!' (Trevor-Roper, 1988). The appearance of many Impressionist works is certainly consistent with the claim. In the 1890s, Monet painted a whole series of images of Rouen cathedral, with the aim of capturing the subtle variations in colour that were characteristic of different times of day and weather conditions. Plate 9 compares a view of Rouen cathedral painted by Monet with a blurred version of the photograph in Plate 8, which has been further processed to reduce the luminance contrast in the image but preserve colour contrast, and so simulate the effect Monet aimed to create. The blurred low-contrast image is plausibly closer in appearance to the painting than to the original photograph.

Are there any facts which can bear out the claim that myopia contributed to Impressionism? Trevor-Roper (1988) reported a survey of 128 members of the Ecole des Beaux Artes in Paris in 1917 (this academy trained many of the Impressionists). Results, summarised in the left-hand bars of Figure 2.4(a), showed that half were myopic, but only about one-quarter were hyperopic.

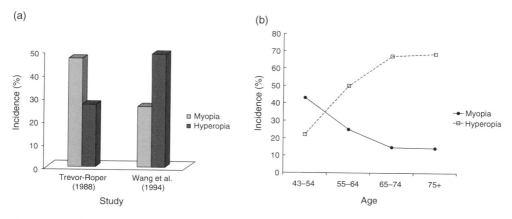

Figure 2.4 (a) Results of a survey of 128 members of the Ecole des Beaux Artes in Paris in 1917, reported by Trevor-Roper (1988), compared with the results of a survey of 4,926 adults aged 43–84 years, reported by Wang et al. (1994). (b) Wang et al.'s (1994) results broken down by age.

A much more recent survey of 4,926 adults in the general population aged 43 to 84 years by Wang et al. (1994) found the opposite pattern, also summarised in Figure 2.4(a); a greater prevalence of hyperopia. At first sight, therefore, the data are consistent with the claim that there was an unusually high incidence of myopia in the Impressionists, who may have just painted what they saw (if they avoided spectacle correction).

However, one must look at the data more closely. Figure 2.4(b) breaks down Wang et al.'s (1994) data into age bands. Hyperopia is more prevalent in the general population only in older age groups. Below an age of 54 years, myopia is actually more prevalent (the rise in hyperopia with age is due to hardening of the lens, as mentioned earlier). If the artists surveyed in 1917 were mostly below the age of 54 years, then the prevalence of myopia among them is no more than one would expect in the general population. Unfortunately, Trevor-Roper (1988) did not report statistics on the age distribution of the artists surveyed, although according to the Institut National D'Etudes Demographiques (http://www.ined.fr), life expectancy in France at the turn of the century was below 50 years of age. Hence, the case for myopia as a factor in Impressionism is unproven. In any case, myopia has presumably been a fact of human life for millennia, yet Impressionism only emerged just over 100 years ago. The Impressionist movement should be seen in its proper art historical context, as outlined in the previous chapter. One might argue plausibly, nevertheless, that myopia offered a convenient tool for promoting a certain way of looking at the visual world, when the time was right.

Astigmatism: the El Greco fallacy

Astigmatism is caused by a specific defect in the eye's optical system. If the curvature of the cornea or lens is not perfectly spherical, but slightly oblong (like the curvature of a dessert spoon), then light from a point in a scene is not focused as a point on the retina, but is spread out or blurred along an axis to create a dash rather than a dot. Contours in the image that are parallel to the blur axis will appear sharp while contours running perpendicular to it will appear blurred. Many people possess a small degree of astigmatism that can be compensated by a 'cylindrical' correction in their optical prescription (a lens that has the opposite curvature asymmetry to that in the affected eye).

As mentioned in the previous chapter, the sixteenth-century artist known as El Greco frequently depicted human figures with elongated bodies and relatively small heads. It has long been argued speculatively that the elongation apparent in El Greco's figures is due to astigmatism in his eyes, or to the distortion introduced by over-correction with a cylindrical lens (Anstis, 2002; Marmor & Ravin, 2009). There are several serious flaws in the argument. Firstly, the elongation cannot be caused by the astigmatism itself, because that condition causes blur, not shape distortion. Secondly, if El Greco had seen shapes as more elongated than they really were (perhaps due to wearing a distorting lens), then he would also have seen his drawings of those shapes as more elongated than they really were. As a result, the drawings should have the same (correct) proportions as the shapes, despite the distortion. In effect, the distortion should apply equally to everything that is seen and so have no effect. Finally, Anstis (2002) reported an experiment in which a participant wore a distorting lens for two days, during which his or her drawing accuracy was assessed repeatedly. He found that copied shapes were always drawn accurately, despite the lens (as expected on the basis of the foregoing argument). Shapes drawn from memory were initially distorted, but the distortion gradually declined and after two days there was none left. The participant apparently adapted to the distortion and was able to apply some internal correction for it. Therefore, there is no evidence to support the claim that El Greco's elongated figures were due to astigmatism. The elongation was almost certainly a stylistic choice, which reflected the Mannerist period in European art that was in the ascendancy during El Greco's lifetime.

Cataract

Clear vision requires an adequate supply of light at the retina. One might think that there is generally an abundance of light, at least during the day, yet paradoxically the retina is starved of light at most light levels and needs to capture as much as it can. Even in a healthy eye, only 10% of the light that enters the eye is actually absorbed by the photoreceptors (Land & Nilsson, 2002). The rest is lost due to scattering and absorption by various other structures making up the eye. Further losses because of optical defects can be disastrous for vision. Many elderly individuals suffer from cataract, an opacity in the lens that causes image blur, decreased retinal illumination and veiling glare. Blue wavelengths are absorbed preferentially by the lens. Cataract gives the pupil a characteristic milky appearance and is partly caused by exposure to the ultraviolet radiation in sunlight (Robman & Taylor, 2005). Claude Monet and Mary Cassatt both suffered from cataract that affected their paintings (Marmor & Ravin, 1997). Monet's cataract was first diagnosed in 1912, and its effect is clearly evident if one compares paintings of the Japanese footbridge in his garden at Giverny executed in 1899 and c.1920 (Plates 3 and 10). The later work lacks definition and is much more abstract. It is possible that these changes reflect a progression in artistic style, or advancing age (Monet was over 80 years old by the time he executed the later paintings). However, they are at least consistent with the consequences of cataract. Monet's letters remove any doubt. In 1922 he wrote:

My poor eyesight makes me see everything in a complete fog. It's very beautiful all the same and it's this which I'd love to have been able to convey.

He complained about changes in his colour vision. Reds appeared muddy and pinks dull; things generally appeared yellowish. The prescription of eye drops gave a temporary improvement. Later in 1922 he wrote:

I can now see everything in my garden. I'm overjoyed at my perception of every colour in the spectrum. (Quotes taken from Elliott & Skaff, 1993.)

But the respite was temporary. Monet underwent surgery to remove the lens in his right eye in 1922, but the corrective glasses he needed to wear afterwards caused image distortion (as many spectacles do) and he struggled to cope: 'the distortion and exaggerated colours that I see are quite terrifying' (quoted in Elliott & Skaff, 1993). Monet's paintings that can be dated reliably to his post-operative period show a return to the style and colour palette that is typical of his work from 1917 and earlier.

Monet's friend and fellow artist Mary Cassatt was diagnosed with cataract in 1912 when she was 68 years old. By 1915, her poor eyesight prevented her from working and she underwent cataract surgery in 1917. The surgery proved to be unsuccessful and she was forced to stop painting entirely. It is difficult to identify changes in Cassatt's artistic output that can be attributed confidently to cataract, perhaps because she stopped working when she recognised that she could not maintain her preferred style.

Retinal defects and their consequences for art

Retinal degeneration

Edgar Degas was undoubtedly myopic because, apparently, he had been refused entry into military service on account of it. The effect can arguably be seen in some of his paintings, in which foreground elements are rendered in detail but background elements are quite indistinct (Elliott & Skaff, 1993). He probably also suffered from a progressive retinal disease that caused particular damage to the central retina (Marmor, 2006). As described earlier, the central retina contains the bulk of the cone photoreceptors that are essential for acute vision in bright conditions. Hence, degeneration in the fovea would have made it very difficult for Degas to resolve detail, both in the visual scene before him and in his work. Degas' friend and colleague Walter Sickert reported that he complained 'he could only see around the spot at which he was looking, and never the spot itself'. Changes in Degas' artistic style mirror what one would expect from a progressive loss of central vision. Earlier work in the 1870s contained precise detail and carefully rendered shading, while later work in the 1880s and 1890s lacked detail and was dominated by relatively coarse hatching (Figure 2.5). Degas' infirmity may well have led him consciously to change his subject matter and style. Working in his studio from photographs rather than from life may have been a response to his growing myopia, although Degas may have been inclined to embrace this new technology more than other artists. His failing sight may also have been a decisive factor in his later preoccupation with sculpture.

Georgia O'Keeffe was diagnosed with degeneration of the central retina in 1964, at the age of 77 years old. She likened the problem to a cloud that had entered her eyeball (Marmor & Ravin, 2009). She employed studio assistants in order to cope with the problem, who commented that 'bare patches of canvas were overlooked... Sometimes she painted the same area twice.' Some of O'Keeffe's last works were simplified, almost abstract watercolours. As with Degas, she turned to a tactile art form, in her case pottery.

Figure 2.5 (a) 'Young Spartans Exercising', Hilaire-Germain-Edgar Degas, c.1860. (b) 'Russian Dancers', Hilaire-Germain-Edgar Degas, c.1899.

Colour deficiency

Human ability to perceive and discriminate colour is based on the trichromatic nature of the cone photoreceptors, described earlier in the chapter. Each of the colours that we can perceive is represented in the brain by a set of just three numbers, which relate to the activity levels of the three cone types. If an individual lacked one of the cone types, or if the absorbance curves in Plate 6 were somehow defective, then his or her ability to see colours would be compromised because the numbers coding colours in the brain would be corrupted. Such an individual would not be totally blind to colour, despite the common label to that effect. However, the range of colours he or she could perceive and discriminate would be relatively narrow compared to an individual with a complete set of fully functional cone photoreceptors. Thus, the more accurate description is colour deficiency. A crucial aspect of artists' perceptual judgement is their ability to match colours, such as when they mix paint pigments in the proportions required to match the colour of an element in the visual scene before them. Colour-deficient individuals make significant errors in this task, at least in the eyes of most other people (because colour vision is entirely subjective, there is no objectively 'correct' colour). Two colours that appear identical to someone with colour deficiency will often appear very different to a person with normal colour vision. About 5%–10% of the general population has some form of colour deficiency. The vast majority of them are male because of the way the deficiency is transmitted genetically. The most common form of colour deficiency is known as deuteranomaly, in which the sensitivity curve for M-cones is shifted to longer wavelengths so that it is much closer to the L-cone curve than normal. The most marked perceptual consequence of this shift is a tendency to confuse hues in the red-green part of the spectrum.

Given the incidence of colour deficiency in the general population, it is plausible to assume that at least some artists over the centuries had a form of colour deficiency. One survey of practising artists in Dresden reported by Marmor and Lanthony (2001) found an incidence of 9%. Pickford (1969) tested the colour vision of 223 art school students in the UK and found a normal incidence of deuteranomaly (5.4% of men and less than 1% of women). However, there are few documented cases of colour deficiency in well-known artists. There is some evidence that artists with defective colour vision confine themselves to working in monochrome. The artist Charles Meryon is thought to have had a colour deficiency, but he established a successful career in etching (Ravin et al., 1995). Cole and Nathan (2002) report the case of an amateur artist with severe deuteranomaly, which is instructive regarding the problems such individuals would face when using colour. To assess his problems they gave him an oil painting of a semi-abstract landscape and asked him to copy it as exactly as possible. His most obvious area of difficulty was in reproducing greens and yellow-greens. Subtle pinks were painted as pale greens and he had a tendency to confuse pale green and white. Saturated greens appeared to have little colour. He remarked that he would have had much less difficulty if he had been told which tubes of colour the original artist had used. This strategy echoes that used by a professional artist, Jens Johannsen, interviewed by Marmor and Lanthony (2001). He also had deuteranomaly and relied on a formula that had been given to him by his tutors at art school, which allowed him to select tubes of paint that would be appropriate for viewers with normal colour vision.

The landscape painter John Constable has long been suspected of colour deficiency because of the small gamut of colours characteristic of his work and the predominance of grey-green tones. Similarly, J. W. M. Turner's work contains a predominance of yellowish-red tones. However, any attempt to diagnose an artist's colour deficiency on the basis of his or her work, while entertaining, is highly dubious. Colour-deficient painters know the names of their tubes of paint and can learn the colours of natural objects and surfaces from individuals without colour deficiency. Furthermore, the use of a restricted palette may well reflect an artistic choice based on the desired colour balance of the composition. In Pickford's (1969) survey of colour deficiency in art students, one defective out of the seven found did not even know of the defect. He reports that the remainder 'showed surprising powers of adaptation, partly as a result of realizing their difficulties consciously and learning to avoid colours which would give rise to difficulty'. It is impossible to know what colours are seen by any colour-deficient individual. Equally, a normally sighted individual cannot explain the difference between red and green to a colour-deficient individual. Colour is inherently subjective.

Summary

Good eyesight is clearly crucial for visual art. The human eye gathers light from the outside world and brings it into focus onto a sheet of light-sensitive photoreceptor cells lining the inside surface of the eye. Rod photoreceptors mediate vision in night-time conditions, and cone photoreceptors operate during daylight. Human ability to discriminate light wavelength in daylight is based on a comparison of responses in three different classes of cone photoreceptor, which are sensitive to wavelengths in the blue, green and red regions of the visible spectrum. Neural interactions in the retina create two channels of processing. The achromatic channel carries information about local luminance contrast, and the chromatic channel carries information about colour contrast. This division into two processing channels has major consequences for the depiction of spatial detail and colour variation in visual art.

Accommodation defects limit the eye's ability to resolve spatial detail; either nearer objects appear blurred and far objects appear sharp (long-sightedness), or nearer objects appear sharp and far objects appear blurred (short-sightedness). Some believe that the distinctive style of the Impressionists can be attributed to their short-sightedness, but there is little convincing evidence to support the claim. On the other hand, cataracts, which block the transmission of light through the lens, are known to have affected the work of Monet and Cassatt, while degeneration in the central retina had a major impact on the work of Degas and O'Keeffe. Although up to about one in ten artists may suffer from a deficiency in colour vision, without systematic assessment it is extremely difficult to ascribe idiosyncrasies in the artistic use of colour to deficient colour vision.

3   Art and the brain

Introduction

The outermost surface of the human brain is covered by a thin sheet of neurones called the neocortex or cerebral cortex. The sheet fits inside the skull only because of its extensive folds, rather like an umbrella furled up inside a case. The cerebral cortex is only 3 mm thick but has a total surface area of over 2 m^2 when unfolded and contains about ten thousand million (billion) brain cells. It covers the brain like the shell of a nut, or the bark of a tree (cortex means bark or shell in Latin). The cortex is larger in humans than in any other species and is thought to endow us with uniquely human attributes.

The brain is divided vertically front-to-back into two hemispheres, one on each side of the head, which are interconnected by a massive band of nerve fibres called the corpus callosum. Anatomists subdivide each half of the cerebral cortex into four lobes, named as the frontal, parietal, temporal and occipital lobes after the bones that lie above them (Figure 3.1). The frontal lobe is at the front of the head behind your forehead, and the occipital lobe is at the back. The parietal and temporal lobes occupy the territory at the side and top of your head. A key feature of the cortex is specialisation of function. Like a medieval town in which different trades gather in different neighbourhoods – spice merchants here, money lenders there – small, circumscribed regions of the cortex specialise in serving particular mental functions. About one-fifth of the cortical surface is devoted to primary sensations (vision, sound, touch, balance, smell and taste) and to movement control. The rear-most part of the occipital cortex, known as the primary visual cortex (V1), receives input from the eyes and is responsible for vision, while a narrow strip of the cortex running side-to-side over the head from ear to ear

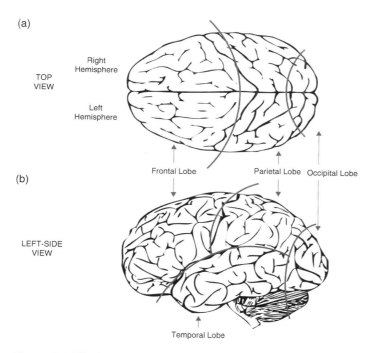

(a)

Right
Hemisphere

TOP
VIEW

Left
Hemisphere

Frontal Lobe   Parietal Lobe   Occipital Lobe

(b)

LEFT-SIDE
VIEW

Temporal Lobe

Figure 3.1 The human brain, viewed from above (a) and from the left-hand side (b). The cerebral cortex is divided anatomically into four lobes: frontal, parietal, temporal and occipital. One-fifth of the cortex is devoted to primary sensory and motor functions; the remainder is devoted to secondary or higher-level cognitive functions. All of these cortical regions play a role in art, as revealed by cases of brain damage.

receives sensory input from the body surface and mediates our perception of touch. Outside of these primary sensory areas, the remaining four-fifths of the cortex specialises in secondary cognitive functions. Research has shown that each lobe performs a specific set of tasks. The frontal lobe is essential for controlling and planning behaviour (and is the most recently evolved of the four lobes); the temporal lobe processes sounds and also specialises in visual recognition; the parietal lobe processes body sensations and is also essential for guiding selective attention to stimuli; and the occipital cortex is devoted to visual processing.

Art emerged with the human species, so one might expect that it is closely dependent on cortical function. But how close is the link between art and the brain? Visual aesthetics is abstract and ineffable; it is almost impossible to capture adequately in words. One might argue that artistic creation and appreciation are so intellectual, so complex and so remote from any specific brain function that a consideration of neural processes is irrelevant to understanding human artistic experience. On the contrary, there is an intimate relationship between brain function and visual art, as the clinical cases in this chapter reveal. Zeki (1999) argued very persuasively that art is a product of the brain and, as such, it must conform to the brain's organisational and functional principles. A truly comprehensive understanding of visual art, therefore, must incorporate an appreciation of its neural substrate. Zeki (1999) coined the term 'neuro-aesthetics' to describe the scientific study of the neural basis of visual art.

Visual information processing and art

The population of neurones that specialise in processing visual information in the human brain occupies the entire occipital cortex. Such a heavy commitment to visual processing reflects not only the importance of the sense of sight but also the complexity of the problems to be solved when trying to make sense of visual images. An effective strategy for solving a complex problem is to break it down into smaller, simpler parts that can be solved separately, either one after the other in sequence or in parallel. The cortex employs such a strategy when processing visual information. The problem of understanding a complex scene is made more manageable by separating out the different attributes of the visual scene and analysing them in different subdivisions of the visual cortex. Spatial form, colour, movement and depth are each handled by different populations of cortical neurones. The primary visual cortex or V1 is the starting point for the division of labour. The electrical activity it receives from retinal ganglion cells (see the previous chapter) carries information about all of the attributes in the visual scene. V1 sorts and sifts this activity, parcelling out signals relating to form, colour, movement and depth and distributing them to different groups of neurones. These V1 cells then send the signals to specialised areas of the secondary visual cortex in the occipital lobe. For example, an area known as V4 specialises in the analysis of colour information, while an area known as MT specialises in analysing motion.

Specialisation is a fundamental feature of cortical processing and can be found even in individual cortical neurones, which are each highly selective in terms of the visual stimuli to which they respond. For instance, a given cell may respond to red but not to other colours. Such colour-selective cells are invariably indifferent to movement. Another cell may respond only to movement in a specific direction but not to colour. Yet other cells may respond to contour orientation, regardless of colour or motion direction. Figure 3.2 illustrates the kind of processing hierarchy that is thought to produce such specialisation.

Figure 3.2(a) shows an array of photoreceptors in the retina and two ganglion cells connected to a subset of photoreceptors. The ganglion cell on the left is connected to only seven photoreceptors. Light falling on the central photoreceptor (light) excites the activity level of the ganglion cell, while light falling on the ring of photoreceptors surrounding it (dark) inhibits the activity level of the ganglion cell. Thus, the ganglion cell's output reflects a balance between central excitation and surround inhibition. Consequently, the cell does not respond to light that falls evenly across all the photoreceptors that feed it but does respond when the central photoreceptor receives more light than the surrounding photoreceptors. In other words, the ganglion cell responds best to spatial variations in illumination, or luminance contrast. The set of photoreceptors connected to the ganglion cell defines its 'receptive field', the area of retina within which light must fall for the cell to respond (either with an increase or a decrease in activity). The concentrically organised receptive fields illustrated in Figure 3.2 are known as 'centre-surround' receptive fields for obvious reasons. The ganglion cell on the left is connected to only seven photoreceptors, so its receptive field is very small. This means that the cell responds only to very fine-scale spatial detail: very thin lines or sharp edges that fill part of the small receptive field. The ganglion cell on the right has the same organisation as the one on the left but it receives inputs from many more photoreceptors (in this example, almost forty), so its receptive field covers a relatively large area of retina. It still responds best to variations in illumination because some of the photoreceptors supply excitation and others supply inhibition, but now the variation must be at a coarser scale if the ganglion cell is to respond. Notice that the best light stimulus for the left-hand receptive field would be a very small spot of light of about the same diameter as a single photoreceptor. On the other hand, the best stimulus for the right-hand receptive field would be a much larger spot covering seven or eight photoreceptors. Note that this larger spot would swamp the entire receptive field of the left-hand ganglion cell and so produce no response from it. Therefore, different ganglion cells respond best to different levels of spatial detail. The anatomy of the retina is arranged so that ganglion cell receptive fields near its centre tend to be very small, like the left-hand one in Figure 3.2, while those further out into the periphery of vision tend to be relatively large. This variation in receptive field size has fundamental consequences for visual art, which will be discussed in the next two chapters.

Ganglion cell fibres leave the eye to form the optic nerve and terminate in a large mass of cell bodies in the centre of the brain called the lateral geniculate nucleus. Signals are relayed from there to the primary visual cortex, as illustrated in Figure 3.2(b). The majority of cells in the primary visual cortex respond

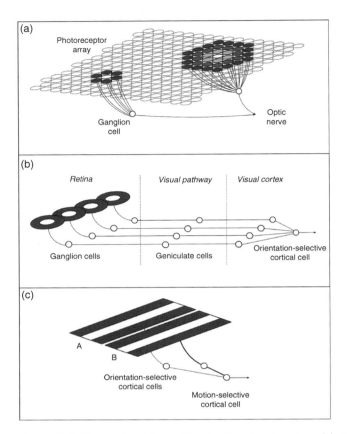

Figure 3.2 Processing hierarchies in the visual cortex. (a) Each ganglion cell receives activity from a small collection of photoreceptors, defining the cell's 'receptive field' on the retina; some of the activity is excitatory and some is inhibitory (indicated by shading). (b) Groups of ganglion cells collectively supply input to an individual cortical cell; the receptive field positions of the ganglion cells are arranged so that the cortical cell responds best to elongated contours at a specific orientation on the retina. (c) Small groups of orientation-selective cortical cells with adjacent receptive fields provide input to other cortical cells that code the movement of contours.

best to elongated contours, by virtue of the fact that the receptive field is itself elongated. The contour's orientation must match the angle of inclination of the receptive field in order to generate a strong response. Different cortical cells have different preferred orientations. In at least some cortical cells, the elongated receptive field is a consequence of the cell receiving inputs from a number of different ganglion cells, the individual receptive fields of which fall along a line on the retina, as illustrated in Figure 3.2(b) (Hubel & Wiesel, 1962). The receptive field of these relatively simple cortical cells contains zones that produce excitation (light in Figure 3.2) and zones that produce inhibition (dark in Figure 3.2), which are derived from the excitatory and inhibitory zones of the ganglion cell receptive fields that feed them. Hubel and Wiesel (1962) labelled these cells 'simple cells'. Many cortical cells have more complex preferences, because they receive inputs from several simple cortical cells. Hubel and Wiesel (1962) called these cells 'complex cells'. Complex cells are typically tuned to contours at a specific orientation, because they receive inputs from several simple cells that all prefer the same orientation and have receptive fields in nearby retinal locations. The receptive field of such a complex cell is necessarily larger than that of the individual simple cells that feed it.

Some complex cortical cells respond selectively to movement of contours in a particular direction. Selectivity for the direction of movement can arise as follows. The signals that pass between neurones along nerve fibres (the lines in Figure 3.2) travel at a specific speed known as the fibre's conduction velocity, and this velocity can vary between one nerve fibre and the next. Consider the complex motion-selective cortical cell shown in Figure 3.2(c). It receives inputs from two simple cell receptive fields, A and B. If the conduction velocity of the signal from A (thin lines) is slower than the conduction velocity of the signal from B (thick lines), then the complex cell would respond best to contours that actually move from A to B (at the appropriate speed). Such a contour first arrives at A and the signal begins its relatively slow journey to the cortical cell. In the meantime, the contour moves on and arrives at B, so triggering a second response, which also travels towards the cortical cell but catches up with the response from A because of its higher conduction velocity. The two signals therefore arrive at their destination together and combine to create a large response in the cortical cell. On the other hand, when the contour moves in the opposite direction from B to A the two signals arrive at very different times (because the signal from A occurs later and also travels more slowly), so the resultant response is very weak. Selectivity for motion detection is hard-wired into the response of many cells in the visual cortex. A range of perceptual phenomena in motion processing can be related directly to activity in these motion-selective cells; some examples of particular relevance to art will be discussed at length in Chapter 6.

Figure 3.2 illustrates how neural circuits in the cortex can create cells that respond only to specific orientations or motion directions. Other neural circuits can create cells that respond selectively to particular colours or to specific stereoscopic depths. These kinds of specialised circuits allow each cell (and entire populations of similar cells) to discard information about some visual attributes and focus on extracting the essence of other attributes. Processing of different attributes advances through the cortex both in parallel and in series. Figure 3.2(a) illustrates parallel processing: different ganglion cells process information at different spatial scales simultaneously, either fine-scale detail (left-hand cell), or relatively coarse detail (right-hand cell). Figure 3.2(b) illustrates sequential processing: circularly symmetrical ganglion cell receptive fields are combined at the next step in the sequential analysis to create an elongated, orientation-selective receptive field. Figure 3.2(c) has elements of both parallel and serial processing: different orientation-selective cells process different contour orientations in parallel (regardless of motion), but their activity also feeds forward to create motion selectivity in specialist cells.

An intriguing aspect of visual processing in the brain is that the specialist areas for processing colour, motion and so on do not converge on a single, super-ordinate 'master' area that collates and interprets their output to create a single coherent representation of the entire visual scene. Instead, each area has multiple connections with other areas. These interconnections should ensure that the representations of different visual attributes that are constructed in different areas are knitted together in a coordinated fashion. Although there is no super-ordinate area to represent the entire visual scene, cells in the temporal cortex do represent significant components of the visual scene, namely large-scale patterns and objects. A group of cells in an area of the temporal lobe called the fusiform gyrus appears to focus specifically on coding human faces (Kanwisher & Yovel, 2006). Adjacent areas of the temporal cortex contain cells that respond selectively to other kinds of complex shapes and objects. Therefore, visual information processing in the brain begins by breaking down the scene into multiple, piecemeal representations of individual visual attributes, and then constructs representations of larger shapes and objects, but does not create a single representation of the entire scene as such.

Visual art is shaped by the modular architecture of visual processing in the brain. Zeki (1999) and Livingstone (2002) argue that visual attributes that are singled out for modular processing have primacy in visual art, in the form of art that focuses on specific attributes to the exclusion of others. The accomplishment of these artworks bears witness to the parallel, modular nature of visual processing in the brain. An obvious example is the isolation of visual form information in monochrome art such as drawings, etchings and woodcuts. On the other hand, the work of the Impressionists focused on exploring colour phenomena rather than precise spatial form and detail. Other artworks appear intended specifically to tap into the human motion processing system; the Futurist art movement aimed to convey the dynamic nature of human and mechanical movement using static forms which, as later research has shown, stimulate neural motion processes in the brain (movement in art is discussed in Chapter 6).

The distinction between painterly and linear art introduced by the art historian Heinrich Wolfflin in 1915, and described in Chapter 1, seems to map onto information conveyed by different processing modules in the visual system. To recap, painterly compositions are dominated by indeterminate patches of colour and tone, often with little clear form, while linear works use clearly defined lines and edges to convey composition, rather than colour or tone alone. Painterly aspects of art may be conveyed by colour processing neurones in the brain, whereas linear characteristics may reflect the response of form processing neurones. The artist's ability to isolate these two characteristics in his or her work may have its root in the modularity of colour and form processing in the brain.

Neurones in the occipital cortex respond to raw sensory attributes such as contrast, colour, contour orientation and movement direction, without regard to the meaning of the scene or the identity of the objects in it. Meaning is represented only at higher levels of neural analysis in the temporal cortex. The potency of certain forms of modern abstract art, which one might call sensory art, depends in part on their ability to isolate and amplify the raw sensory qualities that are signalled by specific populations of neurones in the occipital cortex. Op Art and kinetic art create powerful stimuli for occipital motion processing cells (Op Art is discussed in Chapter 6); Mark Rothko's deeply saturated blocks of pure colour are ideal stimuli for colour-selective cells; Piet Mondrian's linear compositions offer ideal signals for the orientation-selective cells illustrated in Figure 3.2(c) (Zeki, 1999); and Jackson Pollock's drip paintings may refer to the statistical properties of natural textures to which occipital neurones are tuned (this idea is discussed at length in Chapter 9). Even when modern art does contain meaningful elements, in some works the artist appears deliberately to set this meaning into conflict with primitive sensory qualities and, in so doing, draws attention to the fragmented nature of visual processing, the separation between sensory qualities and meaning. The Fauvists used recognisable forms but rendered them using unnatural colours, which do seem to interfere with cortical object processing (Zeki & Marini, 1998; Plate 4 – see colour plate section). The unnaturally massive scale of Chuck Close's portrait paintings and Ron Mueck's sculpted human figures is detected and conveyed by occipital neurones but presents a challenge to our visual memory of the much more modest actual scale of human faces and bodies; early processes in the occipital cortex would assert 'this object is *huge*', while later processes in the temporal cortex assert 'no, it's a human being, it cannot be so huge'. Sheer scale alone can have a massive impact. Feelings of awe evoked by immersive art installations such as James Turrell's light works, or Miroslaw Balka's black chamber (Tate Modern, UK, 2009–2010), may derive, at least partly, from the overpowering effect that *ganzfeld* phenomena have on basic sensory responses in the brain (Avant, 1965): sudden blackness at one extreme, an all-encompassing flood of light at the other, which overwhelms the sensory cortex.

Lesions

In neuropsychology and neurology, the relationship between brain structures and their function is inferred from studying the behavioural consequences of damage. Some clinical cases involve lesions (areas of damage) caused by traumatic injuries or vascular accidents (strokes due to blockage or leakage in blood vessels); others involve neurodegenerative disease that destroys brain tissue. Different areas of the brain deal with different aspects of cognition, so the pattern of cognitive impairment that results from damage and disease depends on the specific functions performed by the affected brain tissue. Damage in one cortical area may result in an inability to produce language (known as Broca's aphasia), while damage in a different area may cause paralysis that affects a particular muscle group. Because visual processing consumes such a large area of the cortex, localised damage can produce a whole range of defects in visual perception depending on the visual tasks performed by the damaged areas. The process of creating visual art draws in many diverse areas of the brain, not just those involved in vision, and hence damage and disease can have many different consequences, which are very revealing about the links between the brain and art. This section describes the impact of lesions on visual art and the following sections consider the effects of neurodegenerative disease.

Damage to the primary visual cortex results in complete blindness in at least part of the visual field, as one might expect given its role as the sorting-house for all visual processing. The extent of blindness is proportional to the area of damage in the cortex. However, damage in secondary areas of the occipital cortex causes more subtle, highly specific losses in visual ability, which relate to the specific attribute processed in each area. The affected individual retains the ability to see, but some particular aspect of visual experience is disordered or absent entirely. The most widely reported case involving an artist centres on an individual who lost the ability to see and paint in colour following a road accident (Sacks & Wasserman, 1987), a condition known as achromatopsia.

However, this case is problematic because it has not been subjected to proper scientific scrutiny and no circumscribed area of cortical damage has been identified. However, other cases of achromatopsia have been traced to damage in the area of the occipital cortex known to specialise in colour processing (V4; Gegenfurtner, 2003). Damage in MT, on the other hand, causes a highly selective deficiency in motion perception (Zihl et al., 1991). In another less well-known case, occipital damage resulted in a condition called hemimicropsia, an apparent reduction in the size of objects presented on one side of the visual field (Cohen et al., 1994). The patient was an art teacher who had suffered a stroke. The investigators reported his problems as follows:

The patient complained, however, that objects falling in his left visual field appeared somewhat shrunk and compressed. He felt it particularly difficult to appreciate the symmetry of pictures. When drawing, he spontaneously tended to compensate for his perceptual asymmetry by drawing the left half of objects slightly larger than the right half... In a sample of six spontaneous or corrected drawings of symmetrical objects, linear measures in the left half were on the average 16% larger than the corresponding measures in the right half. The patient did not mention any anomaly of colour or movement perception, which were not further explored.

Postmortem examination following the patient's death two years later, from an unrelated illness, revealed that the stroke had destroyed a region in the lower part of his occipital cortex. Another artist who suffered a stroke in a region of the occipital cortex that borders on the temporal lobe had great difficulty in recognising images of objects and in interpreting complex visual scenes, a condition known as visual agnosia (Wapner et al., 1978). As a result of his problems with recognition, the artist's drawings would often elaborate certain details on objects and omit others (Figure 3.3). They lacked the structure and coherence that comes from a complete understanding of the visual scene.

It is important to bear in mind that these patients were otherwise entirely normal. Cognitive abilities such as language, memory and attention were unaffected, because the cortical areas responsible for these functions were spared from damage. However, they lacked some specific aspect of visual function that had dramatic consequences for the art they produced, and knowledge of the condition did not allow them to overcome the problem by force of will.

Damage in the parietal cortex, particularly on the right side, is associated with a perplexing clinical condition called unilateral neglect. The patient fails to respond to stimuli and events that are located on one side of the visual space, typically the left side, and seems to deny the very existence of that half of space. They dress one

Figure 3.3 Drawing by an artist suffering from visual agnosia. Parts of the plane are detached, or missing. (From Wapner et al., 1978.)

half of their body, sleep on one side of the bed and eat from one side of the plate. When asked to draw a flower, only petals on the right-hand side are drawn. A clock-face is rendered with all the hour numbers crowded into one side of the face. The condition is thought to result from damage to neural circuits in the parietal cortex that mediate our ability to attend selectively to specific areas of space. Unsurprisingly, unilateral neglect has dramatic consequences for art. An affected artist will frequently neglect to draw anything at all on the left-hand side of a picture. Despite years of experience and an awareness of the condition, artists find it extremely difficult to overcome the tendency to ignore one side of space. A well-known example is the artist Anton Raederscheidt (Butter, 2004), who suffered a stroke in the right parietal cortex. A sequence of self-portraits clearly indicates the difficulties he had in representing the left-hand side of his face (Figure 3.4). Detail on the left is missing or poorly structured.

Figure 3.4 Self-portraits by Anton Raederscheidt, an artist who suffered unilateral neglect following a stroke in the right parietal cortex. The paintings tend to occupy the right-hand half of the canvas, and the left-hand side of his face lacks detail and structure. (From Butter, 2004.)

Dementia

Dementia is caused by degenerative disease processes that destroy cells and neural pathways in the cerebral cortex. It is very diverse in terms of its anatomy, neuropathology and clinical manifestations. Dementia can attack all four lobes of the cortex to varying degrees and can have drastic consequences for all aspects of cognition. However, art does not rely exclusively on any one lobe, brain region or hemisphere but engages multiple areas of the brain. Thus, many artists are able to cope with some degree of damage and to maintain an acceptable level of productivity, skill and artistic quality for years after the onset of neurodegenerative disease. Nevertheless, deficits do emerge, and the pattern of deficit associated with brain damage reflects functional specialisation in the associated brain regions. It can also be revealing about the source of artistic creativity.

Alzheimer's disease

Alzheimer's disease (AD) is the most common form of dementia, causing brain cell death and shortages in the neurotransmitter chemicals that mediate the passage of information between cells. AD is a progressive disease and gradually takes over more and more of the brain. Patients show problems in memory, attention and movement coordination, as well as mood swings (depression, anger and frustration) and a tendency to become socially withdrawn. In the more advanced stages of AD, patients are incapable of looking after themselves, leading to institutionalisation.

The artist William Utermohlen was diagnosed with AD at the age of 61 years. Brain imaging showed generalised atrophy of both cerebral hemispheres. His self-portraits show a progressive loss of structure and detail. Indeed, later portraits are barely recognisable as human (Crutch et al., 2001; see Figure 3.5). On the other hand, Fornazzari (2005) studied the paintings of a professional artist after the onset of AD and found that much of her skill remained intact. Eight months prior to institutionalisation there was evident difficulty in conveying size, proportion and detail. Nevertheless, her work was still very proficient despite the marked deterioration in other cognitive abilities characteristic of AD. Rankin et al. (2007) conducted a case-controlled study of artistic production, with quantitative assessment of patients' output by a group of independent raters. Patients were asked to draw a vase of flowers, a room at home (from memory), a self-portrait using a mirror and an abstract representing

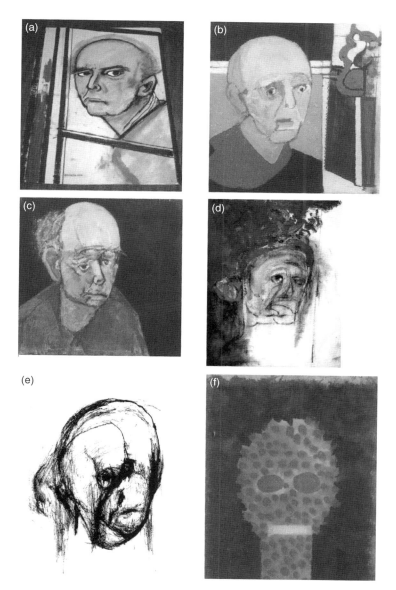

Figure 3.5 Self-portraits produced by William Utermohlen, an artist diagnosed with Alzheimer's disease at the age of 62 years. Aged (a) 60 years; (b) 62; (c) 63; (d) 64; (e) 66; (f) 65. (From Crutch et al., 2001.)

emotion. Age-matched controls also completed drawings. Raters judged the drawings for content, technique and expression. AD patients were divided into two groups on the basis of their drawings. One group resembled controls in terms of their drawing proficiency, and the other group produced work that was more simple and abstract and involved fewer colours. Their flower drawings were judged as rather bizarre. Perhaps the more severe problems observed in William Utermohlen's work arose because his disease involved generalised atrophy, whereas the patients in Rankin et al.'s (2007) study were in the early stages of AD.

Frontotemporal dementia

Another form of dementia called frontotemporal dementia (FTD) has very different consequences for art. This form of dementia affects the frontal and temporal lobes, as its name suggests, but there is little damage to the occipital cortex that serves basic visual functions. Individuals with FTD suffer from lack of self-control, an inability to plan and organise their lives and impaired speech, although they have relatively little abnormality in visual perception. Variants of FTD that particularly affect the temporal lobe are associated with heightened interest in art and greater artistic creativity in patients with little or no previous experience in art (Mendez, 2004). One case reported in the literature concerns a businessman who had no previous record of artistic output.

At age 58, he became verbally repetitive, anomic, and disinhibited. He changed clothes in public parking lots, shoplifted, and insulted strangers. He remained sensitive to light and showed heightened visual awareness to his environment. Although he had shown no previous interest in art, at 56 he began painting for the first time. (Miller et al., 1996.)

His painting style developed over the following eleven years, winning awards at art shows. His work concentrated on brightly coloured, cleanly defined shapes with hard edges. General deterioration had set in by the age of 67 years and this may be related to increasing damage to the temporal lobe.

FTD produces dramatic changes in artistic style in professional artists. One artist trained in Western art and Chinese brush painting was diagnosed with FTD at the age of 57 years (Mell et al., 2003). Initial brain scans showed moderate atrophy in the frontal lobes and mild atrophy in the temporal lobes. Her artistic style underwent dramatic change as the disease progressed. Earlier work displayed a restrained, elegant style. Later work became wilder, freer and more complex, dominated by an emotional and impressionistic style (Figure 3.6).

Rankin et al. (2007) also studied FTD patients in the case-controlled study described earlier. The work of FTD patients showed disordered composition and more facial distortion, was judged as more bizarre and involved less mark-making than that of the controls. FTD highlights aspects of art production that rely on the frontal lobes, namely planning and organisation. The drawings of

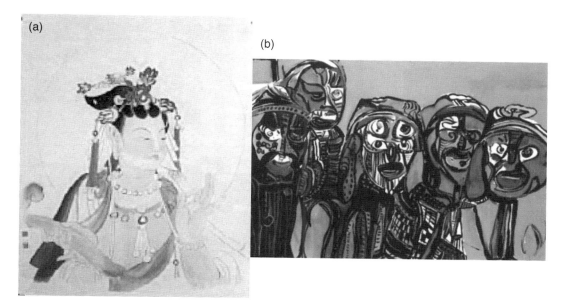

Figure 3.6 Progressive changes in style by an artist diagnosed with frontotemporal dementia. (From Mell et al., 2003.)

FTD patients show deficient organisation and an inability to convey appropriate detail and representational content, which contrasts with the milder deficits seen in AD, at least in its earliest stages.

Savant artists

Individuals with developmental disabilities sometimes possess surprising artistic skills that may shed light on the brain processes underpinning art. The rather unkind title of idiot–savant was first coined by Down in 1887 and refers to individuals with generally low cognitive and/or social abilities but some specific skills (Pring, 2005). A small number of individuals diagnosed with autism display exceptional artistic skills. Autism is a condition that affects how an individual interacts with other people and the world around them. It is a spectrum condition in which different autistic individuals share common characteristics but the particular mix and severity of characteristics varies from person to person. Autistic individuals have difficulty in understanding other people and social situations. They struggle, for example, to understand facial expressions and other non-verbal social signals. They are often socially withdrawn and uncommunicative and have a tendency to engage repeatedly in particular routines. A person with autism may also show heightened sensory sensitivity, so that loud sounds or flashing lights cause anxiety or even pain.

A small number of autistic individuals have been described as 'savant artists' because of their exceptional artistic abilities. Three individuals in particular have been studied in the literature, known as Nadia, EC and Stephen Wiltshire. Nadia was able to produce remarkable sketches of horses from the very early age of three and a half years (Selfe, 1997). Her drawing skills did not change significantly during her childhood and she gave up drawing at the age of 12 years. EC had much better language skills than Nadia but was, like her, diagnosed as autistic. He also shows remarkable drawing skills and continues to draw in adulthood. He tends to use the same background in all of his drawings and does not scale his compositions properly so that they fit onto the page. He depicts depth well, but investigations indicate that this is not due to an understanding of the rules of perspective (Mottron & Belleville, 1995). Stephen Wiltshire is particularly attracted to drawing buildings. As with Nadia and EC, he predominantly uses black and white drawings with very little use of colour, but his work is outstandingly skilful and realistic.

Savant artists do not seem to display the creativity, experimentation and development that is normally associated with artistic practice. They do show exceptional drawing skills and visual memory, but their art is lacking in abstraction and innovation. Perhaps there is a disconnection in their brains between processes that build simple visual representations of shape and contour and those that form higher level, more abstract and symbolic representations of meaning and identity. Pring (2005) describes an explanation of autism known as 'weak coherence' as follows:

The theory proposes that the normal drawing together of diverse information to construct higher-level meaning is disrupted. Instead processing, perceptual and conceptual, is piecemeal and attention to local parts occurs at the cost of attention to global, Gestalt-like processes. (Pring, 2005.)

Gordon (2005) argues that this explanation has implications for art:

Autistic artists make no assumptions about what is to be seen in their environment. They have not formed mental representations of what is significant, and consequently perceive all details as equally important. Also they do not impose visual or linguistic schema, so essential for quickly forming concepts when the information provided is incomplete. (Gordon, 2005.)

Conversely, normal-functioning individuals often have great difficulty in drawing, and this may reflect the dominance of their conceptual processing. Most people tend to draw what they know, not what they see, while the converse applies in autism. The difficulties associated with drawing are explored in greater detail in the next chapter.

Specialisation for art?

A long-standing, speculative view of the cortex is that the left hemisphere specialises in rational thought and language, while the right hemisphere specialises in artistic creativity. There is a grain of truth in the idea, because there is undoubtedly some degree of hemispheric specialisation in the brain. In particular, language is predominantly a left-hemisphere function, in both left- and right-handed individuals, while visual and spatial skills are associated with right-hemisphere processing. However, neurological case studies of art highlight the importance of interactions between the lobes that subdivide each hemisphere, rather than between the hemispheres. Communication between the frontal and temporal lobes seems to be important for regulating creative drive, as indicated by the compulsive interest in art shown by individuals with FTD (Flaherty, 2005). Recent brain imaging research highlights the importance of connections between the frontal and temporal lobes, as well as those between the left and right hemispheres (Takeuchi et al., 2010). Art is a supremely complex activity, so it should not be surprising that it engages all points of the compass, so to speak, in the brain. It requires integration of information along both front-to-back and side-to-side routes in the brain.

The case of Willem de Kooning presents a good example of the complex relationship between brain function and art. De Kooning was a leading exponent of abstract expressionism in the post-World War II era but, by his mid-70s, his artistic output had dwindled away as a result of alcoholism, poor nutrition, depression, amnesia and, at least later on, dementia (Espinel, 1996). However, after concerted effort by his family and friends during which time he abstained from alcohol, adopted a balanced diet and took daily exercise, de Kooning's artistic output resumed. He re-visited his earlier work to pick up the strands of his creative technique and, in his late 70s and early 80s, he produced hundreds of paintings. The later work was visibly different from his earlier output, more sparse, with a change in compositional complexity and colour balance. These late paintings did not meet with the critical acclaim that de Kooning's earlier work had attracted; but nevertheless they demonstrate that even a severely compromised nervous system is capable of marshalling considerable reserves of artistic creativity and energy.

Summary

Art is considered by many to be the highest form of human expression, and philosophers used to argue that higher mental capacities such as artistic appreciation occupy their own domain, entirely detached from the animal flesh and bone of the body. However, neuroscience reveals that art can no longer be considered in isolation from the brain. The cerebral cortex is responsible for all human mental activities, including those relating to art. Each cortical hemisphere, left and right, is divided anatomically into four lobes (frontal, parietal, temporal and occipital), which have distinct cognitive functions.

Specialisation of function means that damage or disease in different cortical lobes has distinct consequences for visual art. Vision occupies the entire occipital lobe, where specialisation of function extends even to individual neurones. Visual attributes such as shape, colour and movement are analysed in parallel by separate populations containing many millions of neurones. Thus, damage to the occipital lobe causes blindness or severely disordered visual perception, depending on the location and extent of tissue loss. The frontal and temporal lobes are important for planning, organising and controlling behaviour, so damage to these regions produces deficiently organised art and poorly controlled artistic impulses. The parietal lobe (particularly on the right) is responsible for selective attention; hence damage here leads to a condition in which the artist ignores the left-hand half of the world and to crowding marks on the right of the canvas.

Therefore, art is a whole-brain activity, and characteristics of visual art ranging from the raw sensory qualities of abstract paintings to a compulsion for creative expression can all be linked to the complex division of the cerebral cortex into specialised subsystems and to the interplay between them.

4 Perceiving scenes

Introduction

During the Italian Renaissance, painters acted partly as interior decorators, creating frescos, murals and easel paintings with which rich patrons decorated the rooms of their grand villas. The aim was to treat the picture frame as a window opening that offered a captivating glimpse of a realistic visual world. In order to achieve the illusion of a window, artists had to solve the problem of projecting a three-dimensional world onto a flat, two-dimensional picture plane. The problem of perspective projection was solved in the early fifteenth century by Fillipo Brunelleschi and Leon Battista Alberti. Leonardo da Vinci described the solution as follows:

Perspective is nothing else than seeing a place [or objects] behind a plane of glass, quite transparent, on the surface of which the objects behind that glass are to be drawn. These can be traced in pyramids to the point in the eye, and these pyramids are intersected on the glass plane.

Figure 4.1 illustrates Leonardo's description. The viewer's eye is positioned at O, and light rays from the top surface of the cube create a pyramid of sight with its apex at O and base defined by the points ABCD at the corners. A plane surface FGHI (Leonardo's transparent window) intersects the pyramid to form a perspective projection of the surface, abcd, as a two-dimensional image. The laws of linear perspective define the shape, size and disposition of all the elements in the scene on Leonardo's window. The image formed on Leonardo's window corresponds to the image that would be captured by a camera positioned at O (apart from the inversion caused by the camera's lens). In a sense, therefore, the aim of

Figure 4.1 Perspective projection. From the observer's viewpoint at O, the top surface of the cube (ABCD) defines a 'pyramid of sight', which intersects a transparent Leonardo window (FGHI) to create a perspective projection of the surface (abcd). (From Pirenne, 1970, Figure 7.1, page 73.)

the representational artist is to create a painting that corresponds to the perspective projection captured by a camera positioned at the eye.

In some respects the eye *is* a camera, as discussed in Chapter 2. Both eye and camera use a lens system to register an image of the visual world on a two-dimensional light-sensitive surface (in fact, cameras have a flat image surface, while the inside of the eye is curved and hence does not create an exactly equivalent image; but the central part of the ocular image does approximate a projection, which is equivalent to that in a camera). One might imagine, therefore, that the two-dimensional retinal image gives the artist a head-start in the process of creating a flat, perspective projection of the scene. However, this view is very far from the truth. As Pirenne (1970) observed, the eye is a peculiar optical instrument in that it forms an image that is not actually intended to be seen. The retinal image itself is not accessible to conscious scrutiny but merely supplies the raw material for the massively complicated brain processes that mediate our perceptions of the objects and surfaces in the scene. A tendency to conflate the retinal image with perception is at the root of a common misunderstanding, which leads to such questions as: How can we see an upright world from the inverted retinal image? Does the brain turn the image to the correct orientation? No inversion is required, because we do not see the retinal image inside the eye, we see surfaces and objects out there in the world. Even when you see a retinal after-image created by a very bright object such as a camera flash, it appears to be projected out onto a surface in the visible scene, not inside the eye.

Specialised cells in the eye convert the pattern of brightness and colour in the image into a neural code that is transmitted up the optic nerve towards the brain (as outlined in the previous chapters). The brain constructs internal representations of a stable three-dimensional world from the transitory, two-dimensional images that flicker across the retina. The representations are held as patterns of activity in the millions of neurones that make up the brain's visual system, and these patterns of activity are the objects of perceptual experience, not the retinal image. By virtue of the stability of these representations, the visual world usually appears to retain its layout and objects retain their shape, despite the dramatic changes in the retinal image that can result from a simple change in viewpoint. For instance, if you place a simple object such as a book on a table top and then walk around and away from the table to view the book from different angles, the projected shape of the book on your retina will change radically with each change of viewpoint, yet you have no problem in perceiving the same book-shaped object in every view. In fact, the different views may appear to be more similar than they really are, as discussed later. The processes by which the visual system performs this trick are largely hidden from conscious awareness (hence the confusion between images and perception). Artists therefore face a formidable problem; in order to depict a visual scene, they must undo all these sophisticated but hidden processes and try to retrieve the original two-dimensional image upon which they depend. This chapter focuses on the perceptual experiments that have gone some way towards revealing the nature of these hidden processes and so have shed some light on the methods artists use to solve the problem.

You see what you choose to see

On the basis of subjective impressions, almost everyone believes that they experience a richly detailed visual world, which is complete, accurate and persisting, indeed almost photographic. Yet it is a well-known and easily demonstrated fact in vision science that when we look at a visual scene, we actually see very little of it in any detail at all. As described in Chapter 2, the cone photoreceptors in the eye are distributed very unevenly across the retina and are packed tightly into the region that corresponds to central vision. Moreover, the receptive fields of ganglion cells vary markedly in size across the retina (see Chapter 3 and Figure 3.2 for a description of receptive fields). Receptive fields are very small in the centre of the retina but large out in the retinal periphery. The eye's ability to resolve fine spatial detail relies upon tightly packed cones and small receptive fields, so visual resolution declines rapidly with distance from the fovea, as demonstrated in Plate 11 (see colour plate section).

The left-hand image in Plate 11 shows Jan Gossaert's 'The Adoration of the Kings' (1510–1515); detail is equally sharp everywhere. The right-hand image has been blurred progressively outwards from the centre (the head of the Madonna), to simulate the progressive loss of visual acuity at locations away from a centrally fixated position, caused by unequal spacing in retinal photo-receptors and variations in receptive field size. To verify the plausibility of this manipulation, fixate the head of the Madonna in one image and then in the other; the two images should appear equally sharp. However, when you shift fixation in the right-hand image, the peripheral blur in it becomes apparent. In order to see any details of the angels or the dogs in the sharp image, one would have to shift fixation to bring the relevant area of the painting onto the fovea.

As mentioned in Chapter 2, we make eye movements three or four times in every second of the waking day. Most are rapid shifts in gaze direction called saccades ('jerks' in French), which take about one-tenth of a second to execute. Vision is suppressed while the eyes are actually moving from one position to the next. This effect is known as saccadic suppression and it minimises the retinal image smear that would otherwise be perceptible during saccades. To demonstrate saccadic suppression to yourself, stand in front of a mirror and transfer your gaze from one eye to the other; you will not be able to see your own eyes move, nor will you see any other movement in the image while your eyes are moving. If you stand in front of a friend and ask them to transfer their gaze between your eyes while you are looking at their eyes, their eye movements will be clearly visible. Saccadic eye movements are so frequent and essential because visual acuity is tightly restricted to the retinal fovea.

Restricted visual acuity need not prevent one from building a full, high-resolution representation of the entire visual scene in one's head, to which one could refer while rendering the scene on canvas. It would be a matter of knitting

Figure 4.2 The eyes could execute a series of fixations to build up a complete, high-resolution mental image of the painting in Plate 11 (see colour plate section). Each circle represents a possible fixation position, with arrows tracking the sequence of fixations.

together the scene from the individual stored snapshots provided by a series of fixations around the image (Figure 4.2). Such a strategy clearly would require a high-capacity visual memory in order to store the contents of several fixations. Cognitive psychologists have discovered the surprising and controversial fact that such a strategy is impossible, at least for humans, because we do not actually have a high-capacity, high-resolution visual memory. On the contrary,

(a)   (b)

Figure 4.3 Two views of Piazza San Marco in Venice, which are identical except for one change in part of the scene.

we hardly appear to retain anything at all from one glance to the next. One experimental technique involves presenting two images one after the other in alternation on a visual display, separated by a short interval containing a blank screen (which simulates the effect of saccadic suppression). The two images are identical except for a single change introduced by the experimenter. Typically, a scene element is deleted or displaced. If observers are capable of storing each image in visual memory, it should be a trivial task to spot the change. In fact, the change is often extremely difficult to find – so difficult that the effect is called change blindness (Resink et al., 1997). The change is much more easily spotted if it occurs in an element that is relevant to the observer's goals and expectations, or involves an element that tends to grab the attention automatically. As an illustration, Figure 4.3 shows two photographs of Piazza San Marco in Venice; see if you can spot the difference between them before reading on.

Did you notice that one image is missing the right-hand dome on the Basilica di San Marco? Now compare the intact image in Figure 4.3 with Canaletto's painting of Piazza San Marco, executed 250 years before the photograph was taken (Figure 4.4). Although Canaletto is often regarded as a painter of 'photographic' scenes, and many believe that he worked from images captured by an optical device (discussed later in the chapter), he frequently departed from strict photographic accuracy. As Venice is preserved largely intact as it was centuries ago, it is possible to check Canaletto's work against the original scene. In the case of Piazza San Marco in Figure 4.3, Canaletto made at least two significant changes. Can you spot what they are? Firstly,

Figure 4.4 A view of Piazza San Marco by Canaletto, painted c.1758. Compare it to the right-hand photograph in Figure 4.3.

notice that the campanile is taller and thinner in the painting than in reality (the original campanile collapsed in 1902, so the present structure is not the one painted by Canaletto, but it is a faithful replica). Secondly, Canaletto omitted the three flagpoles that stand in front of the Basilica, although he did include them in other works.

In change blindness research, the experimental participant is explicitly instructed to look for changes between two otherwise identical images. While it is informative about cognition, this task bears little relation to, say, life drawing or painting. Ballard et al. (1995) used an experimental protocol that is a little closer to the processes involved in life drawing or painting. The participant's task is to copy a pattern of coloured blocks presented on a computer display, using a mouse. The display is divided into three areas, as illustrated in Plate 12. The 'model' area contains the pattern to be copied, say eight blocks randomly arranged within a 4 x 3 grid. The 'resource' area contains the blocks to be used, and the 'workspace' area is where the model is to be assembled. The participant uses the computer's mouse to 'pick up' blocks from the resource area and 'drop' them onto the workspace (a familiar drag-and-drop operation for regular computer users). The instructions are to copy the pattern as quickly and accurately as possible. The experimenters recorded the participant's eye movements while they were performing the task. They found that participants completed the task in a very stereotypical way, which indicated that information about the model was acquired incrementally or just in time during the task rather than *in toto* at the outset and committed to memory. Participants frequently made more than one fixation in the model area when copying a single block. The most common sequence of fixations was: model – resource (pickup) – model – workspace (drop). The first fixation on the model presumably identified the next block to copy. Then the eyes moved to the resource area where a block was picked up. Rather than going straight to the workspace area to drop off the block, which would require a memory of where the selected block was located, the eyes first went back to the model, presumably to recover the location of the selected block. Thus, the least amount of information was committed to memory. It could be argued that not all of the fixations on the model were essential but reflect the fact that the eyes had to wait for the hand movements controlling the mouse to catch up. However, the researchers found that if participants were obliged to use memory because the display was removed after a short time, only two blocks could be copied without error.

Furthermore, in a follow-up experiment (Hayhoe et al., 1998), the researchers actually changed the colour of one or more blocks in an unworked area of the model while the eye was in the process of moving towards it. Remarkably, relatively few of these changes were noticed by the experimental participants. When *all* unworked blocks were changed at once, participants were generally more aware of the change but still greatly underestimated their extent. In most cases, the participant was aware of only one block change, whereas all seven blocks had actually changed. Generally, changes were more noticeable when they occurred during an eye movement that was mid-way through a copying operation ('2' in Plate 12) rather than just prior to the start, indicating retention of at least some information about a selected block across saccades.

The surprising results of these experiments reveal that, rather like fast-food, one's mental representation of each visual scene is made to order, just in time for immediate needs, rather than assembled beforehand and retained in its entirety as a mental 'photograph'. In the case of fast-food, just-in-time manufacture requires less storage space and ensures that the food is always fresh. Similar considerations apply in the context of natural vision. Just-in-time processing guarantees that the information is as up-to-date as possible. Furthermore, given the finite capacity of the visual pathway to process and store information and the relative stability and predictability of the real world (objects do not disappear spontaneously or change identity, except during a magician's performance or a psychology experiment), it would be wasteful to carry around high-resolution representations of previously seen parts of the scene in the brain continually. If a piece of information about the visual scene suddenly becomes important, one only needs to look at it, because it is probably still there. Other research shows that only relatively abstract, general features of the scene are usually retained, known as scene gist in the scientific literature. You may remember, for instance, the general layout of your desk and what kind of items you keep on it, but may be unable to remember the precise arrangement of the items. If you need a pen, it is a simple matter to look at the desk to find one. Similarly, you may need to look at the computer keyboard quite often while typing in order to locate specific keys, even though you have used it many times before.

Artists cannot circumvent the inherent limitations of the visual system that are revealed by these experiments and, knowingly or unknowingly, they must adopt strategies to cope with the limitations if they aim to work closely from life (or even from a photograph). The natural way to cope with limited retention of detail is to make frequent eye movements; this is the strategy spontaneously adopted by the participants in Ballard et al.'s (1995) experiment. Indeed, artists do appear to make very frequent eye movements between the visual scene and their work. Cohen (2005) found that trained artists make more frequent eye movements than non-artists when drawing from a model. Typically, they fixate for periods of 1.5 seconds. Furthermore, Cohen (2005) found that the rated accuracy of drawings produced by artists and non-artists was higher for those who made more frequent eye movements. Therefore, it seems that increasing the rate at which gaze alternates between the work and the subject can go some way towards mitigating the limited capacity of visual memory. On the other hand, strict accuracy is not always the aim in working from life. Cohen (2005) recounts the advice of two celebrated artists. Degas apparently stated that if he were to open an art school, he would locate the model and the students on separate floors so as to force them to work from memory; Ingres apparently advocated 'Never work from nature. Always from memory'. Clearly, every time artists transfer their gaze from a visual scene to their work, they must rely on memory inevitably, and its limitations can have an impact even over time-scales as short as a second or so.

You know what you see

As you move around a visual scene, the images of the objects in the scene change dramatically as your viewpoint shifts. Shapes deform as view angle changes, as described earlier in the example involving a book placed on a table top. Retinal image size shrinks as an object recedes into the distance; image size halves with each doubling of distance. Despite these gross changes, your perception of object properties remains fairly stable. People do not appear to become midgets as you watch them walk into the distance; a book does not appear to become trapezium shaped when you place it on a table. This general tendency to perceive stable object properties is called perceptual constancy and it is clearly a useful feature of the sensory systems in most circumstances. Perceptual constancy in apparent size and shape depends on information in the image that indicates depth and distance. The converging lines in Figure 4.5 indicate a gallery extending into the distance. The three statues in each image appear to be positioned at different distances from the viewer along the gallery. Consequently, the statues on the right appear to be equal in objective size despite the fact that their sizes in the image differ markedly. On the other hand, the three statues on the left appear to be very different in objective size although their image sizes are identical. Perceptual constancy mechanisms also play a part in judgements of lightness, colour and movement velocity.

Perceptual constancy, while useful for everyday vision, presents an obstacle for artists attempting to depict visual scenes. Your perception of the objects under view at any given moment does not accord faithfully with the retinal image, but tends to veer towards constancy, namely the object's true shape, size,

(a) (b)

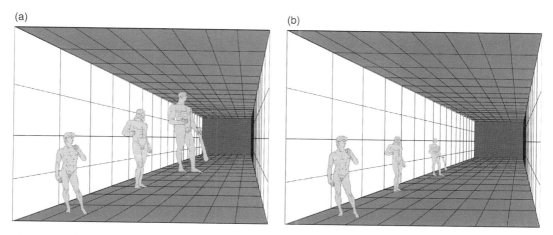

Figure 4.5 (a) The statue on the left is actually the same size in the image as the other two statues, but appears smaller. (b) The statue on the left appears the same size as the others, but is actually larger in the image.

colour and so on. When you view the book on the table top, you know that books are rectangular objects, so your perception of its shape in different views tends to be more rectangular than it actually is in the image. A classic experiment conducted in 1932 measured this effect (Thouless, 1932). Participants in the experiment viewed a flat circular disc (like a coin or plate) placed on a table top, similar to the one depicted in Figure 4.6, and were asked to match the shape of the plate as they saw it with one of a set of discs varying in circularity (as in Figure 4.6). If the observer could disregard their knowledge of the plate's shape completely, they should be able to select the correct matching disc. On the other hand, if their selection was based entirely on constancy, they would select the circular matching disc (because the plate is actually circular). Thouless (1932) allocated a score of zero to matches that were based entirely on retinal image shape and a score of 1.0 to matches based entirely on constancy. The results of the experiment showed that observers selected a shape that was intermediate between the two extreme values. The plate image was not seen as circular, but nor was its shape seen correctly. Interestingly, observers who had received artistic training tended to select discs that were closer in shape to the elliptical image than to a circle, but could not entirely overcome the tendency to base judgements on object knowledge.

More recently, several studies have investigated the link between perceptual constancy and drawing (e.g. Mitchell et al., 2005; Cohen & Jones, 2008). They found that drawings exhibit distortions that reflect perceptual constancy. In one experiment, Cohen and Jones (2008) asked participants to match the shape of a

Figure 4.6 A plate is shown in (a). Which elliptical shape in (b) matches the shape of the plate, as it appears in the image? The closest match is the fourth ellipse from the top.

window seen at an oblique angle in a photograph against outline drawings of rectangles. They found that the shape selected by participants was closer to a rectangle than it was in the image. In addition, the rated accuracy of drawings produced by the participants was correlated with the degree of constancy they showed in the matching experiment.

A further obstacle confronting artists working from life is due to the way in which the brain stores representations of objects in long-term visual memory. The act of recognition involves a process of comparison between the neural representation of an object currently in view and stored representations of known objects held in the brain. Recognition occurs when a match is found between the current representation and a stored representation. This comparison process normally occurs with no perceptible effort, or even delay, which in itself is a remarkable feat achieved by the brain. There is still some degree of scientific debate as to exactly how this highly efficient matching process is implemented in the human brain, but evidence indicates that part of it involves aligning the current view of an object with a small collection of views of that object held in memory. The memorised views of each object are few in number (perhaps six or fewer) and probably quite sketchy, but possess just enough detail for reliable matching. For any given object, the views held in memory are thought to be just sufficient for any other possible view to be considered as a combination of two stored views. For example, the stored views of a given house might include a frontal view and a side view, so any oblique view would be recognised on the basis that it contains elements of both the frontal view and the side view. A number of studies have investigated which views of particular objects seem to be selected for storage in the brain. One experimental technique involves measuring precisely how long it takes a participant to name a particular object seen in a photograph. Palmer et al. (1981) found that certain views of objects support faster recognition times than other views, indicating that those views may be closer to the stored views for those objects. They also found that the faster views corresponded to those rated as being the most prototypical or 'canonical' view of each object as judged by participants in other experiments. Horses and cars, for example, are recognised most easily in three-quarter views, while clocks are recognised best from straight on and the best view of a teapot is a side view. It is plausible to suppose that artistic depictions of objects might reflect the structure of visual memory. When selecting a composition in a still life, for instance, the artist may tend to position objects so that they are aligned with their most prototypical views. When drawing from memory, artists may tend to draw prototypical views. In the act of drawing a particular object from life, the artist may distort the drawing unwittingly so that it accords more closely with a prototypical view than the object before them actually does. There is relatively little experimental evidence bearing on these suppositions, but there is a small amount of evidence that observational drawings of an object from a specific viewpoint may be biased towards a viewpoint that corresponds to the artist's internal canonical representation of the object (Picard & Durand, 2005; Matthews & Adams, 2008). Matthews and Adams (2008) asked experimental participants to draw a cylinder from memory, as a way of accessing the participants' canonical view of this object, and then asked them to draw one from observation of an actual cylinder. They found that each observational drawing was influenced by the observer's preferred canonical view of the object.

Overcoming object knowledge

Constancy and canonical view effects demonstrate that visual impressions tend to be a compromise between the information present in the retinal image and stored knowledge of the objects under view. As the artist and critic Patrick Heron acutely observed in 1955, artists are not immune from the intrusion of object knowledge into mark-making:

The naturalistic painter, directing his gaze into the amorphous, vibrating, rainbow-coloured masses of the natural scene, waits until his mind, sorting out the wild chaotic rush of visual sense data, has found a rough blueprint of the particular scene confronting him among the vast collection of remembered pictures which, like any other painter, he stores in a sort of cerebral reference library. When from this private collection he has extracted a 'naturalistic' tree that roughly corresponds with the palpating mass of multi-coloured dots that he in fact is seeing before him, the naturalistic painter begins the process which the unwary might have called 'copying the scene in front of him', but which I will describe as the process of taking an interior, subjective image from his cerebral library and imposing it upon the external image which his eye transmits to him. (Gooding, 1998, p. 41.)

Traditional exercises such as drawing from upside-down views or mirror images help to break the link between the image and stored knowledge, and so prompt the artist to rely on purely pictorial information in the image (object recognition is known to be impaired using inverted views of objects; Jolicoeur, 1985). Research on perceptual constancy also suggests that constancy takes a short time to build up. Constancy estimates based on Thouless' (1932) matching technique showed less constancy when participants were allowed only a very brief view of the object (Leibowitz & Bourne, 1956). Hence, the frequent eye movements made necessary by the limitations of short-term visual memory discussed earlier may also help to diminish the intrusion of constancy effects as well.

A simple, traditional way to avoid distortions introduced by object knowledge is to measure the relative sizes of different elements in the scene using a thumb pressed against a pen or brush held at arm's length. The measured relative sizes of the elements are then transferred to the artwork. Alberti himself described a more sophisticated mechanical aid which took the form of a grid stretched across a window, through which the artist could view the scene and then transfer it square-by-square onto a corresponding grid drawn on a canvas. Grids of this kind are still used commonly by artists, especially when they are working from photographs. The American photorealist artist Chuck Close uses such a system to create startlingly realistic, gigantic portraits from photographs of his subjects.

The Dutch painter Johannes Vermeer is also celebrated for the photographic quality of his paintings, although they were executed over 200 years before the advent of photography. Vermeer was widely admired during his lifetime, but only thirty or so surviving paintings have been attributed to him. The majority are small paintings of interior scenes containing up to three human figures. An example is shown in Plate 13 ('Young Woman Standing at a Virginal'). Despite a lack of documentary evidence, many believe that Vermeer used a device known as a camera obscura (*camera obscura* means dark room in Latin) as an aid to create his realistic interiors. The camera obscura is a precursor to the modern camera. It is a chamber with a small opening on one side by means of which an image of the outside world is projected onto the opposite wall. A simple camera obscura contains only a pin-hole opening, while more sophisticated devices employ a lens. Such devices were available during Vermeer's lifetime, although their main practical purpose was to observe solar eclipses in safety. Provided that it was large enough, however, an artist could use a camera obscura to trace out the image projected onto its interior wall, or even paint directly from the projected image. How strong is the evidence that Vermeer used a camera obscura? Steadman (2001) reconstructed the three-dimensional geometry of the rooms depicted in eleven of Vermeer's interiors by working backwards from the two-dimensional image in each painting (certain assumptions were required, such as that the rooms, windows and furniture were rectangular). He found that recognisable pieces of furniture, which appear in several paintings, remained constant in estimated size. The pattern of floor tiles across large areas interrupted by figures or furniture is also precisely correct and consistent. Indeed, Steadman's (2001) measurements point to the use of the same room in a number of different paintings. Steadman went further and created real three-dimensional reconstructions of the room. He calculated the precise location and size of the projected image that Vermeer would have used in each painting and found that, in each case, it agreed almost exactly with the actual size of the painting. Thus, the evidence for Vermeer's use of a camera obscura is convincing.

Vermeer is by no means the only artist to have been linked with the use of optical devices. Canaletto is also widely thought to have used a camera obscura to create his almost photorealist images of Venice (Kemp, 1990). However, as you saw in Figure 4.4, Canaletto departed from strict pictorial accuracy in many of his paintings and, in some cases, the use of an optical device would have been out of the question because of the viewpoint (in some paintings it is in the middle of the Grand Canal). Canaletto was trained as a theatrical scenery painter, so he probably knew a great deal about creating accurate perspective projections without the aid of a device. Nevertheless, detailed examination of some paintings does indicate use of a camera obscura (Bomford & Finaldi, 1998). Tantalisingly, the Museo Correr in Venice holds a camera obscura bearing his name, but its provenance is uncertain.

The artist David Hockney believes that from the fifteenth century onwards many artists have used optical devices such as the camera obscura, in fact many more than have been acknowledged previously, including Caravaggio and Velasquez (Hockney, 2001). Optical devices create living projections from which artists can produce drawings and paintings. There is little documented evidence because, he argues, artists are inclined to be quite secretive about their working methods. There is also some reluctance to discuss the use of optical devices, because of feelings that it would constitute 'cheating'. Hockney rejects this accusation as follows:

Let me say here that optics do not make marks, only the artist's hand can do that, and it requires great skill. (p. 14.)

The artist must necessarily first select a viewpoint and a composition, even when using an optical device. Then the selection of marks to make from the image requires consummate skill. The image formed by a camera obscura has an almost paradoxical appearance to a modern eye. It is obviously a flat, two-dimensional projection like that on a flat-screen display but there is no pixellation, no perceptible limit to its resolution. The raw material, so to speak, is of supremely high quality and presents the artist with an overwhelming choice of marks to make; it is only the departure point for the artist's journey.

The evident need for such devices through the ages reinforces the main thesis of this chapter, that the inherent properties of the human visual system, as revealed by scientific studies, present the artist with a formidable challenge when he or she sets out to create a representational depiction of a natural scene. This is the real motivation behind aids such as the camera obscura or the Alberti grid, rather than 'cheating' or 'laziness'.

Summary

The overview of visual processing in the brain presented in the previous chapter described how the cerebral cortex breaks the visual scene down into basic sensory attributes, such as form and colour, and then constructs representations of individual shapes and objects. As far as we know, there is no single area of the brain that puts all of the information back together to build a single internal representation of the entire visual scene. This chapter has concentrated on the psychological consequences of this neural architecture, particularly in relation to art. The lack of a whole-scene representation in the brain means artists and viewers of art retain only piecemeal impressions of the visual world, dominated by individual objects and their relatively stable properties. Detail is sharp only close to fixation and, once the eyes have moved away from a point in the scene, very little information about that region is retained in memory. Moreover, perceptual judgements of properties such as size, shape and colour amount to a compromise between the information available in the scene and our stored knowledge of constant object properties. These limitations in perceptual processing can be mitigated by making frequent eye movements to overcome memory limitations and by the use of aids that measure scene geometry and shape to avoid the intrusion of perceptual constancy into the proportions transferred to the picture.

5   Perceiving pictures

Introduction

Assume, as we did at the beginning of the previous chapter, that the aim of the artist is to create a representational painting, which is as close as possible to the light distribution that would be sent to the viewer by the scene itself; a window onto a virtual scene. Even though the artist may be able to use detailed knowledge of perspective projection and optical devices such as the camera obscura, in every case the painting will fall short of an exact facsimile. Instead, it will be a resemblance or approximation to the scene itself. The viewer is almost always aware of the perceptual characteristics of the picture as a flat surface in itself, such as its shape, size and position. The information carried in a picture is also lacking in several important respects, even when the picture is a photograph captured by the highest resolution camera available today or a painting faithfully copied from such a photograph. Natural objects and surfaces have an inherent spatial scale, which we apprehend when we view real scenes. Redwood trees appear massively tall, while the intricate pattern of lichen growing on a rock surface appears tiny. Pictures of objects and surfaces, on the other hand, can be any size; information about absolute scale is lost. In a closely cropped photograph, it may be impossible to distinguish between small ripples in sand, as seen at one's feet when standing on a beach, and massive sandbanks viewed from an aeroplane. We are able to appreciate absolute scale in real scenes because they have three spatial dimensions (width, height and depth), which carry information about absolute distance. When one's gaze shifts between real objects, the lens of the eye adjusts its focus to maintain a sharp image (accommodation, described in Chapter 2) and the two eyes alter their convergence angle so that both are directed at the same object. Changes in focus and convergence angle are brought about by muscles inside the eye itself (which control focus) or those attaching the eye to its socket (which control convergence). Sensory information about the state of tension in these muscles provides the visual system with information about absolute depth, which can be used in judgements of absolute size. For example, a car does not appear to shrink in size as we watch it move into the distance, even though its retinal image size halves with each doubling of distance. Changes in accommodation and convergence indicate the change in distance and exactly compensate for changes in the size of the car's retinal image, so the car appears to remain the same objective size. Pictures, on the other hand, have only two dimensions (width and height); the eyes do not have to adjust their focus or convergence angle as the gaze shifts between objects in the picture, regardless of their depicted depth. Hence, there is no information in the picture that can be used to establish absolute scale with any degree of precision, although recognisable objects in the scene can give an indication of it. Some information in a picture is undeniably informative about the *relative* depths in the scene, such as lines of convergence and changes in relative size, but none of these so-called pictorial cues can specify *absolute* depth and distance. Moreover, any perspective information that is present in the picture will be correct only if the painting is viewed from the correct distance and angle. All other viewing positions introduce distortion.

Plate 14 (see colour plate section), for example, shows an imaginary view of Saint Jerome in his study, by Antonello Da Messina. It is very carefully composed to create the impression that one is viewing a real three-dimensional scene through an archway in the plane of the picture. The centre of projection is a point midway between Saint Jerome's head and the book he is reading. All lines receding in depth, such as those defining his bookcase and the tiles on the floor, radiate from this point, the focal point of the work both conceptually and optically. The visual image formed in your eye while viewing the painting will be optically correct only when you stand directly opposite the focal point, at the appropriate height and distance. All other viewing positions introduce distortion. When you view the painting from an oblique position, slightly to one side or below, for example, the projection lines in it change in accordance with their disposition on a flat surface (the painting), not in accordance with their position in the depicted scene. To illustrate this point, Figure 5.1 (top) shows a perspective projection of a box, such as would be produced either by viewing a real box or by viewing a picture of it from the correct position (a projection on a Leonardo window; see Figure 4.1). The middle image in Figure 5.1 shows a view of the

Figure 5.1 (a) A view of a box (either a real box viewed through a window aperture, or a picture of a box within a frame). (b) An oblique view of a real box through a window aperture. (c) An oblique view of a picture of a box within a frame.

same real box from a slightly oblique angle, in which one of the sides becomes visible. The bottom image shows a correspondingly oblique view of the *picture* of the box. Obviously the oblique view of the picture cannot reveal any more of the box but, instead, distorts the original view in accordance with its projection on a flat picture surface. Similar distortions of projected shape would occur in the painting of 'Saint Jerome in his Study' (Plate 14) when it is viewed from an oblique angle.

Even the most carefully rendered paintings are thus only approximations to real three-dimensional natural scenes (setting aside dynamic properties, which are discussed in the next chapter). Yet the artifice so carefully created by masters such as Antonello Da Messina is rather tolerant of shifts in viewing position and changes in picture size. It does not collapse as soon as one views the painting from the 'wrong' position. Therefore, one might justifiably ask how this is possible. Why are pictures so effective as depictions of real scenes? One answer lies in perceptual apparatus that serves depth perception.

Visual cues in pictures

Antonello Da Messina's 'Saint Jerome in his Study' (Plate 14) is, actually, quite small, measuring 46 cm by 36 cm. The figure of Saint Jerome is approximately 10 cm tall in the painting. If one views the painting in the National Gallery from a typical distance of a metre or so, the projected size of Saint Jerome at the retina of the eye is consistent with viewing a person of average stature from a distance of about 18 m. Yet we do not perceive Saint Jerome as paradoxically small (as a result of our estimation of the viewing distance to the painting), probably because of limitations in the available information about depth in natural images. As indicated earlier, there are a number of visual and non-visual 'cues' that carry information about depth, including perspective lines, retinal size and muscle tension (for accommodation and convergence), but all of these cues operate effectively only over a limited range of distances. Consider the visual size cue just mentioned. Objects that are relatively small in the image are often farther away than objects that are relatively large; thus, other things being equal, smaller objects in the image tend to be further away. But the variation in projected size with viewing distance is highly non-linear. Figure 5.2 shows the projected retinal size of the image of a soccer ball as a function of the ball's distance from your eye. When the ball is relatively close, a small change in distance produces a large change in retinal size, but when it is relatively far

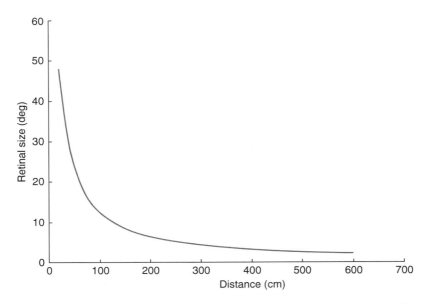

Figure 5.2 Graph showing the variation in the projected image size of a soccer ball at the retina, as a function of its distance from the eye. Most of the variation in image size is confined to distances of less than three metres.

away, an equivalent linear change in distance produces very little change in projected size (the line flattens out at longer distances). In fact, beyond a distance of just a few metres, size variation offers relatively little clue about distance; distance scaling begins to break down. All of the other cues to distance, both visual and non-visual, including stereoscopic information (slight differences between the images in the two eyes) and information from the eye muscles (signalling eye convergence and accommodation), are similarly restricted in their utility to distances within a few metres (Mather, 2009). All we can say is that very distant objects such as mountains that project large retinal images must be relatively large compared to distant objects that project small images, such as houses. Therefore, we are actually quite limited in our ability to judge depth and distance accurately, at least for relatively distant objects. Consider, for example, a tree viewed in the distance. It usually looks quite flat; its width is very apparent but there is little or no impression of front-to-back depth. Most trees are, actually, as deep as they are wide, of course, but we do not perceive them as such due to the limitations of depth perception at a distance. Thus, a flat tree in a picture looks perfectly acceptable.

There is another complicating factor in the use of visual and non-visual cues to judge depth and distance. Different cues vary in their availability and reliability, so no one cue can be relied upon totally. For example, the availability of relative size and perspective information depends on the presence of similar shapes or textures at different distances, such as a line of trees, or a river meandering into the distance, but natural scenes sometimes do not contain these features. A seascape or desert scene, for instance, would contain little of either. To cope with this unpredictability, the visual system seems to be quite flexible in its use of cues, using whatever is available and giving priority to different cues on the basis of their consistency in the scene. Therefore, perception of pictorial qualities such as size and distance is based on interpreting a combination of different cues, which vary in their reliability (Watt et al., 2005). One could argue that we accept the inaccuracies or distortions present in pictures because, provided that they are not too extreme, they are within the range of tolerances that we allow for cue use in natural scenes. The brain processes that achieve perceptual constancy (discussed in the previous chapter) should also tend to cancel out the picture distortion produced by different viewpoints (Vishwanath et al., 2005), and our sketchy visual memory for scene detail also militates against the detection of distortions (discussed further below).

A more extreme view of picture perception argues that pictures are entirely different in kind from natural images and we must learn to 'read' them in the same way that we learn to read written language. Letters and words are arbitrary visual symbols or signifiers for concepts or objects and, in order to read, we must learn the association between the signifiers and the objects. Perhaps pictures too contain arbitrary visual signifiers that we learn to interpret in order to become able to read a picture, or become 'pictorially competent'. Such a view was popular in the middle of the last century, largely inspired by research into the influence of culture on picture perception. The next section evaluates the evidence for cultural transmission of pictorial competence.

Pictures and culture

Scottish missionaries to Africa during the 1800s returned with anecdotal reports that 'natives' were unable to recognise the content of pictures, and these reports led to the view that pictorial competence is culturally transmitted (Deregowski, 1989). Members of cultures that lack pictorial representations such as rural tribes in Africa, it was argued, lack the ability to perceive pictures. There have been relatively few systematic studies of picture perception in non-Western,

Figure 5.3 One of seven pictures used in Hudson's (1960) test of pictorial competence.

rural cultures. The most widely known studies were conducted in the 1960s. Hudson (1960) developed a test of pictorial competence based on simple line drawings such as that depicted in Figure 5.3. Participants were shown each drawing and asked a series of questions such as: What do you see? What is the man doing? Which is nearer the man, the elephant or the antelope? Hudson categorised responses according to whether they displayed an acceptable aware-ness of the three-dimensional relationships in the scene depicted in the drawing. He administered the test to several groups of participants in South Africa and reported that participants who had undergone formal schooling gave more three-dimensional responses than 'unschooled' participants. He concluded that cultural isolation from pictorial representations prevented the development of pictorial competence. Although Hudson's (1960) results are widely cited, the research has significant flaws. Later work failed to replicate some of Hudson's results and also found that participants' responses were heavily influenced by experimental instructions (Jahoda & McGurk, 1974; Hagen & Jones, 1978). Bias effects are very well known in experimental psychology. In the famous case of Clever Hans, a horse was initially claimed to be able to solve simple arithmetic problems by tapping out the answer with his hoof. It transpired that the horse was responding to involuntary cues in the body language of his trainer, who was unaware that he was providing them. Hudson's methodology was based on interpreting face-to-face verbal answers to open-ended questions and it is impossible to rule out bias effects. Two other aspects of Hudson's methodology weaken his evidence for cultural transmission of picture perception. Firstly, Hudson's questions presup-pose that the participant *can* interpret the picture, otherwise it would make no sense to ask about the man, the elephant or the antelope. Secondly, Hagen &

Jones (1978) found that 30% of educated Scots did not give acceptable three-dimensional responses to Hudson's pictures, indicating that the pictures or the questions or both were ambiguous and difficult to interpret even for highly competent viewers. Other studies purporting to show culturally mediated differences in susceptibility to visual illusions (Allport & Pettigrew, 1957; Segall et al., 1963) are similarly contaminated by possible bias effects.

Despite the problems with some cross-cultural studies, there is a convincing case to be made for cultural transmission of one aspect of pictorial competence. Anecdotal reports from missionaries described how 'natives' felt the paper on which the picture was presented, as well as sniffed, crumpled and tasted it. Paper itself was clearly a novel material. A report of a slide show in Uganda in 1904 runs as follows:

When all the people were quietly seated, the first picture flashed on the sheet was that of an elephant. The wildest excitement immediately prevailed, many of the people jumping up and shouting, fearing the beast must be alive, while those nearest to the sheet sprang up and fled. The chief himself crept stealthily forward and peeped behind the sheet to see if the animal had a body, and when he discovered that the animal's body was only the thickness of the sheet, a great roar broke the stillness of the night. (Quoted in Deregowski, 1989.)

Individuals lacking previous exposure to pictures may actually be able to make sense of the content of a picture, but they may fail to recognise the difference between an object and a depiction of the object. Experience may be necessary before this aspect of pictorial competence can emerge, as shown by studies of human infants.

The development of pictorial competence

In a brave experiment two American psychologists, Julian Hochberg and Virginia Brooks, decided to use their own infant to test whether pictorial competence is a learned ability (Hochberg & Brooks, 1961). They intended to raise the infant from birth without exposure to any pictorial representations and then, in a test phase, to assess his ability to interpret pictures. They reported that:

The constant vigilance and improvisation required of the parents proved to be a considerable chore from the start – further research of this kind should not be undertaken lightly. By 19 months of age, the child began actively to seek pictures, and continuation of the restraints became both pediatrically and methodologically undesirable. (p. 626.)

The child had previously learnt the names of many common objects by direct experience of them. Upon testing, spontaneous verbal responses to pictures of the objects were recorded and then transcribed by independent judges. The child's responses to line drawings were perfectly accurate on his first exposure.

Other studies of human infants have found that picture perception does not require learning. Three-month-old infants who have never seen a photograph of their mother before look at it longer than at a stranger's photograph (Barrera & Maurer, 1981). A study by DeLoache et al. (1998) addressed the question of whether infants can distinguish between objects and depictions of objects. Nine-month-old infants tended to explore pictures manually as if expecting them to be real, attempting to feel, rub, pat or grasp the depicted objects. As in the earlier anecdotal cross-cultural research, it seems that experience is not required to make sense of the picture, but is required in order to learn the difference between an object and its depiction. Research on animals such as apes and sheep also finds that they can interpret pictures appropriately without prior experience, but may show a tendency to confuse depictions of objects with the objects themselves (Davenport & Rogers, 1971; Vandenheede & Bouissou, 1994).

Limitations of scene perception

On the whole, research shows that we perceive pictures in the same way that we perceive real scenes; we do not read pictures like we read words. Pictures are interpreted on the basis of the same cues that are used to interpret natural visual images, not on the basis of arbitrary, learned associations. Flexibility in the use of visual cues is essential when interpreting natural scenes, due to the fluctuating availability and reliability of those cues, and this flexibility gives the visual system the latitude to cope with the paradoxes and inconsistencies that occasionally arise in pictures. There is another quirk of the visual system that has an impact on the viewer's perception of an artwork. Plates 15 and 16 illustrate the point well.

At first sight, there may appear to be nothing untoward in the paintings, but all bear closer inspection. Consider the lighting in Domenico Beccafumi's 'The Story of Papirius' (Plate 15). The angle of the shadows cast by the figures in the foreground indicates a light source slightly behind the viewer. However, the shading of the distant reconstruction of ancient Rome, and in the sky, indicates a light source in the far distance. There is a global inconsistency in the lighting, which is not immediately obvious on casual viewing. Careful inspection of other paintings reveals that such an inconsistency in the use of shadows is by no means unique to Beccafumi (Cavanagh, 2005).

One might argue that inconsistencies in painted shadows are not usually apparent because the visual system pays little heed to shadows. It is true that shadows can be omitted almost entirely without destroying the meaning of a picture, as can be seen, for example, in Giovanni Bellini's 'The Blood of the Redeemer' (Plate 1), Andre Derain's 'Barges on the Thames' (Plate 4) and many of Paul Gauguin's paintings. However, the visual system is very flexible in its use of information about shadows, because they vary so much in natural conditions. When present, shadows can have a definitive impact on scene interpretation, as the images in Figure 5.4 demonstrate. The top part of the figure shows two views of a shaded disc against a marbled background. Shading gives the disc the appearance of a sphere lit from high on the left. The position of the disc relative to the background texture is identical in the two views. However, the dark ellipse in each view is seen as a cast shadow, which leads to an impression that the left-hand sphere rests on the marbled surface while the right-hand sphere hovers above it. The bottom part of Figure 5.4 again shows two shaded discs. The only difference between the two discs is in the direction of

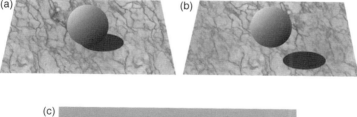

Figure 5.4 Examples illustrating the importance of shadows in visual perception. (a) The shaded disc seems to hover above the surface while in (b) the disc appears to rest on it, due to the difference in cast shadows. (c) The direction of shading alters perceived convexity.

shading. The left-hand disc shades from bright to dark from top-left to bottom-right, while the right-hand disc shades from dark to bright. The left-hand disc is seen usually as a convexity (a bump) while the right-hand disc is seen as a concavity (a hollow), even though the shading information is, actually, ambiguous and could support either interpretation (if you turn the page upside-down, your interpretations of the two discs will probably swap over). The visual system's interpretation of shading seems to be driven by an implicit assumption that any light source is usually above objects in the scene rather than below them. Hence, shading can play a significant role in shape and scene perception, even though global inconsistencies in shading of the kind displayed in Plate 15 are not readily perceived (Ostrovsky et al., 2005).

Turning to Rogier van der Weyden's 'The Exhumation of Saint Hubert' (Plate 16, top), here the global inconsistency is in other depth cues. Perspective lines in different parts of the painting converge on different points. Compare, for example, the perspective in the floor tiles with that in the altar. Notice also the variation in the size of the heads of the figures, which bears little relation to their relative depth in the scene. Faults in perspective projection often go unnoticed unless they are gross errors. Indeed, close inspection reveals inconsistencies in many masterpieces (Cavanagh, 2005; Mamassian, 2008). Kemp (1990) and Hockney (2001) describe a number of other examples of paintings that contain multiple vanishing points, such as Van Eyck's Ghent Alterpiece. David Hockney describes such a painting as a multi-perspective window. Different parts of the painting present different perspectives on the scene. Each human figure is seen straight on, regardless of where they are in the scene. There are differences in scale, such as figure stature, which pay no regard to location in the scene. Everything is seen in close-up, against the picture plane rather than located realistically in a three-dimensional space.

Even when a painting obeys the rules of perspective in having correct vanishing points, departures from geometric accuracy may be present but are largely unnoticed. Joachim Beuckelaer's 'The Four Elements: Fire' (Plate 16, bottom) offers an unusual, extreme wide-angle perspective on an interior scene. The front-to-back lines in the scene (the window frame and the floor tiles, for example) converge accurately on a vanishing point just to the left of the picture in the open door at the back. Such a wide-angle view should distort the shapes of all the objects in the scene, including the people, carcasses, plates and jugs. Circular objects, for instance, would project as ellipses in the image, with the major axis pointing towards the vanishing point. However, the objects in Beuckelaer's scene are rendered with little or no distortion. Yet the disparity between the distorted room and the undistorted objects within it is only mildly disconcerting.

Why are inconsistencies in paintings so difficult to spot? Experimental evidence discussed in the previous chapter shows that visual memory is very restricted. Little visual detail is normally retained from one glance to the next. Instead, the visual system retains an abstract representation of the gist of the scene. This processing strategy is highly efficient but presents the working artist with a challenge, as the previous chapter discussed. It also impacts on our perception of artworks and explains why global inconsistencies of the kind evident in Plates 15 and 16 often go unnoticed by viewers. If the viewer does not retain a single visual impression of the whole scene, they do not have the means by which to detect global inconsistencies, which only become apparent upon careful, serial inspection of small parts of the scene. These inconsistencies do not, of course, exist in real natural images, so there is no need for the visual system to be sensitive to them. The artist, therefore, can afford to ignore certain rules about shading and depth, if that suits his or her purpose in the composition. Indeed the use of Hockney's multi-perspective composition by an artist may be a tacit acknowledgement of the very localised nature of visual experience. As the eyes move about the painting, they arrive at different viewpoints. The scene is not apprehended as a whole, but as one view at a time dictated by the pattern of eye movements.

Visitors to art galleries either glance briefly at an individual artwork before moving on to another immediately, or stop and spend time with it. Research indicates that a brief glance allows the viewer to establish the gist of the scene and no more (Locher et al., 2007). More prolonged scrutiny, as advocated by art historians, is the only way to pick up subtleties in the composition and any liberties that the artist may have taken with the laws of optics.

Reflections

In mirror reflections you see something which is not where it seems to be, a kind of virtual reality. Of course, all representational paintings contain a virtual reality, a visual scene that is not really there. Paintings that include mirrors contain a second order of virtual reality, namely a painted reflection (Jonathan Miller, 1998). Close study of the visual impression created by painted reflections reveals some surprising facets of perception. Turn to the plates and have a look at

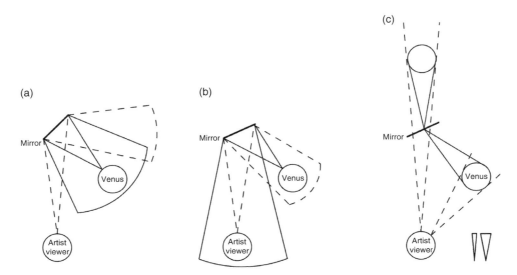

Figure 5.5 Geometry of the mirror reflection in the Rokeby Venus (Plate 5). (See the text for details.)

Velasquez's Venus (Plate 5), commonly known as the Rokeby Venus. How would you describe the scene in this painting? Most viewers would say that Venus is gazing at her reflection in the mirror (Bertamini et al., 2003). Mirrors are often used in this way in visual media (paintings, film, television, theatre) to portray the actor in the scene gazing at his reflection. However, it would be physically impossible for the viewer to see the actor's face in the mirror at the same time that the actor can see his own reflection. Figure 5.5 shows why this is so. The left-hand drawing (a) is a schematic plan view of the scene depicted in the Rokeby Venus. One circle represents the position of the viewer's head, a second circle represents the position of Venus' head and a short, thick black line represents the mirror. The mirror is arranged so that Venus' view in the mirror (thin, solid black lines) includes her own reflection. The viewer is positioned to the left of Venus and, therefore, cannot see Venus in the mirror, but sees only the parts of the scene to her right (thin dashed lines). In the middle drawing (b), the mirror has been rotated to allow the viewer to see Venus in the mirror; Venus, of course, now sees the viewer in the mirror, not herself. Thus, the common interpretation that Venus is gazing at herself in the Rokeby Venus is erroneous. Bertamini et al. (2003) call this common misunderstanding of mirror reflections the Venus effect, for obvious reasons. Jonathan Miller (1998) studied about forty paintings that contain mirrors and Bertamini et al. (2003) contend that over one-third of them incorporate the Venus effect. However, Miller (1998) notes that in Velasquez's masterpiece, Venus is knowingly looking out at the viewer, not at herself:

Velasquez's Venus, who is often described as looking at herself, is more disconcertingly looking at us, enigmatically contemplating the reflected spectacle of someone revelling in a beauty such as hers. (p. 162.)

Other examples in Miller's (1998) book unequivocally exploit the Venus effect, because the mirror appears to be angled towards the subject of the painting, as though they were looking at their own reflection, yet the viewer can see the subject's face in the painted reflection.

The Rokeby Venus (Plate 5) contains another distortion that you may have missed. Consider the size of Venus' head in the painting. The reflection of the head is painted as the same size as the head itself, but this equality would be impossible in a real scene. The right-hand drawing (c) in Figure 5.5 explains why. Again one circle represents the position of the viewer's head and another represents the position of Venus' head. This time there is also a third circle (top) representing the projected position of Venus' head as seen in the reflection visible to the viewer. Notice that the projected distance of the reflected head is over twice as far as the distance to the head itself, from the viewer's position. Consequently, from the viewer's perspective, the head seen in the mirror should be half the size of the head seen directly. The two small triangles in the bottom-right of the drawing show the projected angular subtense at the viewer's eye of the reflection (left) and the head itself (right). The gross scaling error is not usually noticed.

Reflections in many paintings include other errors: extraneous items that should not be visible or omitted items that should be visible (Cavanagh et al., 2008). Research indicates that most people seem to have a relatively poor grasp of the optical properties of reflections. Many people greatly overestimate what should be visible in a mirror from specific vantage points (Croucher et al., 2002). Most viewers find painted mirrors quite convincing, despite the many inaccuracies that frequently are present. Why should this be so? The natural environment in which humans evolved contains very few perfectly flat, reflective surfaces. Furthermore, the factors governing the content of a reflected image are often difficult or impossible to specify; the precise angle of inclination of the mirror relative to the viewer is impossible to determine if one cannot see its edges; and objects may be visible in the mirror that are not visible by direct line of sight. Thus, the visual system has little choice but to be quite tolerant of mirror reflections. Artists, therefore, have considerable licence to depart from strict fidelity in their depiction of mirrors, as you have seen in the Rokeby Venus.

Figure 5.6 'Saint Michael Triumphant over the Devil', Bartolome Bermejo, 1468.

Reflections also tell us about surface properties. Lustre, for example, is the gleam seen on the polished surface of opaque bodies such as metal bowls and armour. The lustre on relatively flat surfaces may actually contain a recognisable reflection. In Bartolome Bermejo's 'Saint Michael Triumphant over the Devil' (Figure 5.6), a miniature reflection of the Heavenly City is responsible for the metallic lustre of the Saint's breastplate. The lustre is immediately apparent, although the content of the reflection itself often goes unnoticed. As discussed earlier, you do not take in everything at once, but only what you choose to see. You cannot apprehend the surface property (lustre) and the content of the reflection simultaneously. Moreover, highlights such as those on polished metal armour or bowls normally move about as we do but clearly cannot move in paintings. Yet we tolerate the lack of movement when we view paintings as we stroll around a gallery.

Where viewers look in artworks

Eye movements are an essential element of human vision, driven by the need to direct objects of interest onto the acute foveal region of the retina (demonstrated earlier in Figure 4.2). The pattern of one's eye movements is usually dictated by the task at hand. When in a kitchen making a cup of tea, for instance, one would execute a series of eye movements to locate the kettle, the teapot, the cup and so on (Land et al., 1999). Some of the earliest research on eye movements while viewing paintings also found that the viewer's scan path (the trajectory of their eye movements) through a picture depended on the information that the viewer sought to extract from the scene (Yarbus, 1967). But when most people view an artwork, there is often no such specific task at hand (unless one is an artist or art historian). Therefore, how do they choose where to look, and do artists design artworks to control fixation patterns? Some clues can be found in the scientific literature. Given the importance of eye movements, it is not surprising that they have attracted a great deal of research over the years. A basic finding is that empty or uninformative parts of the scene are rarely fixated. Instead, viewers concentrate their fixations on the most informative and interesting parts of the scene. The eyes are often drawn to the most salient regions of the scene, which correspond to the areas containing the highest density of features such as edges and bars, or having the highest local contrast (Itti & Koch, 2000). There is also a general tendency for viewers to fixate the centre of a framed image, regardless of its content (Mannan et al., 1997; Henderson, 2003). However, saliency alone does only a mediocre job of predicting where viewers fixate in pictures. The meaning of the picture, and the objects in it, frequently dominate the viewer's scan path (Cerf et al., 2008; Einhauser et al., 2008). Faces are especially powerful attractors of attention. Cerf et al. (2008) found that when a picture contained a face, the viewer's gaze was drawn to it immediately, even when he or she was supposed to be searching for a specific object in the image such as a banana, car or phone. Eyes are particularly important. Birmingham et al. (2009) found that viewers fixated the eye region of the faces in a depicted scene within the first one-fifth of a second of viewing. Face detection is hard-wired in the human brain; there is a population of neurones in the temporal cortex that specialises in detecting human faces. Damage in this region causes a curious clinical condition called prosopagnosia, in which the patient's visual faculties are largely intact but they have a very specific inability to recognise faces, including their own face in a mirror (Farah, 2004).

A clever illustration of the power of eyes in pictures comes from an experiment by Bateson et al. (2006). In many university psychology departments, staff pay for tea and coffee using an honesty (or honour) box, but receipts often fall short of the amount consumed. Bateson et al. (2006) placed a picture banner above the notice detailing the prices in their department. The picture alternated in different weeks between an image of some flowers and an image of a pair of eyes. The amount of money collected in each week was found to depend on the picture present in that week. Takings were significantly higher when the picture contained eyes. Gaze is a crucial form of non-verbal communication in humans and in animals and can indicate dominance or emotional interest (one should never stare back at aggressive dogs or bears). Eye contact is such a powerful social cue that it can influence behaviour even when it is mediated by a picture rather than a real person. Artists exploit the power of eye contact in portraits. Leonardo's famous 'Mona Lisa' gazes back at the viewer enigmatically, while in Holbein's 'Erasmus' (Figure 5.7), the averted gaze signifies detached contemplation. The emotional potency of images of military, political and religious leaders throughout history must partly be a consequence of our instinctive reactions to eye contact, even in pictures. The famous World War I poster urging British men to enlist in the army is dominated by Lord Kitchener staring straight out at the viewer, with a pointed finger for added emphasis.

So great is the human attraction to faces that they are often seen in images that do not contain them at all, a phenomenon called pareidolia (Figure 5.8). Sometimes these imagined faces are interpreted as religious messages. In one famous case, the Virgin Mary was seen in a grilled cheese sandwich by an American called Diana Duyser. The object was eventually sold on eBay for $28,000. Even car design is influenced by the face-like properties of vehicle frontages

Figure 5.7 'Erasmus', Hans Holbein the Younger, 1523.

Figure 5.8 An example of 'pareidolia' in the façade of a house in Switzerland.

(Windhager et al., 2008). Narrow headlamps and a low, wide grille (as in BMW saloons) are perceived as dominant, aggressive and masculine; large headlamps and a narrow grille (as in Minis) are perceived as more child-like.

The Italian artist Giuseppe Arcimboldo exploited pareidolia to create many portraits of faces made from collections of fruit, vegetables, flowers, fish and books. Our extreme sensitivity to faces and face-like configurations is undoubtedly related to the presence of face-processing neurones in the temporal lobe, mentioned in Chapter 3.

Summary

Pictures are inherently paradoxical. They are flat, two-dimensional surfaces, yet artists can create highly convincing representations of real three-dimensional scenes. Two factors contribute to the success of pictures. Firstly, the visual depth cues available in three-dimensional scenes are relatively weak at longer viewing distances, so picture viewers are not aware of the paradox they present. Secondly, viewers are very tolerant of the distortions and inconsistencies introduced by pictorial violations of perspective projection, variability in the use of shadows and errors in the depiction of reflections. This lenience has two sources: it reflects the visual system's flexible use of the inherently unreliable visual cues available in images; and it is also a consequence of a limited visual memory. The brain does not build and retain a single representation of the entire scene under view, so inconsistencies in local pictorial details such as shadows, shapes and reflections often go unnoticed unless the viewer embarks on a detailed point-by-point comparison. Eye contact is a powerful social cue, detected by dedicated neurones in the visual brain, so eyes in pictures exert an inexorable power over the viewer.

There is little evidence to support the old contention that pictorial competence is a culturally transmitted skill similar to the ability to read text, apart from the ability to distinguish between a real object and a depiction of that object.

6   Motion in art

Introduction

Paintings traditionally present a single, static view of the world. Indeed, still life paintings are, by definition, unchanging and inanimate. Portraits also disregard time in the sense that they capture the relatively stable demeanour of the sitter, which conveys their character (refer back to the portrait of Erasmus in Figure 5.7, p. 85). Some paintings do convey the passage of quite long periods of time, particularly narrative paintings that tell a story in a series of episodes integrated in a single composition. Several traditional pictorial devices are available to artists striving to convey the passage of time in a narrative painting. In 'continuous narrative' paintings, the same protagonist appears in several places, often separated by architectural structures that mark out different episodes in the story. Jacopo Pontormo's elegant 'Joseph with Jacob in Egypt' (Plate 17; see colour plate section) presents several episodes from Joseph's life as Viceroy of Egypt. Joseph appears in four locations, always wearing a red cap, lavender cloak and amber tunic. The story begins in the left foreground with Joseph presenting his father Jacob (kneeling) to the Pharaoh. In the right foreground, a messenger presents Joseph with news of his father's illness. In the middle distance, Joseph is shown ascending a staircase with one of his sons to visit his ill father. In the top right, Joseph is shown presenting his sons to his dying father. Pontormo uses subtle pictorial cues of movement to convey the passage of time. Movement always produces a progressive change in position. Notice that the successive episodes in the story unfold progressively across the canvas and into the distance from foreground to middle distance (the figures in the far distance are thought to be references to Joseph's earlier arrival in Egypt to seek grain; Langmuir, 2003).

How can artists convey events that unfold much more rapidly, involving brief bursts of dynamic action? This chapter will explore the techniques that artists use to convey a sense of action and the reasons for their effectiveness. The next section considers techniques used in still images such as paintings (Cutting, 2002), and the subsequent section considers animated images. The success of the various techniques is related to their ability to excite activity in the motion-detecting neural circuits of the visual cortex, which were mentioned in Chapter 3.

Representations of action in still images

Implied motion

In Titian's dynamic composition 'Bacchus and Ariadne' (Plate 18), all of the human figures are captured in the midst of an action. Bacchus in the centre (the god of wine) is leaping towards Ariadne, who is reaching towards a departing ship. The movements are implied by the postures of the actors; we can effortlessly infer or extrapolate their future positions. This kind of representation of motion in a static image is called implied motion in the scientific literature. In order to understand Titian's composition, it is essential to appreciate the movement clues present in the painting. It would be physically impossible for the figures in the scene to remain in their positions for longer than an instant. Stop-action photographs containing implied motion are common place today, but it is remarkable that Titian was able to create such vivid and convincing depictions of implied motion hundreds of years before the advent of photography.

Vision scientists have discovered that static images containing implied motion do stimulate the cells that normally respond to real movement in dynamic images. Recall from Chapter 3 that a region in the temporal lobe of the cerebral cortex called area MT is known to contain many cells that respond selectively to visual movement. Senior et al. (2000) showed participants video clips of objects in motion and clips of the same objects at rest, while they monitored their brain activity using functional magnetic resonance imaging (fMRI; this technique detects tiny alterations in blood flow in the brain, which signify changes in neural activity). They found higher activation in area MT while viewing clips containing motion, consistent with other evidence for the presence of motion-detecting neurones in that area. Then Senior et al. (2000) compared activation while participants viewed *still* images of implied motion with activation while viewing of images not containing any implied motion. Activation was higher in MT when viewing implied motion, indicating that these static images also activated motion-selective cells. Similar results were reported by Kourtzi and Kanwisher (2000). Given that the images depicting implied motion are actually stationary, it seems extremely unlikely that they directly activate motion-selective cells of the kind shown in Figure 3.2(c), because many physiological studies have shown that these cells respond directly only to dynamic images. A plausible possibility is that the cells are activated indirectly via other cells as follows. When a static image is cast on the retina, it triggers a cascade of neural processing operations, which culminates in the creation of object representations in the cortex. In neural terms, the representations correspond to patterns of activity in populations of cells in the temporal lobe, as discussed in Chapter 3. If the shape and disposition of the object imply that it is in motion, then these representations would include assertions that 'the object is moving'. The assertion of motion results in a neural signal being transmitted to motion-selective cells in area MT, making them more likely to respond as if the movement was actually present rather than just implied. Neural cross-talk of this kind is thought to be widespread in the cerebral cortex. As mentioned in Chapter 3, different groups of cortical neurones specialise in handling different visual attributes but, given the highly structured nature of visual images, there is often a high degree of correspondence between the different attributes (shape, colour, movement and so on). Thus, in the interests of maximising the efficiency and reliability of neural processing, different neural groups share their outputs via cross-talk connections. Implied movement in a static image therefore augments the activity of cells that would normally respond to the actual movement that usually accompanies it.

The results of three very different experimental studies are consistent with the cross-talk explanation of implied motion perception. Saygin et al. (2010) recently measured fMRI activation in human area MT while participants heard sentences conveying a sense of motion or stasis, such as 'The wild horse crossed the barren field' versus 'The black horse stood in the barren field'. They found that visual area MT was activated more by hearing motion sentences than by hearing non-motion sentences. Saygin et al. (2010) also measured activation changes in another cortical area not associated with motion processing, to check that the effect really was unique to MT, and found no effect. Therefore, either visually or verbally mediated assertions about object motion can evoke a motion response in the visual cortex. In another study, Lorteije et al. (2006) investigated neural responses to implied motion using a technique that measures visual evoked potentials (VEPs, sometimes called brain waves). In this technique, the participant wears a skullcap lined with a matrix of electrodes, which can pick up tiny changes in voltage associated with brain activity in the underlying region of the cortex. Lorteije et al. (2006) were interested particularly in how rapidly the electrical response to implied motion developed as compared to the response to actual motion. The latter response should occur quite rapidly, as actual motion directly triggers a response in motion-detecting neurones. On the other hand, the response to implied motion should be relatively delayed if it relies on indirect activation via other cells that represent objects. Lorteije et al. (2006) did indeed find a timing difference between actual motion and implied motion responses, which reached a peak at about one-third of a second after the image was presented. In neural terms, this is quite a slow response, consistent with indirect activation. Finally, a perceptual experiment by Winawer et al. (2008) found that inspection of a series of static images, which each contained implied motion, altered the perceived movement of subsequently presented dynamic images. This kind of perceptual adaptation effect is normally produced by inspection of actual motion (described in the next section) and is considered to be a reliable marker for activation in motion-selective cortical neurones (see also Pavan et al., 2011 and Morgan et al., 2012).

For hundreds of years artists had to rely on their powers of observation and their skill to create images containing implied motion. However, the advent of high-speed photography made natural images of implied motion available and introduced a realistic standard against which to compare traditional artistic depictions of implied motion. Galloping horses have long presented a particular challenge to artists. They are traditionally depicted in a 'rocking horse' or 'flying-gallop' pose, as in Figure 6.1; the two forelegs leap forwards while the hind legs stretch backwards. This pose is not merely a convention of Western European art, because it can also be seen in the art of native Americans. However, the early stop-action photographs of Eadweard Muybridge revealed, for the first time, that galloping horses never actually adopt this pose. Muybridge was employed by a wealthy Californian landowner called Leland Stanford in the late 1870s to take action photographs of his race horses, supposedly to resolve a disputed claim that there is a moment when galloping horses have all four feet off the ground. With the help of Stanford's technicians, Muybridge set up a row of twelve high-speed cameras at intervals alongside a track, which were triggered by threads or wires stretched across the track. The resulting photographs of horses trotting or galloping along the track (Figure 6.2, left) revealed that there was indeed a moment when all four feet were off the ground.

Figure 6.1 'A Race on the Round Course at Newmarket', John Wootton, c.1750.

(a)   (b)

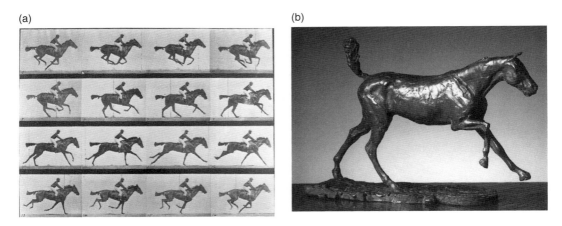

Figure 6.2 (a) 'Annie G Galloping', Eadweard Muybridge, c.1887. (b) 'Horse Galloping on Right Foot', Edgar Degas. (From John Rewald, 1957, *Degas Sculpture: The Complete Works*. London: Thames & Hudson, Plate 3VI.)

Muybridge went on to take many more stop-action photographs of other animals and humans in motion and he toured extensively to exhibit his work (see accounts in Solnit, 2003 and Miller, 2010).

None of Muybridge's photographs of galloping horses show them in a flying-gallop pose, and many of the artists who became familiar with Muybridge's work evidently spotted their 'error'. The flying gallop quickly disappeared from artistic depictions of galloping horses, to be replaced by a pose derived, it seems, from Muybridge's photographs. Edgar Degas' early paintings do employ the flying gallop, but his later work is clearly inspired by Muybridge's photographs. The pose of the sculpture in Figure 6.2 (right), for instance, is almost identical to that in one of Muybridge's frames in Figure 6.2 (left).

Not all artists were so convinced about the artistic validity of the poses revealed by stop-action photographs, and they raise interesting questions about the nature of 'truth' in paintings. The French artist Theodore Gericault was famed for his depictions of horses, and his work included the traditional flying-gallop pose (*ventre à terre* or belly to the ground). Auguste Rodin (1984) defended Gericault's 'error' as follows:

Yet I believe that Gericault rather than the photograph is correct because his horses have the appearance of running. This comes about because the spectator looks from back to front. (p. 32.)

Rodin argued that artists may combine different phases of an action in a single pose, so condensing the impression of several moments into a single image. In Rodin's own sculpture 'Saint John the Baptist', the figure's pose seems unnatural. Saint John is posed as if in mid-stride, with his right leg forward and left leg back, both legs are straight and both feet are flat on the ground. Rodin felt that stop-action photographs of a man in mid-stride, which show the back heel or foot raised, appear unnaturally frozen, having

the bizarre appearance of a man suddenly struck with paralysis and petrified in his pose... (p. 31.)

When questioned on the lack of correspondence between the statue's posture and a real walking human, Rodin replied:

No. It is the artist who tells the truth and photography that lies. For in reality, time does not stand still. And if the artist succeeds in producing the impression of a gesture that is executed in several instants, his work is certainly much less conventional than the scientific image where time is abruptly suspended. (p. 33.)

Ernest Meissonier was well known for the attention to detail evident in his paintings, and he held extensive discussions with Muybridge during the latter's visit to Paris in 1881. However, Meissonier too expressed scepticism regarding the use of Muybridge's poses in art:

For the artist, there exists only one category of movements, those which the eye can grasp. (Quoted in Dagognet, 1992.)

Art was for him a matter of seeing, not knowing. Nevertheless, Meissonier is known to have altered the pose of horses in his work to take account of Muybridge's photographs.

These artists draw attention to the fact that photographic evidence may not correspond to our conscious experience of movement. If the aim of art is to be true to human experience rather than to photography, then photography should not be relevant. However, the ubiquity of photographic images in modern society has created its own, dominant standard of truth, a photographic truth. The debate raises an interesting but unresolved issue regarding implied motion: Do artistic poses that are true to experience evoke a stronger neural motion response than poses that are true to photographs? Only if artistic poses prove more effective than photographic ones can one accept Rodin's and Meissonier's arguments and argue against the primacy of photographic truth.

The French physiologist Etienne-Jules Marey was a contemporary of Muybridge and he pioneered multiple exposure photography in the late 1800s during his research into animal and human locomotion. In this technique, which Marey called chronophotography, a single frame of photographic film is exposed several times at regular intervals during the execution of an action, to leave multiple impressions of the action at different instants in time. The series of figures in different poses is seen as successive positions of the same figure during an action rather than as several entirely different figures. Each pose is only slightly different from the last, owing to the short time interval between them; as the eye scans across the frame, the sequence of poses appears entirely natural, almost as if the eye were tracking an actual moving figure in a series of fixations.

Marey unwittingly laid one of the foundations of an art movement called Futurism (Miller, 2010). Futurism spanned literature, painting and sculpture. In the visual arts, Futurism aimed to give an impression of speed. Cubism had already attempted to depict several different spatial aspects of three-dimensional form in a single image by blending different views into one configuration, such as both profile and frontal views of faces (with a shared eye) in Picasso's portraits. Futurism attempted to represent *action* by showing different phases of movement simultaneously, just as Marey had done in his chronophotographs.

Chronophotographs and Futurist art necessarily contain multiple instances of implied motion. As such, the research outlined earlier indicates that such images should activate motion-processing circuits in the cortical area MT. Kim and Blake (2007) tested this idea. They compared brain scans collected while observers viewed chronophotographs, Futurist art and non-Futurist abstract art. The chronophotographs produced the greatest activation in area MT, while the Futurist art produced more activation than abstracts but only in viewers who had previous experience of Futurist artwork. Going back to Rodin's assertions about photography, it seems that, at least in the case of Futurism, the camera image is more powerful than the artistic image.

An important component of implied motion is forward lean. A human figure stands vertical when at rest but leans forward while walking or running (or skiing: rigid ski boots have forward lean built into them). Forward lean accompanies movement because it helps to overcome inertia and to compensate for wind pressure, so, when present in a static image, it implies motion. This cue seems to be effective even when applied to objects that cannot, in reality, lean forward. Figure 6.3 (left) shows a photograph of a moving vehicle, in which the shape of the vehicle is distorted to create forward lean. The distortion does evoke a vivid impression of forward momentum. Forward lean in photographs of moving rigid bodies is an accidental by-product of camera technology. Many cameras are equipped with a mechanical shutter that advances across the frame as a slit. Consequently, different parts of the image are exposed at slightly different times. If the image contains moving objects, the shutter movement introduces a distortion that depends jointly on the directions of the object, the slit and the camera. In the illustration (Figure 6.3, right), the shutter moves up through the frame while the car moves horizontally. As a result, the lower part of the car is captured on the film slightly before the upper part and slightly further back on the road; hence the apparent forward lean of the photograph. Forward lean is often used in cartoon animation to enhance the impression of speed, even in objects that are not capable of leaning forward.

Motion blur

The sensitivity of the earliest photographic plates was so low that photographers needed to use very long exposures even in bright conditions. Early photographs of city streets are largely devoid of people, not because the streets were deserted but because anything that moved did not leave an impression on the plate before departing the scene. Exposures of less than one-fiftieth of a second became possible only after 1858, twenty years after the first photographs. Unless the exposure is extremely short, a moving object is registered in a photograph as a smear across the image, a blurred ghostly shadow, the extent of which diminishes as the exposure shortens.

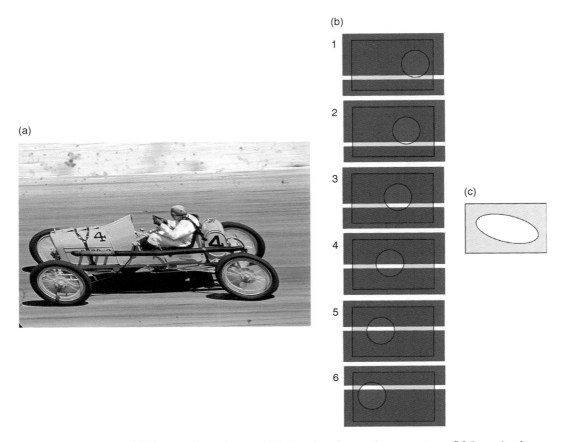

Figure 6.3 (a) Forward lean in a vehicle implies forward momentum. (b) Lean in the photograph is a consequence of the camera's shutter moving vertically through the frame as a thin slit (time advances from top to bottom); the wheel moves leftwards and the shutter moves upwards, sweeping a thin strip of the wheel across the film to form an ellipse (c).

The Impressionists were aware of the presence of motion blur in photographs and exploited it in their work. In Monet's 'Boulevard des Capucines', for instance, the bustle of the boulevard is conveyed by the blurred human figures, which seem to mimic the ghostly smudges in early photographs. In Renoir's 'A Gust of Wind', dynamic brush strokes (not really visible in small photographic reproductions) successfully convey the effect of wind on the meadow.

Motion blur also occurs in the human visual system, because the photoreceptors in the eye cannot respond instantaneously to changes in the light striking the retina. You may recall from Chapter 2 that photoreceptors in the eye fall into two types, called rods and cones. Rods operate in the dark conditions typical of

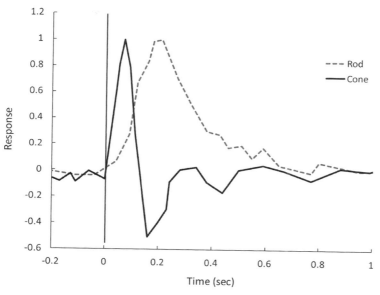

Figure 6.4 The time course of electrical responses in photoreceptors. After a single brief flash of light at time zero (vertical line), photoreceptor responses stretch over a time period spanning at least one-quarter of a second. (Replotted from Schnapf & Baylor, 1987.)

night-time while cones operate in the bright conditions of daylight. Figure 6.4 plots the electrical response of each type of photoreceptor to a very brief flash of light, during the second after the flash. Cones respond faster than rods, but both types of receptor take at least one-twentieth of a second to reach their peak response to the flash. After reaching its peak, the response dies away over a further period of up to one-tenth of a second. Thus, rapid movement of light across the retina leaves a trail of waning photoreceptor responses behind it. The trail of neural activity is perceptible in dark conditions as a bright streak following behind moving lights. The dazzling patterns created by fireworks are largely due to this effect, which is called visible persistence. It was first explained by Isaac Newton:

And when a coal of fire moved nimbly in the circumference of a circle, makes the whole circumference appear like a circle of fire, is it not because the motions excited in the bottom of the eye by the rays of light are of a lasting nature, and continue till the coal of fire in going round returns to its former place? (1730/1952, p. 347.)

Artists sometimes use trails or 'motion streaks' to convey movement. Tim Layzell's '1960 Goodwood TT' (Figure 6.5) is full of motion streaks, which vividly portray the high-speed action in the scene. They are also used in Roy

Figure 6.5 '1960 Goodwood TT'.

Lichtenstein's pop art. Recent research in perception indicates that motion streaks actually augment neural responses to motion in the visual system. Removing them or adding spurious streaks severely confounds motion perception (Burr & Ross, 2002). As in the case of motion implied by shape and pose, motion streaks in static works of art are so effective at evoking a sense of motion because they tap into the cortical neurones that signal motion in dynamic images.

Animation

In the mid-1800s, a number of different mechanical devices were invented, which present the viewer with a series of static images containing actors in a successive series of poses during natural movements such as walking, jumping or running. If the images are presented at an appropriate rate, the viewer experiences a convincing impression of lively, animate movement. The earliest devices used drawings, but once stop-action photographs became available, such as those of Muybridge, it became possible to bring realistic photographs back to life by presenting them as a rapid sequence. By the turn of the century, new devices had been developed to take stop-action photographs and then present them as a motion sequence. Following a meeting with Marey during which he saw a new roll film camera, in 1892 the American Thomas Edison devised a 'kinetograph' camera that used roll film. Crucially, Edison's film had perforations along the edge, which allowed the film to be transported by a toothed sprocket and each frame to be accurately registered in a gate. The dimensions of the film strip have remained unchanged to the present day. Two French innovators, the Lumiere brothers Auguste and Louis, were the first to develop a full system for recording and projecting a sequence of photographs on a strip of celluloid film. Their innovation led to the silent film era.

Early silent films were shot and projected at a rate anywhere between 16 and 24 frames per second (fps), although the standard rate was supposed to be 16 fps (Brownlow, 1980). Projectionists could vary frame rate by varying the speed at which they turned the hand crank on the projector. Kevin Brownlow quotes from a 1915 projectionist's handbook, which points out that the speed at which each scene was recorded 'may – and often does – vary widely. . . One of the highest functions of projection is to watch the screen and regulate the speed of projection to synchronise with the speed of taking.' Silent films were almost always shown slightly faster than they were shot, perhaps to enhance the sense of dynamism in the action, although exhibitors often changed projection speed to suit their screening schedules. Recording speeds above 24 fps were avoided because they used too much film and film stock was not fast enough to cope with the resulting short exposure times. However, with the advent of sound it became essential to adopt a single, precisely defined frame rate in order to keep sound and vision in synchrony, and 24 fps was selected as the standard speed, sufficient to produce a realistic impression of animate movement.

Motion pictures grew to become the dominant visual art form of the twentieth century, now viewed by millions of people around the globe every day either in a cinema, on television, or increasingly on small mobile devices such as telephones. Why do motion pictures exert such a powerful grip on the viewer? This section considers why a succession of still images is experienced as continuous movement, while the next section explores the importance of motion for understanding the world and the subtle power it exerts over art.

The traditional explanation for the perception of motion pictures is 'visible persistence'. You have read about visible persistence earlier in the chapter; photoreceptor responses persist for a short time after a visual stimulus is extinguished (Figure 6.4). Persistence of vision supposedly explains the perception of motion pictures as follows:

The brain holds an image for a short period of time after it has disappeared, so it is possible to construct a machine that can project a series of still images quickly enough so that they merge psychologically and the illusion of motion is maintained. (Monaco, 2009, p. 130.)

This explanation is appealing intuitively and relies on a well-established and easily demonstrated phenomenon, namely persistence of vision, so it reappears regularly in discussions of motion pictures. However, it is completely incorrect. Persistence blends or averages successive images together so that they appear simultaneous (think of Newton's circle of fire); thus, it can only ever destroy an impression of movement, not create it. An impression of movement requires that the successive positions of the moving object be registered as separate events, so that they can be compared to infer motion direction. Once successive positions are combined into a single image by persistence, it becomes impossible to deduce (hence perceive) movement direction.

If you have read Chapter 3, you will be familiar with the correction explanation for motion picture perception: responses in motion-selective neurones in the visual cortex. As illustrated in Figure 3.2(c), each of these neurones compares information arriving from two adjacent locations on the retina. By virtue of the neural connections between the retina and the cortex, each motion-selective neurone responds only to motion across the retina in one direction, not the opposite. Motion-selective neurones basically detect sequential activation of adjacent retinal locations. Motion pictures contain shapes and objects that shift position discretely from one frame to the next in the sequence. Provided that they are not too large, these position shifts are an effective stimulus for motion-sensitive neurones. The resulting response creates the usual conscious experience of movement and the motion picture appears to come to life.

Powerful evidence that motion-selective neurones mediate our perception of movement, and of motion pictures, comes from an effect called the motion after-effect. It was first reported by the ancient Greek philosopher Aristotle and has been rediscovered several times since (twice in the nineteenth century). The Czech physiologist Jan Evangelista Purkinje described it very well in 1820 as follows:

Another form of eye dizziness can be demonstrated if one observes a passing sequence of spatially distinct objects for a long time, e.g. a long parade of cavalry, overlapping waves, the spokes of a wheel that is not rotating too fast. When the actual movement stops there is a similar apparent movement in the opposite direction. (Quoted in Wade & Verstraten, 1998, p. 4.)

The eye dizziness Purkinje described is now called the motion after-effect or MAE, and usually lasts only a matter of seconds after the cessation of movement, although it can be dramatic and compelling in its intensity. The MAE is seen only after one maintains steady fixation on a stationary point in the scene so that consistent movement is allowed to sweep across the retina. Furthermore, the illusory reversed motion is apparent only in the area of the visual field that was previously exposed to real movement. These two requirements may explain the rarity of MAEs in everyday experience. The occurrence of the MAE is thought to be closely associated with activity in motion-selective cortical neurones. Animal studies have shown that the responsiveness of these cells declines during steady stimulation and takes some time to recover to normal levels after the stimulation ceases (Petersen et al., 1985). Our ability to perceive movement relies on a comparison between the outputs of direction-selective cells tuned to different directions; we perceive the direction corresponding to the tuning of the most active cells at any given moment. Exposure to movement in a particular direction depresses the activity of cells tuned to that direction, skewing the pattern of responses across the whole population of cells to favour cells tuned to the opposite direction. As a result, we see the opposite direction of movement even in the presence of a stationary pattern (Mather et al., 2008). Thus, the MAE can be viewed as the perceptual signature of prior activation in motion-selective cortical cells. Tellingly, the movement seen in motion pictures is also capable of producing a vivid MAE, although only when the frame-to-frame displacement is relatively small (Banks & Kane, 1972). There is no known way that visible persistence alone would be capable of producing an MAE.

As discussed previously, early cinematographers settled on a frame rate of 24 fps because it produced an acceptable visual impression of movement without using up too much film. However, at this presentation rate there is a distracting level of flicker because the light beam from the projector is interrupted by a shutter twenty-four times every second while the film is being advanced through the film gate onto each successive frame. Flicker becomes imperceptible only at interruption rates in excess of about fifty flashes per second (domestic lamps flicker at fifty flashes per second), hence cine projector shutters were designed to interrupt the light passing through each frame once or twice while the frame was stationary in the film gate (this interruption also protected the film from the searing heat of the projection lamp). In this way, the movie would still contain twenty-four frames of *animation* per second but the *flicker* rate would be raised to an undetectable 48 or 72 flashes per second. Visible persistence explains why high flicker rates are not perceptible. Photoreceptor response is so sluggish

(Figure 6.4) that responses to individual flashes blend together and, as a result, cannot be distinguished. It is important to appreciate that visible flicker is entirely separate from motion perception, and a conflation of the explanations for the two effects may account for the erroneous attribution of motion picture perception to visible persistence. Motion perception is achievable at a presentation rate of 24 fps, while apparent continuity (lack of flicker) requires a presentation rate of about 50 fps. The different temporal requirements of these two percepts reinforce their separate origins in the visual system.

Action perception

Motion pictures activate specialised neurones in the visual cortex that evolved to detect movement in the retinal image. Motion detection represents only the first step in a sophisticated, multi-level processing system. Survival depends on the correct interpretation of any motion in the scene. Was it caused by a natural force, such as wind causing a tree branch to sway, or gravity forcing a rock to fall down a slope, or was it caused by an intentional agent, such as the movement of a predator? Clearly, we must understand the causes of events in order to deal with them appropriately, and visual motion is a vital source of evidence. Humans are hard-wired to interpret visual motion in ways that promote our understanding of the world.

Consider the two movies illustrated by the sequences in Figure 6.6. Both contain simple animations of geometrical shapes. On the left, a circle moves in a straight line towards a triangle and stops at the point where it meets the triangle, which then starts to move along the same trajectory as the circle. On the right, the circle and triangle are in the same initial positions but, in this movie, the triangle starts to move before the circle reaches it, and moves rapidly along a curved path. Observers perceive these two movies very differently (Scholl & Tremoulet, 2000). In the left-hand movie, the circle appears to collide with the triangle and so cause it to move. In the right-hand movie, the triangle appears to move with the intention of fleeing from the circle before the circle arrives. The first movie is an example of perceptual causality and the second is an example of perceptual agency. In one case, we attribute the contingency between the movements of the shapes as due to simple mechanical causation and, in the other case, we attribute it to an animate, intentional agent. In both cases, the attribution does not rely on prior knowledge of the objects because they are arbitrary geometrical forms. Causality was first studied by a

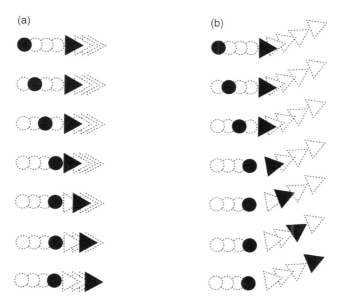

Figure 6.6 Animation sequences that create an impression of mechanical causality (a) or agency (b). Successive positions are denoted by dotted outlines.

Belgian psychologist called Albert Michotte (1963), while agency was first studied by Heider and Simmel (1944).

Perception of causality and agency is fast, automatic and sensitive to basic visual properties such as the precise timing and distance relationships involved in the pattern of movement. Mechanical causality is usually perceived when visual movement obeys Newtonian laws, such as motion along a simple linear or curved path, with acceleration or deceleration that is consistent with a collision or gravity. Movement that does not obey Newtonian laws because it involves unpredictable changes in speed and direction, or is not prompted by direct contact between objects, tends to be perceived as intentional. The shapes in Figure 6.6 are arbitrary; any shapes would suffice. What matters is how the shapes move, not prior knowledge of the likely behaviour of particular shapes. Even a single moving object can create the visual impression that it is animate and intentional, based solely on its pattern of movement. Tremoulet and Feldman (2000) found that simultaneous changes in speed and direction were sufficient to convey an impression of agency even in a single spot. Jonathan Miller (2010) used a poem by Robert Frost to illustrate our capacity for perceiving agency in simple movement patterns:

> A speck that would have been beneath my sight
> On any but a paper sheet so white

Set off across what I had written there.
And I had idly poised my pen in air
To stop it with a period of ink
When something strange about it made me think,
This was no dust speck by my breathing blown,
But unmistakably a living mite
With inclinations it could call its own.
It paused as with suspicion of my pen,
And then came racing wildly on again
To where my manuscript was not yet dry;
Then paused again and either drank or smelt –
With loathing, for again it turned to fly.
Plainly with an intelligence I dealt.
It seemed too tiny to have room for feet,
Yet must have had a set of them complete
To express how much it didn't want to die.
It ran with terror and with cunning crept.
It faltered: I could see it hesitate;
Then in the middle of the open sheet
Cower down in desperation to accept
Whatever I accorded it of fate [...]
I have a mind myself and recognise
Mind when I meet it in any guise
No one can know how glad I am to find
On any sheet the least display of mind.

As Miller (2010) points out, scientists would not concur with Frost's attribution of *conscious* intent to a mite. Nevertheless, the poem offers a lyrical illustration of the capacity of the human brain to infer agency from the simplest of movements. The automatic, stimulus-driven nature of causality and agency perception is a strong indication that they are mediated by hard-wired, stimulus-tuned cells in the visual system. Research studies show that even infants as young as six months of age can discriminate between animations containing causal and non-causal events (Leslie & Keeble, 1987). Brain imaging studies find that the perception of causality and agency is associated with activity in the temporal and parietal lobes, including areas that are known to be involved in other aspects of motion perception (Blakemore et al., 2003; Schultz et al., 2004).

In the movies illustrated in Figure 6.6, the perceived agent is a simple shape. It is also possible to perceive a single agent defined by a constellation of shapes, which move in different directions and at different speeds, as long as the pattern of movements is appropriate. Johansson (1973) created animations that contained twelve disconnected bright spots moving against a uniform dark background. The spots were actually small flashlight bulbs attached at the major joints of an assistant dressed in tight-fitting dark clothing. A movie camera was used to film the assistant's movements in complete darkness. When naïve observers were shown a still-frame from the movie, they could not form a coherent interpretation of the twelve isolated lights. On the other hand, when the movie was played they quickly and spontaneously reported seeing an agent, a moving human figure, and correctly recognised the particular activity involved, whether it was walking, running, gymnastics, dancing and so on. Johansson (1973) named motion patterns that are characteristic of humans and animals 'biological motion'. He later reported (Johansson, 1976) that perception of biological motion in his movies was extremely rapid. Exposures as brief as one-fifth of a second were sufficient. Johansson concluded that detection of biological motion, therefore, must involve hard-wired neurones, and argued that the initial stage of processing was accomplished by motion-detecting neurones of the kind described earlier in this chapter and in Chapter 3. The later stages involve neurones that process information about body shape as well as motion (see reviews in Johnson & Shiffrar, 2012). Very young infants are able to see biological motion (Simion et al., 2008), and individual cells that respond only to biological motion have been found in the temporal cortex of the monkey (Perrett et al., 1990). Furthermore, brain imaging studies confirm that biological motion perception is associated with activation in the human temporal cortex (Grossman & Blake, 2002).

Laboratory studies of perceived causality and agency reveal that visual motion alone is sufficient for humans to draw inferences about the contingencies between events, the chain of causation or intent of an active agent. This ability is hard-wired and does not require any knowledge or understanding of the objects involved. As a result, when you view a silent movie in which Charlie Chaplin kicks someone in the backside, your understanding of the chain of causation is immediate and automatic and does not rely on familiarity with Charlie Chaplin or his behavioural tendencies. Viewers effortlessly attribute intentionality to objects that are normally considered to be inanimate, such as desk lamps, provided that they move appropriately (skilfully exploited in John Lasseter's short film entitled 'Luxo', released in 1986). Effortless perception is a hallmark of efficient, specialist neural processes. Our understanding of movies is guided by the hidden hand of sophisticated motion processing systems in the brain.

Op Art

Optical Art or Op Art was an abstract art movement of the 1960s that employed simple visual forms designed specifically to evoke pronounced visual stimulation. The precise, mathematically regular patterns in Op Art appear to shimmer, flicker and move before the eyes, sometimes in a disturbing and unstable way. One of the foremost exponents of Op Art is Bridget Riley. Figure 6.7 (left) shows an example of her work.

The term Op Art was first employed in an article in *Time* magazine on 24 October 1964, which carried a report on a new exhibition called 'The Responsive Eye', due to open at New York's Museum of Modern Art in 1965. The term is unfortunate in the sense that all visual art is 'optical'; Op Art aimed specifically to provoke primitive visual disturbances, but these disturbances are necessarily perceptual, not optical. Op Art exploited contemporary advances in our knowledge of how the brain processes visual information and perhaps was also an expression of the uncertainty and disturbance created in society by the rapid scientific advances of the time. Figure 6.7 (middle) shows an example of the kind of disturbing pattern studied in the scientific literature (MacKay, 1957).

Op Art rapidly became part of consumer culture and was adopted by fashion houses for their designs. Figure 6.7 (right) is a design created by the Japanese artist and designer H. Ouchi (1977). The heyday of Op Art was undoubtedly the 1960s, but visual scientists have, only recently, devoted some attention to explaining the varied visual effects it provokes. Scientific explanations fall into two categories. The first kind of explanation attributes at least some of the

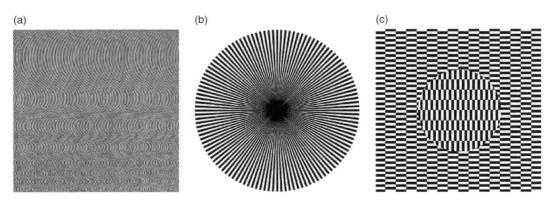

(a)   (b)   (c)

Figure 6.7 (a) 'Fall', Bridget Riley, 1963. (b) A pattern similar to that used by MacKay (1957). (c) An Ouchi pattern (Mather, 2000).

visual disturbance in Op Art to fluctuating accommodation. As you read in Chapter 2, changes in the eye's point of focus are effected by altering the shape of the lens inside the eye. Ciliary muscles around the rim of the lens squeeze or stretch the lens to alter its shape and thus its focussing power. The eyes continuously adjust focus in order to maintain a sharp image on the retina, by hunting for the lens shape that minimises blur at the retina. Campbell and Robson (1958) argued that, during this process of continuous adjustment, different segments of the circular ciliary muscle contract at slightly different times, introducing some degree of astigmatism (unequal blur at different pattern orientations, discussed in Chapter 2). Fluctuating astigmatism may account for the shimmer and jazzing seen in certain Op Art patterns. Changes in focus also produce very slight changes in image magnification (if you require spectacle corrections, changes in image magnification can be dramatic when you wear them), which may produce visual disturbances.

The second kind of explanation for the shimmering, mobile quality of Op Art relies on eye movements. The eyes are continually in motion. Even when you attempt to maintain rock-steady fixation, the eyes make tiny involuntary saccades as well as slow drifts in position. These eye movements create image motion on the retina, which triggers activity in the cortical motion-detecting neurones described earlier in the chapter. Retinal motion is an inevitable consequence of all eye movements, of course (unless the eyes are closed), whether voluntary or involuntary, and the visual system is mostly able to attribute retinal motion signals correctly, either to movement of an object in the world or to movement of the eyes and head. Consequently, the world does not normally appear to become unstable or mobile every time you move your eyes. However, it has been argued that the visual patterns employed in Op Art are especially difficult for the brain's compensation mechanisms to cope with. Finely spaced lines forming waves or stripes at different orientations produce complex patterns of retinal motion, which do not correspond in any straightforward way to the eye movements that produced them. Small errors in compensation may arise, which means that part of the retinal motion is not attributed appropriately to the eye movements that generated them. The result is apparent movement in the Op Art pattern.

The accommodation and eye movement explanations of Op Art effects are not mutually exclusive, and experimental evidence indicates that both can play a part in the visual experiences evoked by Op Art. Zanker et al. (2003) found that motion effects were reduced but not abolished when patterns similar to Op Art designs were viewed through a small pinhole that almost eliminates accommodation. On the other hand, when the designs are imprinted on the retina as an after-image using a high-intensity flash, so preventing any retinal motion, apparent motion effects disappear. Mather (2000) and Zanker et al. (2010) report further evidence that errors in retinal motion attribution are responsible for the apparent motion seen in some Op Art patterns. Anomalous motion signals generated by eye movements are also the likely explanation for the powerful movement sensations generated by Akiyoshi Kitaoka's well-known 'Rotating Snakes' pattern (Fermueller et al., 2010).

Summary

One might think that artistic images depicting motion come alive through an act of imagination, by means of an intelligent understanding of how bodies move. However, the results of many research studies permit us to draw a more specific and remarkable conclusion: both static images and movies are so effective because they automatically trigger neural responses that are normally generated by natural moving images. In paintings, motion can be implied by the pose of figures and the placement of objects in the scene. The motion blur visible in photographs can also be employed in paintings to convey a sense of movement. Op Art offers another example of the power of static images to trigger activity in motion-sensitive areas of the brain. In movies, rapid presentation of a series of static images is extremely powerful in evoking an impression of movement, which is virtually indistinguishable from real, natural movement. The traditional explanation of motion picture perception, based on visible persistence, is erroneous. Movies work so well because they excite motion-detecting cells in the brain, which are usually stimulated by natural movement. Viewers effortlessly attribute contingencies between moving elements in a movie to mechanical causation or intentional behaviour, and this ability is also intimately associated with specialised neural networks in the temporal lobe whose function is to help us to understand causation in the visual world.

Plate 1 (a) 'The Blood of the Redeemer', Giovanni Bellini, 1460–1465. (b) 'Saint Catherine of Alexandria', Raphael, 1507.

Plate 2 'Landscape with the Marriage of Isaac and Rebekah', Claude, 1648.

Plate 3 'The Water-Lily Pond', Claude-Oscar Monet, 1899.

(a)

(b)

Plate 4 (a) 'Barges on the Thames', Andre Derain, 1906. (b) Untitled, Mark Rothko, 1950.

(a)

(b)

Plate 5 (a) 'The Toilet of Venus', Diego Velasquez, 1647–1651. (b) 'Hunters in the Snow', Pieter Brueghel the Elder, 1565.

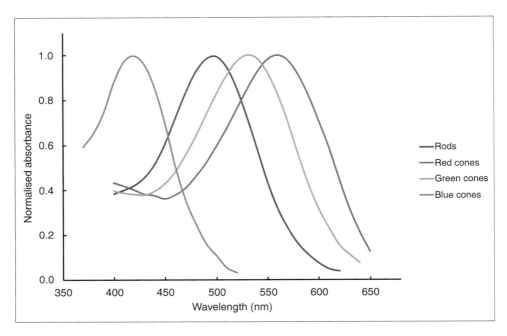

Plate 6 Absorbance spectra of human photoreceptors: short-wavelength 'blue' S-cones (peak: 420 nm); medium-wavelength 'green' M-cones (peak: 534 nm); and long-wavelength 'red' L-cones (peak: 564 nm). Rods all have the same absorbance (peak: 498 nm).

(a)   (b)

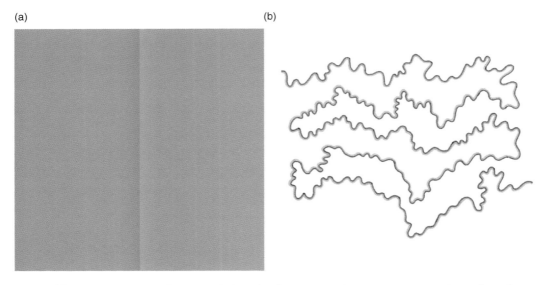

Plate 7 (a) The Craik-O'Brien illusion. A dark-to-bright contrast edge separates two regions of equal lightness, but perceptually one side appears darker than the other. Place a pencil along the edge to reveal the true lightness of the two regions. (b) The watercolour effect (Pinna et al., 2001). The two regions on either side of the contour appear different in hue, but the difference is actually confined to the edge itself.

(a)

(b)

Plate 8 (a) A photograph of Rouen cathedral. (b) The same photograph, digitally processed to preserve chromatic variation (colour) but remove achromatic variation (luminance).

(a)

(b)

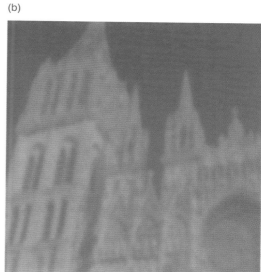

Plate 9 (a) 'Rouen Cathedral at the End of the Day, Sunlight Effect', Claude-Oscar Monet, 1892. (b) The view of Rouen cathedral from Plate 8, after the application of spatial blur and luminance contrast reduction.

Plate 10 'The Japanese Bridge', Claude-Oscar Monet, 1919–1924.

Plate 11 Demonstration of the variation in visual acuity with retinal location. (a) Jan Gossaert, 'The Adoration of the Kings', 1510–1515. Detail is equally sharp everywhere. (b) The same painting, but progressively more blur has been added away from the centre of the image, to simulate the decline in visual acuity away from central fixation. When you fixate the head of the Madonna, the two images appear equally sharp.

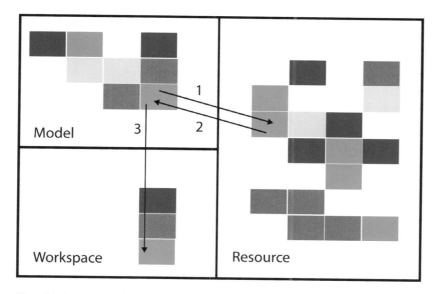

Plate 12 A computer-based copying task used to investigate visual memory. The participant creates a copy of the model in the workspace area by 'picking up' blocks from the resource area using the mouse and 'dropping' them into the workspace. The arrows indicate successive fixations while copying one green block. The first fixation shift (1) takes the eyes from the model to a block for pick-up. Before going to drop it off (3), the eyes return to the model (2).

Plate 13 'Young Woman Standing at a Virginal', Johannes Vermeer, 1670–1672.

Plate 14 'Saint Jerome in his Study', Antonello Da Messina, 1475.

Plate 15 'The Story of Papirius', Domenico Beccafumi, c.1520.

(a)

(b)

Plate 16 (a) 'The Exhumation of Saint Hubert', Rogier van der Weyden, c.1430.
(b) 'The Four Elements: Fire', Joachim Beuckelaer, 1570.

Plate 17 'Joseph with Jacob in Egypt', Jacopo Pontormo, 1518.

Plate 18 'Bacchus and Ariadne', Titian, 1520–1523.

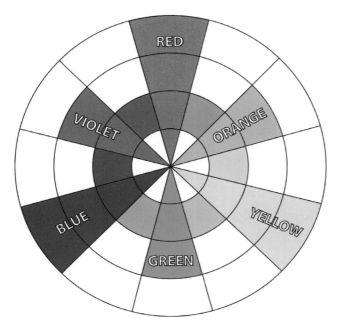

Plate 19 Artist's colour wheel, which summarises the rules of subtractive colour mixture. The outer ring contains three primary colours (red, blue, yellow); the middle ring contains three secondary colours (orange, green, violet) produced by mixing adjacent primaries; and the inner ring contains six tertiary colours produced by mixing adjacent primary and secondary colours.

Plate 20 'The Bedroom', Vincent Van Gogh, 1888–1889.

7 Colour in art

Introduction

As Chapter 1 made clear, a major function of painting from antiquity to the nineteenth century was the representation of nature. In this regard, colour is traditionally viewed as an essential component because it brings visual art closer to nature. In 1528, the Renaissance courtier Baldassare Castiglione recorded a conversation on the relative merits of the figurative arts as follows:

And do you think it a trifle to imitate nature's colours in doing flesh, clothing and all the other things that have colour? This the sculptor cannot do; neither can he render the grace of black eyes or blue eyes, shining with amorous rays. He cannot render the colour of blond hair or the gleam of weapons, or the dark of night, or a storm at sea, or lightning and thunderbolts, or the burning of a city, or the birth of a rosy dawn with its rays of gold and red. In short he cannot do sky, sea, land, mountains, woods, meadows, gardens, rivers, cities, or houses – all of which the painter can do. (Quoted in Castiglione, 1528, p. 80.)

Since the earliest cave paintings 30,000 years ago, artists have used pigments to add natural colour to their work. Prehistoric painters used earth pigments such as charcoal bound with water (or saliva) to create yellow ochre, red ochre and black hues. The Egyptians introduced bright greens and blues using pigments derived from natural minerals, which were washed, ground and bound with gum or animal glue to create a painting medium. They also introduced vegetable dyes. Other colours were created by ancient Chinese, Greek and Roman artisans. Various binding agents were used to hold the pigment together as a painting medium, including wax, resin, water and egg. From the fifteenth century onwards, walnut and linseed oil gradually replaced egg as the binding agent preferred by many artists. Acrylic paints became available in the middle of the twentieth century, in which acrylic resin emulsified with water is used as a binder and thinner.

The binding agent selected by the artist has a profound effect on the finished artwork. It defines the distinctive characteristics of watercolour, egg tempera and oil paintings. Fast-drying egg tempera, for example, lends itself to a precise linear style, such as that seen in early Italian Renaissance work by Fra Angelico and Botticelli. Slow-drying oils, on the other hand, allow the seamless blending of colour and tone, which characterises chiaroscuro, such as that seen in late Renaissance work by Raphael (Plate 1; see colour plate section), and the painterly works by later artists such as Rembrandt (Figure 1.3).

Pigments are common to all artists' paints and, even in the modern age of synthetic pigments, some paints still contain pigments that were first used hundreds of years ago. For instance, Winsor and Newton still make Rose Madder Genuine from the root of the madder plant (Barnett et al., 2006). What is the physical basis of colour in pigments and their mixtures? As outlined in Chapter 2, most light sources emit energy in light waves that vibrate at a broad range of different frequencies or wavelengths (frequency corresponds to the number of vibrations per second, while wavelength specifies the distance between adjacent peaks in the wave). Light wavelength is the basis for colour vision; the shortest wavelengths appear violet and, as wavelength increases, colour progresses to blue, green, yellow, orange and finally red at the longest wavelengths. The most dramatic natural demonstration of the relationship between wavelength and colour can be seen in rainbows. When the sun is at your back, water droplets in the distance reflect the sunlight back towards you. As light rays enter and leave each droplet they are bent or refracted by an amount that depends on their wavelength; shorter wavelengths are bent more than longer wavelengths. Therefore, when the reflected rays of sunlight reach the eye, different wavelengths arrive from slightly different directions, creating the vivid bands of colour.

All pigments absorb some light wavelengths and reflect others, and the colour appearance of a pigment depends on the reflected wavelengths that reach the eye. Figure 7.1 shows the relative amount of light reflected by two artists' pigments. The horizontal axis is light wavelength in the visible spectrum (measured in nanometres) and the vertical axis is the relative amount of light reflected. One pigment (solid line) reflects mainly short wavelengths and

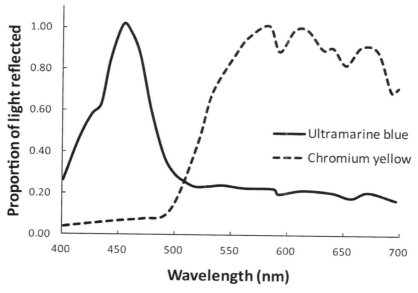

Figure 7.1 Proportion of light reflected as a function of wavelength for two artists' pigments, one blue and the other yellow (based on data plots in Livingstone, 2002).

therefore appears blue, while the other (dashed line) reflects medium and long wavelengths and appears yellow. When two or more pigments are mixed together, the colour appearance of the mixture depends on the wavelengths reflected jointly by all of them. Hence, pigment mixtures necessarily reflect less light than the individual pigments, because each pigment absorbs its own portion of the wavelength spectrum in the incident light. In this sense, pigment mixing is called subtractive mixing; the addition of more pigments can only ever result in less light being reflected from the mixture. The colour appearance of specific pigment mixtures is predictable and reproducible. When blue and yellow pigments are mixed, for example, only medium wavelengths are spared by both, so the mixture has a greenish hue.

Artists use the pigment wheel to summarise the rules of subtractive pigment mixing (Plate 19). The three primary colours (red, blue and yellow) cannot be created by mixing any other pigments. The secondary colours (orange, green and violet) are created by mixing pairs of primary colours. The tertiary colours are created by mixing pairs of primary and secondary colours and so on. In this context, one can also consider white and black as primary colours, because artists use them in mixtures to adjust colour appearance. For example, a pink can be created by mixing red and white, while a brown can be created by mixing yellow and black. The pigment wheel in Plate 19 illustrates some of the colours that can be created by mixtures of three primaries but, in practice, most painters use many more basic colours in their palette than the minimum. Matisse is said to have used seventeen, while Van Gogh used nine (Fryer, 2006).

When artists decide which colours to use and where to place them in the work, their choices inevitably are governed by the properties of the neural systems that mediate colour vision. This chapter will first survey the neural machinery in the brain that serves colour vision and then discuss how this neural substrate influences the use of colour in art.

Colour in the brain

It is important to bear in mind that the colour relationships illustrated in the pigment wheel in Plate 19 are determined purely by the *physical* process of subtractive pigment mixing. The pigment wheel reveals nothing about the *physiological* process of colour analysis by the visual system. Pigment mixtures are used to manipulate the wavelengths that predominate in the spectrum of light reflected from paint. Those dominant wavelengths shape our colour experience, but the particular mix of pigments needed to create them is immaterial and unknowable as far as the visual system is concerned and a purely technical matter for the artist. One can think of the relatively broad spectrum reflected by a pigment mix as an envelope covering all the wavelengths supplied by the constituent pigments. All the visual system receives is the envelope. It cannot know what wavelengths each pigment contributed to the shape of the envelope. Furthermore, the reflectance spectrum is only the starting point for colour processing in the brain and, ultimately, has only an indirect relationship to the colours we actually perceive.

Visual scientists define colour vision as the ability to distinguish between lights of different spectral composition, regardless of intensity. Such an ability is a great asset in a world full of natural surfaces that vary intrinsically in terms of their propensity to absorb some wavelengths in the spectrum of the incident light and to reflect others (known as spectral reflectance). An organism possessing colour vision can discriminate between objects on the basis of their different spectral reflectance properties. Leaves, for instance, contain chlorophyll, which reflects predominantly in the region of the spectrum at 555 nm. Ripe fruit and berries, on the other hand, contain flavonoids that reflect most strongly at long wavelengths above 600 nm. Our primate ancestors may have evolved colour vision because it allowed them to discriminate and identify edible leaves and ripe fruit on the basis of the spectral composition of the light they reflect (Osorio & Vorobyev, 1996); leaves are usually perceived as green while ripe fruit and berries are seen as red. Changizi et al. (2006) have argued that the evolution of primate colour vision may also have been influenced by the importance of discriminating the emotional state of fellow beings. Blushing and blanching in the face are significant indicators of emotional state, and detection of these signals requires a fine-tuned ability to judge redness. Changizi et al. (2006) point out that primate species which possess three cone types tend to have bare faces, while those with inferior colour discrimination due to the presence of only two cone types tend to have furry faces.

The task of estimating an object's spectral reflectance is actually extremely complex, for reasons that will become apparent later; as a result, the neural analysis of colour involves two stages. Firstly, the visual system analyses the spectral composition of the light arriving at the eye from different places in the image. Then it attempts to take account of prevailing lighting conditions in order to produce a stable estimate of the spectral reflectance of the visible surfaces.

Representing spectral composition

The human retina possesses three classes of cone photoreceptor, which absorb light preferentially in different parts of the visible spectrum (Plate 6). S-cones absorb most light at short wavelengths (420 nm), while M-cones and L-cones absorb at medium to long wavelengths (534 and 564 nm, respectively); the colour names of the different cone types should be considered as convenient labels rather than accurate descriptions of spectral colour. You may recall from Chapter 2 that the visual system assigns the processing of different aspects of the retinal image to different populations of cells, often called channels of processing (borrowing terminology from telecommunications systems, which carry different TV and radio stations in different transmission channels). In the case of colour, one processing channel handles achromatic information (shades of grey) and another two channels carry two kinds of chromatic information (colour). The three cone classes are used to construct these three processing channels by combining their responses in different ways. The neural activity in each channel takes the form of a balance or difference signal between opposing pairs of colours (Figure 7.2(a)). The luminance (L) or black-white channel combines information from all three cone receptor types to produce a signal

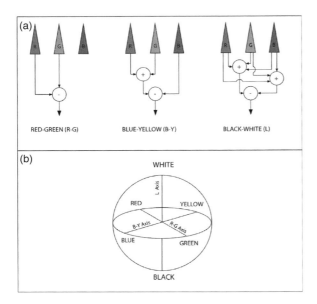

Figure 7.2 Colour processing in the human visual system. (a) The three-cone photoreceptor classes (L- or R, M- or G, S- or B) combine to create three separate channels: the achromatic or black-white luminance channel (L) and two chromatic channels, red-green (R-G) and blue-yellow (B-Y). (b) The three channels represent three independent axes in perceptual colour space. Each colour we perceive occupies a unique location in the three-dimensional space, specified by just three numbers or coordinates (corresponding to activity levels in the three channels).

that balances black against white. The red-green (R-G) channel uses only the M- and L-cone types to balance red against green, while the blue-yellow (B-Y) channel uses all three receptor types to balance blue against yellow (the combined action of M- and L-cones equates to a response in the yellow part of the spectrum). Therefore, our colour experience varies along just three perceptual dimensions or axes (Figure 7.2(b)), namely the luminance axis (L), the red-green (R-G) axis and the blue-yellow (B-Y) axis.

In an abstract sense, one can say that each of the thousands of colours that we perceive is coded in the brain by just three numbers, which correspond to the neural activity in each of the three channels (L, R-G and B-Y). Each triplet of numbers specifies a unique location along the three independent axes shown in Figure 7.2. The nature of human colour experience is constrained fundamentally by the three axes of perceptual colour space. Notice that because the axes involve antagonistic pairs, any given colour can be biased towards either one or the other colour in each pair, not both together: either red or green, blue or yellow, black or white, but not both at the same time. On the other hand, it is possible to perceive colours that are combinations of *different* pairs. For example, a combination of predominant red and blue yields violet; a combination of red and yellow yields orange; or a combination of red and white yields pink. This coding scheme is rather like the scheme used for specifying geographical location in map coordinates. Each location can be specified uniquely by just three numbers, namely longitude, latitude and elevation. A given location can be towards the north or towards the south, but not both. At the same time, it can be either towards the east or towards the west. We attach unique colour labels to specific locations in colour space just as we attach place names to specific geographical locations. All the visual system knows about a colour is its location in colour space; it cannot deduce what physical combination of pigments or lights brought the visual system's response to that location. This makes it possible for an artist to produce an apparently perfect match between a colour in the world, such as a deep blue sky, and the colour of a pigment mix on his or her palette; the pigment mix produces the same three numbers in the head as does the colour of the sky (such pairs of colours are known technically as metameric colours).

Perceptual colour space is defined in terms of six cardinal or primary colours representing the extremes of the three colour axes, namely black, white, red, green, blue and yellow. As far as the physical properties of light are concerned, there is nothing special about the wavelengths corresponding to these colours, so why has human colour vision evolved to create these three particular dimensions? Several research studies have analysed the spectral reflectance curves of natural colours and surfaces such as grass and wood, and assessed how many different colour axes would be needed in order to represent them economically and accurately for the purposes of discrimination and recognition. These studies find that only three axes are required, which bear a close similarity to the axes of human colour vision (Lennie & D'Zmura, 1988; Lee et al., 2002). Thus, the L, R-G and B-Y channels are ideally suited to inform the visual system about the spectral composition of light reflected from natural surfaces.

Representing spectral reflectance

The evolutionary utility of colour vision is based on the fact that natural surfaces can be discriminated and identified by their characteristic spectral reflectance. One might think that all the visual system needs to do to complete this task is to estimate the spectral composition of the light reflected from a surface. If, for instance, there is a lot of red light reflected from the surface, then the object can be labelled 'red' (for example, a ripe fruit or berry). Actually, the task of colour vision is more difficult than this. The difficulty arises from the fact that reflected wavelengths depend not only on the properties of the surface but also on the wavelengths in the incident light, which fluctuate in natural conditions. If there is relatively little energy at red wavelengths in the incident light, then even the ripest fruit or berry cannot reflect much red light. Atmospheric conditions and time of day can both have a dramatic effect on the wavelength composition of natural light and, therefore, on the wavelengths available to be reflected from any surface. When the sun is low on the horizon, for example, natural light contains a preponderance of energy at red wavelengths and many different surfaces will reflect a lot of red light. Thus, in order to estimate colour reliably, the visual system must take into account the prevailing lighting conditions as well as the preponderance of energy at different wavelengths arriving at the eye from reflective surfaces. Fundamentally, colour vision depends on a comparison between light arriving at the eye from one patch in the visual scene and light arriving from surrounding patches. Therefore, a berry will look red not because of the absolute amount of energy at red wavelengths that the eye receives from it but because the berry reflects more energy at red wavelengths than do neighbouring surfaces. Regardless of how much energy the illuminating light contains at red wavelengths in absolute terms, berries look red because they always reflect relatively more energy at red wavelengths than adjacent leaves.

Exactly the same ratio comparison takes place in all three channels. Take the black-white channel: assume that you have in your hand a piece of chalk and a piece of charcoal. The chalk looks lighter than the charcoal, regardless of lighting conditions; it looks white both in sunlight and in moonlight. Yet the absolute amount of light coming off the charcoal in sunlight is likely to be greater than the amount of light coming off the chalk in moonlight. What matters is not the absolute amount of light coming off each object but the *relative* amount. Chalk always reflects more light than charcoal at any given light level, so it always looks lighter. The ratio comparison reinforces the point that colour is a mental computation.

The chromatic ratio computation of colour is performed by neurones in the visual cortex. You may recall from Chapter 3 (Figure 3.2) that cells in the visual cortex only respond when a visual stimulus is presented in a small circumscribed area of the retina in the eye, which is called the cell's receptive field. Some visual stimuli falling within a given cell's receptive field excite the cell, while others inhibit it. A group of cells in the cortex responds to colour or chromatic edges specifically (Conway et al., 2002). A given cell may respond only to edges that are red on one side and green on the other. Other cells respond only to edges that mark a change from blue to yellow.

Crucially, such cells respond only when there is a change in colour across the edge. Moreover, they respond to colour differences even when there is no luminance difference across the edge. In other words, the edge is defined by a change in colour without a change in lightness: an 'equiluminant' edge.

The earliest perceptual demonstration that colour is based on a comparison between one patch in the scene and neighbouring patches was made in 1789 by the French mathematician Gaspard Monge (Mollon, 2006). During a lecture to the French Academy of Sciences, he invited fellow members of the academy to view various objects through a piece of translucent red glass (such glass transmits only red wavelengths, hence its red appearance). When a white object was viewed through the red glass it continued to look whitish, despite the fact that the glass prevented all but red wavelengths from reaching the eye. There was one condition for obtaining the phenomenon: there should be several objects of different colours in the scene. What mattered was not whether light from the white object contained a lot of red light (which it did) but whether it contained a greater preponderance of red light than other objects in the scene (which it did not). If the red glass was placed at the end of a long tube through which the viewer saw nothing but the white object, then the object appeared red. As Monge himself realised in 1789:

So our judgments of the colours of objects seem not to depend uniquely on the absolute nature of the rays of light that paint the image of them on the retina; our judgments can be altered by the context and it is likely that we are influenced more by the ratio of particular properties of the light rays rather than by the properties themselves, considered in an absolute manner. (Quoted in Mollon, 2006, p. 299.)

Another consequence of colour computation in the visual system is the phenomenon of coloured shadows. The shadow of an object viewed under red light looks green, even if the shadow region is illuminated only by white light. The shadow appears green when it is a surface that reflects proportionately less red light than the surrounding red-illuminated surface. In a similar fashion, the shadow of an object viewed under yellow light looks blue even though the shadow region does not contain a preponderance of blue light.

Colour in art

A number of consequences for art flow directly from the architecture of colour processing in the visual system. The independence of luminance and chromatic processing makes it possible for artists to create successful compositions entirely in monochrome; colour is not an essential element of meaningful representations. Correspondingly, it is also possible for artists to create works that are defined predominantly by chromatic variation, with relatively little luminance variation. However, it is very difficult (some would say virtually impossible, even in a laboratory setting) to remove luminance variation completely, due to the extreme sensitivity of the visual system to even the slightest change in luminance. Nevertheless, the Impressionists were particularly adept at isolating pure colour as much as is humanly possible by eye. Monet was a master of this technique, which is most dramatically apparent in his depiction of the shifting surfaces of lakes and seas and in his series of paintings depicting the cathedral at Rouen. The chromatic channel has low spatial resolution, so paintings that minimise luminance variation appear to shimmer and lack clarity (Chapter 2 and Plate 9). Monet even captured the phenomenon of coloured shadows on his canvases, painting exactly what he saw. In his series of paintings depicting haystacks, the shadows cast by the haystacks are almost invariably rendered in a colour that is complementary to the sunlit field and haystack.

The purest and most vivid colours that we perceive correspond to those lying at the extremes of the perceptual colour axes: blue, yellow, green, red, white and black. Independent neural coding of the three axes means that when a colour lies at the extreme of one axis, say red, but at the neutral point of the other axes, then the neurones sensitive to its complement (green in this case) will be maximally suppressed and neurones signalling the other axes should be inactive (although it should be borne in mind that real-world pigments are unlikely to target the axis extremes with high accuracy). In this sense, the perceptual primaries create the purest colour sensations available. National flags around the world are dominated by these colours. The French *Tricolore* has inspired many other flags and actually contains an anchoring colour from each of the three perceptual axes: red, white and blue. The close psychological association between the opposing chromatic primaries is apparent in the historical use of language. Medieval French used the word *sinople* for both red and green. The terms *bloi* and *caeruleus* could refer to either blue or yellow. Such confusions also occur in other languages in Europe, Asia and Africa (Gage, 2006).

The perceptual primaries figure prominently in the paintings of many masters. The presence of one primary is often offset by including its complement to endow the composition with balance and harmony. Vermeer often used a palette based on harmony between blues and yellows, as can be seen in Plate 13. In his most famous painting, 'Girl with a Pearl Earring', the girl's head-dress is rendered in only two colours, blue and yellow. Both Henri Matisse and Piet Mondrian also made extensive use of compositions containing complementary primary colours. Vincent Van Gogh studied the laws of colour and made careful, systematic arrangements of complementary colours in his work. In his bedroom paintings (Plate 20), the blue of the walls and door is complemented by the yellow of the bed and the chair, while the red tones of the blanket and floor are balanced with the green of the chair covers, towel and floor in-fills. Even the smallest details conform to the scheme: the green towel and the chair covers contain fine red stripes.

It is fascinating to re-visit Raphael's 'Saint Catherine' (Plate 1) with the perceptual primaries in mind. Not only does Raphael include all four cardinal or primary colours, perhaps as a reference to the purity and harmony of Catherine, but he arranges them along two perpendicular axes that mirror the axes of colour space. The red-green pair is arranged across Saint Catherine's body from her lowered left arm to her raised right arm, while the blue-yellow axis runs from her right hip to her left shoulder. Raphael's older contemporary Leonardo da Vinci is acknowledged as the first artist to advocate a colour scheme based on all six perceptual primaries (Harkness, 2006). Raphael studied Leonardo's work, so his use of all four chromatic primaries may have been inspired by Leonardo. The arrangement of the clothing forms a colour circle; moving clockwise from the red of Catherine's left arm, the composition moves into yellow, then the green of the right arm and finally the blue of the bodice. The circular harmony may have been intended as a reference to Saint Catherine's emblem, namely the wheel of her martyrdom, also visible in the painting. This painting may represent the first time a perceptual colour wheel was depicted in a work of art.

Some artists deliberately avoid the use of complementary colours in order to achieve the effect they desire. In her colour paintings, Bridget Riley often avoids the direct opposition of complementaries:

If there were, the colour energy would be locked up in the complementary contrast, as though in a straightjacket. It is released by instability, a free floating flux. (Kudielka, 1999, p. 95.)

In some paintings she uses a palette in which green is opposed by violet and pink (which lie on either side of the red complement on the colour circle). The missing complementary is evoked by the colours actually present.

In the pointillist technique practised by the Neo-Impressionist Georges Seurat, colour is applied to the canvas as many small, discrete dots. Viewed close up, the individual dots of colour are discriminable as separate marks. But at a distance, they merge together to create a new colour. The technique circumvents the traditional laws of subtractive mixture, because the colours seen at a distance result from optical or additive mixing, somewhat similar to the additive mixing that occurs in modern colour printing. The rules of additive colour mixing are entirely different from those of subtractive mixing. For example, a subtractive mixture of blue and yellow pigments yields green, because only green pigments are spared (as described earlier). An additive mix of blue and yellow light, on the other hand, yields a grey; the wavelengths in the two colours add together, so the resulting spectrum is relatively broad and neutral. The pointillists argued that their technique produces more vibrant colours. Livingstone (2002) agrees that pointillist paintings are lively and vibrant, but argues that the effect is not due to optical mixing but to the use of discrete dots. As mentioned previously, the chromatic channels are quite weak in their ability to resolve spatial detail. Therefore, at certain intermediate viewing distances, pointillist paintings appear simultaneously as optical colour mixes (via the chromatic channels, which cannot resolve individual dots) and as collections of discrete dots (via the achromatic channel, which can resolve the dots). Dots may be dominant wherever one happens to fixate the painting, while additive mixture dominates away from fixation (due to the uneven resolution of the retina illustrated in Figure 4.2). Each fixation shift produces a new combination of resolution and mixing. This shifting, dual quality gives pointillism its vibrancy; there is no drama caused by the colour mixes themselves.

Summary

Colour is traditionally viewed as an essential component of visual art because it adds to its natural appearance. Colour analysis in the brain aims to estimate the stable spectral reflectance of visible surfaces in the face of changeable lighting conditions. At the first stage of neural colour processing, the wavelength composition of the retinal image is analysed in terms of three opponent pairs of colours (red-green, blue-yellow and black-white), creating three independent perceptual colour axes. At the second stage, surface colour is estimated by comparing the wavelength composition of light arriving at each location in the image with that arriving at adjacent locations, to take account of general illumination effects.

Red, green, blue, yellow, white and black produce the purest, most vivid colour experiences in art because they represent the extremes of the perceptual colour axes, although they have no special status in any purely physical sense. The independence of the three opponent colour axes allows artists to focus their compositions on only one or two of the axes. The opposing colours in each axis interact perceptually to create phenomena such as colour contrasts, complements and coloured shadows. In the interests of compositional balance and harmony, artists often use arrangements of complementary colour pairs. When balance is not desired, complementary pairs are avoided.

8   Visual aesthetics and art

Introduction

During the two millennia before the advent of modern conceptual art, with its emphasis on ideas and intellectual qualities, visual aesthetic pleasure was considered to be a core element of one's experience when viewing visual art. Indeed, beauty was at the very core of the British Aesthetic Movement in art during the late 1800s. Aesthetic judgements are not, of course, restricted to visual art but are also made about natural visual forms such as faces, landscapes and flowers, and about manufactured forms such as buildings and machines. All of these judgements are closely tied to the sensory qualities of the object: its visual attributes such as shape, texture, colour, movement and so on, as well as other attributes such as smell and touch. Moreover, aesthetic judgements are also central in other art forms such as music, literature, opera and dance. Aesthetic judgement is such a fundamental aspect of human experience that it has been considered from the perspective of many different disciplines including philosophy, cultural studies, history and anthropology. This chapter will focus on the insights that can be gained from the scientific perspectives of modern psychology. It will ask how scientific principles can deepen our understanding of aesthetic appreciation in visual art.

Firstly, it will be useful to recognise one of the salient differences between art historical and scientific approaches to the subject. Art historians often focus on individual works or artists, exploring the provenance of an artwork, discussing the formative influences on the artist, or perhaps analysing the particular techniques used in the works. Many deep insights can be gained from such case studies, although they necessarily focus on the unique qualities of individual artists and artworks. The scientific method employed in psychology, on the other hand, typically samples a broad range of individual cases. Data are often collected from a large cohort of experimental participants, who are exposed to a great many visual stimuli. Results are collated across participants and stimuli. Data analysis involves a search for patterns in the relationship between behaviour and physical stimuli – a search for unity in diversity. The aim is to build a general theoretical structure that can explain all the observed patterns and predict the patterns that would be obtained in new experiments. As such, one might complain that scientific approaches to art do little more than search for the lowest common denominator. This may be true to some extent, but a full understanding of a complex, multi-faceted set of behaviours requires an appreciation both of the factors that unite them and of those that make them unique. Both individual and group-based approaches can make a valuable contribution to our understanding. All scientific inquiry is based on established empirical methods for collecting data from large samples, in the form of procedures for making controlled observations that take account of issues such as sampling bias and statistical reliability. Such methods have a long history in psychology, and a particular set of empirical methods were developed over one hundred years ago, specifically for the study of aesthetic judgement.

Empirical aesthetics

The modern field of Experimental Psychology largely owes its origin to Gustav Fechner, who was a German physicist working at Leipzig University in the 1800s. One of his interests was in how humans make fine perceptual discriminations between similar stimuli, such as two slightly different weights or two lights of different intensity. He devised several empirical techniques to measure the 'just noticeable difference' (JND) between two stimuli, defined as the smallest change in sensory stimulation that can be detected reliably. A colleague at Leipzig, Ernst Weber, had previously found that these judgements were remarkably consistent and lawful. He discovered that the JND is a constant fraction or percentage of the original stimulus level, typically of between 1% and 8%, depending on the stimulus involved. To detect a small change in the intensity of a light, for example, intensity must change by approximately 8%; to detect a change in the saturation of a red light, saturation must change by 2% (Teghtsoonian, 1971). Fechner extended Weber's work as follows. He argued that if one started with the smallest amount of stimulation that could be detected (the dimmest light or the smallest degree of colour saturation) and began adding physical increments to it, which were equally discriminable by an observer because they correspond to the JND (for example, increasing light level in steps of 8%), one would create a stimulus series that was spaced at equal intervals along a subjective, psychological scale of perceived magnitude. Each stimulus is only just discriminable from the previous one. The scale is highly non-linear because, as stimulus level rises, progressively larger physical increments must be added at each step to maintain the JND. For example, if light intensity is initially at 100 physical units, then the constant JND increments would be: 8.0, 8.64, 9.33, 10.08, 10.88, 11.76 units and so on. Fechner thus devised a simple mathematical law relating mental events (equal perceptual intervals) to physical events (stimulus increments), a *psychophysical* law. Fechner's experimental methods to measure JNDs became known as psychophysical methods, and variants of them are still widely used in experimental psychology.

In his later work, Fechner applied the new psychophysical approach to aesthetic judgements, reasoning that such judgements should be amenable to measurement in the same way as judgements of brightness, saturation and so on. His aim was to reveal the laws that relate objective measures of aesthetic judgement to physical properties of the sensory stimulus. In 1876, Fechner described three empirical techniques for studying aesthetic judgement:

Method of production. The participant is asked to produce an artwork that conforms to their taste.

Method of choice. The participant is asked to compare artworks with respect to their 'pleasingness'.

Method of use. Artworks are examined under the assumption that the most commonly observed characteristics will be those that meet with the most widespread approval.

Modern studies in empirical aesthetics predominantly employ the latter two methods (although McManus et al., 2011, use an interesting variant of the *Method of production*). A study employing the *Method of choice* may present the participant with a number of experimental trials, each containing a different pair of artworks. In each trial, the participant is asked to select the member of each pair that they find most pleasing. Binary choices of this kind are used very commonly in scientific studies of perception. Presentation order is randomised to ensure that choices are driven primarily by the images themselves rather than by certain biases that are not related to the images, such as a preference for the first image in each pair, or the left-hand image, or images presented early in the study rather than late, and so on. Binary choice data are also amenable to well-established statistical analysis techniques. However, data from binary choice experiments can reveal only a limited amount of information about aesthetic preference; they can show which images are preferred over others, but they cannot indicate just how beautiful (or ugly) the images are judged to be.

An alternative implementation of the *Method of choice* attempts to remedy this limitation. The participant is shown only one artwork in each trial and is required to rate it along a scale of 'pleasingness' or aesthetic merit from, say, 1 to 10. Using this technique, one can be confident that ratings provide some measure of aesthetic pleasure, but rating scales have their own limitations, which relate to the verbal descriptors attached to the scales. If the scale descriptors range from 'the ugliest artwork ever' to 'the most beautiful artwork ever', then participants are very unlikely to use ratings near the extremities and there is a consequent danger that ratings cluster around the middle of the scale. On the other hand, if the 10-point scale covers a less extreme range, say from 'very ugly' to 'very beautiful', participants may feel unable meaningfully to discriminate between small differences in scale, such as a one-point difference between a '5' and a '6'. Thus, no method is perfect, and different techniques have their own virtues and limitations.

Whichever technique is used in the *Method of choice*, scores can be compared against a physical measurement of the properties of the artworks, in an attempt to infer the nature of the psychophysical law relating preference or rating to physical stimulation. It is up to the researcher, of course, to decide which physical measure to apply to the artworks, perhaps based on a theory regarding the source of aesthetic pleasure. For example, if the researcher has a theory that symmetrical compositions are the most attractive, then the theory can be tested by first assembling a collection of artworks that differ in terms of a physical measure of symmetry and then collecting a preference or rating score for each artwork to determine whether the data can be predicted by measured symmetry.

Theories of visual aesthetic beauty

Aesthetic judgement essentially involves a judgement regarding beauty. What makes a painting beautiful? Historically, theories of beauty were divided into three camps. *Objectivist* theories argue that beauty is an inherent property of an object that induces a feeling of pleasure in the perceiver. This kind of theory is associated with philosophers such as Plato and Kant (Pluhar, 1987) and has led many to search for the properties that signify beauty such as balance and proportion. *Subjectivist* theories take the opposite view, arguing that 'beauty is in the eye of the beholder'; it is an idiosyncrasy of the perceiver and their culture, a socio-cultural construction (Englis et al., 1994). Both kinds of theory are untenable because they lack an essential element of the beauty equation: judgements of beauty inescapably involve both a perceiver *and* an object. Yet the objectivist approach denies the role played by the perceiver in the judgement. On the other hand, according to the subjectivist approach the properties of the perceived object are irrelevant. An adequate theory of aesthetic judgement must surely find a role for both the perceiver and the object. Thus, modern *Interactionist* theories argue that beauty emerges from the interaction between the two. Consistent patterns in the way perceivers relate to objects result in some objects being judged more beautiful than others. Reber et al. (2004) advocated the view that "beauty is in the processing experiences of the beholder" (p. 378), to emphasise the idea that beauty judgements are determined jointly by objective stimulus properties and the perceiver's cognitive and emotional processes. Leder et al. (2004) proposed a detailed interactionist theory of aesthetic judgement that breaks down the underlying cognitive processes into a series of stages comprising perceptual analysis, memory integration, classification and aesthetic evaluation.

Traditional philosophical concepts of aesthetic judgement view it as a special process that is distinct from the appraisal of everyday things. The philosopher Emmanuel Kant argued that pure aesthetic judgement comes only from 'disinterested' appraisal that is detached from considerations of practical utility (Pluhar, 1987). Classical art sought to promote a disinterested attitude in the viewer by defining clear borders between the artwork and the real world: the frame surrounding a painting, the pedestal supporting a sculpture, or the stage hosting a performing art. Once isolated in this way, attention could be focused purely on the internal attributes of the object: its self-sufficiency, completeness, unity and so on (Bearleant, 1993). As will become clear later in the chapter, scientific evidence indicates that the classical disinterested view of aesthetics is untenable. Aesthetic appraisal of everyday things such as objects, people, buildings and landscapes shares much in common with the appraisal of artworks.

Empirical studies of visual aesthetic preference

The interactionist theory predicts that there should be consistent patterns in human aesthetic judgements that relate to specific stimulus properties, because they are rooted in universal human cognitive faculties. There is convincing evidence to support the prediction. Consider aesthetic judgement of facial beauty. One study (Cunningham et al., 1995) used Fechner's *Method of choice*: 97 participants were shown 48 photographs of female faces, each presented for 30 seconds. Upon each presentation, the participant was required to rate the photograph on an 8-point scale ranging from 'very attractive' to 'very unattractive'. Forty-six of the raters were white American, 38 were Asian and 13 were Hispanic. A total of 43 were male and 54 were female. The 'target' photographs included Asian, Hispanic, black, European and American women. Results showed no statistically reliable difference between the ratings of male and female raters. Nor were ratings affected by the ethnic origin of either the raters or the targets. One might argue that ratings were similar because all the raters had been influenced by Western cultural standards of beauty, despite their different ethnic origins. To test this possibility, Cunningham et al. (1995) conducted a second experiment using the same procedure as the first but the raters were 38 Chinese-speaking students at Chung-Yuan University, Taiwan, who had very limited exposure to Westerners. Results again found no reliable difference between male and female raters and high levels of agreement with the ratings from the first study.

Therefore, it seems that standards of facial beauty are fairly universal. Such a conclusion does not deny that cultural factors can also play a role in beauty, but one cannot ignore the fact that human beings are predisposed to find some forms more visually appealing than others. Cunningham et al. (1995) took measurements from the rated photographs to assess the stimulus attributes that were associated with high scores. They found that large eyes and a small chin were particularly important. Other more extensive investigations into the physical features of attractive faces have identified three general factors (Rhodes, 2006). Firstly, the face should be balanced and symmetrical. Secondly, it should be sexually dimorphic, so female faces should have fine, soft features such as a petite jaw-line and full lips, while male faces should have strong features such as a prominent, angular chin and broad jaw. Finally, and somewhat surprisingly, the face should be an average face. Typical faces, which are closer to the population average, are consistently rated as more attractive than distinctive faces, even after other factors such as symmetry are accounted for.

Not only are judgements of facial attractiveness universal, they also seem to be innate. Research reveals that babies have an innate capacity to find and track face-like patterns in the visual world. Even nine minutes after birth babies can apparently track a face. Fechner's *Method of choice* can be employed in studies using young infants. In this case, the experimenter presents the infant with two faces side-by-side and measures the amount of time he or she spends looking at each face. One study (Slater et al., 1998) measured the relative time babies less than three days old looked at each of two faces that had been rated independently as 'attractive' or 'unattractive' by adults. The agreement between adult ratings and infant preferences, as indicated by their looking time, was very high: infants looked at the attractive faces for almost twice as long as they looked at the unattractive faces.

Chapter 10 will consider the question as to why facial attractiveness might be universal and innate but, in the present context, the main point is that judgements of facial beauty are universal, innate and related to specific stimulus features, as one would expect on the basis of interactionism.

Basic artistic preferences also seem to be universal. In the 1990s, two Russian émigré artists in the United States, named Vitaly Komar and Alexander Melamid, embarked on a satirical quest to discover the artistic preferences of the American population. They employed legitimate scientific methodology: a professional market research company polled a representative sample of 1,001 Americans, administering a standard questionnaire containing 102 questions on fine art preferences. Komar and Melamid had ostensibly set out in the 1970s

to show that Soviet society, in spite of government propaganda, had many contradictions; that there were different circles, even classes; that, in spite of revolution, everyone was not more or less same socially. Here in America, before we got results of poll we thought we would have to paint different pictures by income, by race. Instead, we made surprising discovery: in society famous for freedom of expression, freedom of individual, our poll revealed sameness of majority. (Wypijewski, 1997.)

The questionnaire has since been administered to thousands of people in ten countries across several continents. A surprising picture of uniformity emerges. At least in terms of their questionnaire responses, people the world over seem to prefer the same kind of art. The respondents represent a broad spread of human cultural and artistic traditions, namely North America (USA), Europe (Germany), Africa (Kenya) and Asia (China). In all four continents, the overwhelming majority of people professed a preference for paintings of outdoor scenes rather than indoor scenes and that these scenes should contain both animals (either domesticated or wild) and people. In answer to the question 'Which type of outdoor scene appeals the most?', the consistent preference was for open, rural scenes containing water, rather than forests or manufactured landscapes (Figure 8.1).

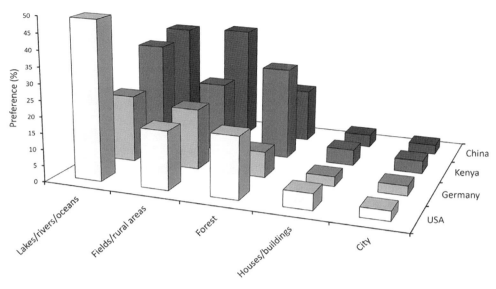

Figure 8.1 A summary of responses in four countries to Komar and Melamid's question: 'Which type of outdoor scene appeals the most?'

The overwhelming majority also agreed that art should be 'relaxing to look at', rather than 'jumbled up and confusing'. The striking uniformity in responses offers support for the universality of aesthetic preferences. It is remarkable how often the world's most popular paintings contain all the elements highlighted in Komar and Melamid's survey – predominantly open rural scenes containing both animals and humans. Claude's landscapes (Plate 2) and Brueghel's outdoor scenes (Plate 5), for example, are widely regarded as among the greatest paintings in the Western tradition, and their paintings tend to contain all of these elements. Humans and animals often occupy the foreground, with trees in the middle distance giving way to an open landscape often containing water, sometimes with peaks or crags in the far distance. Brueghel added distant crags to his views of European lowlands purely for aesthetic effect. Evidence of human habitation, in the form of buildings, is almost always present as well. Preferences for these pictorial elements are unlikely to reflect culturally transmitted standards based on Western art, as they were expressed strongly in all populations surveyed, including African and Asian respondents. Scenes containing trees, mountains and water, with humans and perhaps animals, are also a common theme in Chinese landscape art.

Landscape architects such as Lancelot 'Capability' Brown were adept at catering for these universal preferences in creating garden designs that contain undulating open spaces broken up by clumps and belts of trees, incorporating water features such as lakes and streams. Our positive response to certain elements in a natural landscape, whether a painting or a garden, is so powerful and deeply rooted that it can actually impact on our physical well-being. Patients recovering from surgery in hospital recover faster and require less analgesic medication when their room has a view out onto a natural scene rather than onto a brick building (Ulrich, 1984).

The biological root of aesthetic judgement

The universality of aesthetic judgement indicates biological roots and an evolutionary origin. These roots can be traced to their source by picking up another key feature of aesthetic judgement, its reward value. Visual beauty gives pleasure to such an extent that many people actively seek it out. They visit galleries, go to movies and buy artworks (or reproductions) because of the pleasure they experience. Rewarding stimuli have been studied extensively in biological psychology. How does aesthetic pleasure fit into the general biological context of reward and motivation?

In a biological context, rewards can be defined as stimuli that positively reinforce behaviour, meaning that they increase the likelihood that the behaviour will be repeated. Food, water and sexual stimulation are well known as primary rewards, which can produce intense feelings of pleasure. Animal studies have identified a particular neurotransmitter called dopamine and a 'reward circuit' in the brain that seem to control reward-related behaviour. The circuit includes neurones in brain regions called the orbitofrontal cortex (OFC) and ventral striatum. Animals have been found to self-administer chemicals that mimic the effects of dopamine. Drugs which cause humans to experience a 'high', such as cocaine, are known to stimulate dopamine release (Ikemoto & Panksepp, 1999).

Recent studies of the neural basis of pleasure in humans have used non-invasive brain imaging techniques. Human fMRI studies have found that food- and sex-related sensory stimuli produce activation in the reward circuit previously identified in animal studies (McClure et al., 2004). The OFC receives direct connections from several regions of the sensory cortex, including visual, olfactory, gustatory and somatosensory areas, so it is well placed to play a role in processing the reward value of sensory stimuli.

Recent brain imaging studies have explored the pattern of brain activation that accompanies the aesthetic appraisal of artworks. If the traditional view of aesthetic judgement as disinterested is correct, then there is no reason to expect any correspondence between brain activation when judging artworks and activation patterns when judging food- and sex-related stimuli. To assess whether aesthetic judgement is part of a more general object appraisal process, Brown et al. (2011) collated the results of 93 neuroimaging studies of aesthetic appraisal across multiple sensory modalities, including both art objects and non-art objects. They found consistent overlapping areas of activation in the OFC. There was no evidence of any specific activation pattern associated with art objects as opposed to non-art objects. They concluded that aesthetic appraisal of art is mediated by the same brain processes that serve aesthetic appraisal of objects that have survival value, such as food sources. fMRI studies using faces (Aharon et al., 2001), abstract patterns (Jacobsen et al., 2006), photographs (Yue et al., 2007) and paintings (Kawabata and Zeki, 2004; Vartanian and Goel, 2004) all find activation in the reward circuit that correlates with aesthetic pleasure, as well as activation in other areas such as the visual cortex and parietal cortex. The activation of the latter brain areas is not surprising, as aesthetic judgement must involve elements of introspection, decision-making and memory. However, activation of the reward circuit demonstrates that aesthetic judgement is not a purely intellectual exercise. It taps into the same basic drive mechanisms as food and sex.

In one study (Kawabata & Zeki, 2004), a group of participants judged the aesthetic merit of 300 paintings. The experimenters then selected a subset that were representative examples of paintings judged as beautiful, neutral or ugly. When a second group of participants were shown these samples while in an fMRI scanner, the extent of activation in the OFC cortex was found to depend on aesthetic merit as measured in the earlier experiment. In another study, participants assigned preference scores to a series of photographic scenes in terms of mystery (the likelihood that something new would be visible from a different vantage point), vista (how wide was the view), natural versus urban, complexity and intelligibility (Yue et al., 2007). Preference judgements along these different dimensions were quite consistent, and images that were highly preferred generated more activity in the ventral striatum than images that were least preferred.

Thus, aesthetically pleasing images really are rewarding in the same general way that food and sex are rewarding. To appreciate why aesthetic pleasure may be rewarding, it is useful to know a little more about the function of the reward circuit. Mobile creatures operate within strictly limited resources in the sense that they must balance food intake against energy expenditure while, at the same time, taking steps to avoid danger and to perpetuate their genes. This balancing act requires the organism to make decisions continually about what to do next, because each decision inevitably has a cost and may have a benefit. In order to reach these decisions about how to allocate time and energy, selecting which action to take at any given moment, all animals must place a relative value on alternative behaviours (sensory inputs and motor outputs). The alternatives may have little in common in terms of the neural structures involved, the resources required and their consequences. The individual is torn between diverse fundamental needs, such as: Do I search for a potential mate, or some food? Therefore, how does he or she reach a decision when the alternatives are so different? In order to solve this problem, the brain needs a common internal currency for assigning expected relative value to each of the alternatives, its reward value. Actions can then be selected on the basis of their relative reward value at that particular time. The job of the reward circuit in the brain is to compute expected reward value, so it plays a crucial role in all moment-to-moment decision-making (Montague & Berns, 2002). Perhaps our conscious awareness of the pleasure or 'rush' we experience from a particular behaviour whatever that may be, such as viewing a particular scene, is the subjective expression of the reward computed for that action; a kind of running commentary on the brain's internal decision-making, the currency exchange. Although we may feel that we do things because they are pleasurable, it may well be the case that this experience of pleasure is actually a consequence rather than a cause, a by-product of the hidden neural processes that underpin our decision-making.

The next question to ask is why aesthetic pleasure is part of the reward economy at all. What role does aesthetic appraisal play in the give-and-take of survival? The modern life sciences are underpinned by Darwin's theory of natural selection, which proposes that new biological design features emerge in a species only if they improve the chances of reproduction. Features that improve a creature's chances of avoiding predation or of finding a mate or of selecting nutritious food clearly have adaptive value and will become part of our genetic inheritance. Aesthetic experiences must have evolved as part of a motivational system that steers humans towards certain forms of visual stimulation in preference to others. What adaptive value might be attached to aesthetic experiences? As part of a general reward processing system, aesthetic experiences may relate to a number of biologically important needs including survival, energy conservation and reproduction. The concept of affordance provides a useful framework for thinking about how aesthetic judgement relates to biological need.

Aesthetic affordance

Neuroimaging evidence described earlier in the chapter indicates that the aesthetic appraisal of objects cannot be detached from their utility. The psychologist J. J. Gibson coined the term 'affordance' to describe the properties of an object that determine just how it could be used:

The affordances of the environment are what it offers to animals, what it provides or furnishes for good or ill. (Gibson, 1977, p. 68.)

For example:

- Does a particular object afford support for body weight and, therefore, can act as a seat?
- Does a particular substance afford eating or drinking?
- Does a particular creature afford a particular kind of interaction, whether sexual, predatory, nurturing, competing or cooperating?

The environment is full of thousands of different things, some of which may be unknown to a particular individual. Yet novel objects or unfamiliar creatures need to be assessed promptly if appropriate action is to be taken. An ability to perceive their affordances rapidly would help to ensure survival in a challenging world. Hence, all creatures seem to possess a perceptual system that can seek out and assess affordance independently of object categorisation and knowledge. For example, a novel object can be perceived as affording a seat even if it is not recognisable as a chair, provided that it has certain visual properties (size, surface orientation, position and so on). An unfamiliar surface can be perceived as affording support for one's body weight and, therefore, is safe to stand on (or swing from). It is still not known exactly how perceptual systems evaluate affordance, and relatively little research has been conducted to shed light on the issue.

Affordances can be either beneficial or detrimental to survival. A food source, for instance, has positive affordance (it affords eating), but a precipice has negative affordance (it affords falling). It could be argued that a function of the reward circuit described earlier is to evaluate affordance; in other words, to compute how positive or negative is the affordance of a specific thing or creature. Positive affordance is associated with anticipated reward. Because objects that are evaluated as having positive affordance should be associated with an anticipated reward (comfort, safety, satiety), they should be pleasurable to behold; they should be aesthetically pleasing. Hand tools are an excellent example of the close association between aesthetically pleasing form and useful function. At an exhibition in London's Design Museum to celebrate his work, the British interior designer Sir Terence Conran remarked:

I have never seen an ugly hand tool, it's a perfect example of form and function coming together to produce something that not only works, but is also aesthetically beautiful.

For his 80th birthday, Conran's company Benchmark Woodworking Ltd presented him with a tool case containing a display of woodworking tools that are undeniably both aesthetically beautiful and highly functional (Figure 8.2). The aesthetic pleasure evoked by these and many other well-designed artefacts such as kitchen utensils, furniture, cars and so on may relate to their perceived affordance, the anticipated reward from using them successfully to complete a task. Of course, beautiful form does not always follow function. Some designs may appear attractive but perform their intended task very poorly, as discussed at length by Norman (1998). The arrangement of controls on a car dashboard, a telephone, a remote control unit, a microwave oven or whatever may appear visually appealing in its simplicity, regularity and coherence but may make the object very difficult to use. The problem here is that an object may offer several affordances, which are perceived via different visual attributes. Functionality may be indicated by features signifying that the object is wieldy, comfortable, powerful and so on, while visual forms that are well composed, coherent and organised afford highly efficient processing by the visual system (discussed in the next chapter). The two sets of visual attributes need not coincide, so some designs may compromise functionality for the sake of visual form. The most successful designs are those that combine both a high degree of perceived utility with a coherent, well-organised visual form.

The general point is that aesthetics is linked biologically to utility or affordance, not detached from it in the traditional philosophical sense. The next two chapters reveal how the concept of aesthetic utility or affordance applies equally well to natural forms, to their representation in artworks and to artworks themselves. Certain aspects of landscape (actual or depicted) may be attractive

Figure 8.2 A tool case containing a collection of woodworking tools, presented to Sir Terence Conran by his company, Benchmark Woodworking Ltd.

because they afford safety and survival, while some human features (again, actual or depicted) may be judged as beautiful because they afford successful reproduction and healthy offspring. Artworks may be valued as objects to the extent that they afford efficient processing by the brain, as well as reliable judgements of mate quality.

Summary

The scientific method employed in psychology involves a search for patterns in the relationship between art and perception across a range of artworks. This approach complements the traditional art historical approach, which emphasises individual case studies. Empirical methods introduced in the nineteenth century, such as the *Method of choice*, allow researchers to make objective measures of aesthetic judgement and to relate these measures to the physical characteristics of visual images.

Many such studies have found that aesthetic judgements are universal and innate, as expected on the basis of an interactionist approach to aesthetics, which acknowledges the importance of both object properties and consistent patterns of human cognition. Studies of brain activation are not consistent with the traditional concept of aesthetics as disinterested appraisal. Instead, data reveal that the aesthetic appraisal of everyday things such as objects, people, buildings and landscapes activates the same neural processes as those involved in the appraisal of artworks. The perceived aesthetic value of a thing may be tied, at least partly, to its utility or affordance.

9 Visual aesthetics and nature

Introduction

The previous chapter concluded that aesthetic preference is tied, at least in part, to utility or affordance. If the human aesthetic sense did evolve as part of a reward system for satisfying certain biologically important needs, then it must be closely linked to visual features in the natural environment. Humans evolved not to function in the environment of modern civilisation, which emerged only in the last few thousand years, but in the environment of the Pleistocene era. For two million years humans existed and evolved as Pleisto-cene hunter–gatherers. Survival depended on foraging for edible plants and hunting animals. It was a relatively mobile, nomadic existence that relied upon the resources available in the local environment. Bands of hunter–gatherers perpetually moved on to new locations with the changing seasons and with the depletion of local resources. The first point of enquiry in the search for the natural origin of visual aesthetics is this ancient environment. Perhaps the demands of this ancestral lifestyle still drive our aesthetic preferences. The artist Henri Matisse remarked that 'art imitates nature'. The mimetic theory of art described in Chapter 1 views art as an idealised imitation of nature, a distilled essence of natural aesthetic beauty. To what extent does aesthetic appreciation of art spring from judgements about ancient natural forms? This chapter considers the question from the viewpoint of modern research on landscape preference and visual statistics.

Landscape art

Landscape art has a long history extending back at least to Roman frescos. It developed as a distinct artistic genre from the sixteenth century onwards. Representations of natural scenes gradually became more realistic, and the landscape itself became the main subject, rather than a backdrop to a portrait or a narrative scene. In Europe, landscape art differed between northern and southern artists, perhaps reflecting the local environment. In the north, artists such as Cranach the Younger, Altdorfer, Durer and Brueghel (Plate 5; see colour plate section) depicted dense forests, mountains and vast horizons. In the south, the predominant motif was rolling countryside, a cultivated landscape dotted with ancient ruins or farm buildings. By the seventeenth century, painters such as Claude (Plate 2) had developed a set of conventions for depicting idealised or classical landscape scenes. The painting was usually divided into a series of receding depth planes. Tall trees occupied the middle distance, giving way to a distant view of mountains. People and perhaps animals were often placed in the foreground. Water in the form of a lake or river was a common element, as was a blue sky and low sun partially obscured by dramatic cloud formations. Evidence of human habitation took the form of a distant farmhouse or villa, or perhaps a temple or classical ruin. Some of these elements recur in landscape art of the nineteenth century, such as paintings by Constable and Corot. By this time, 'a peaceful scene, with water in the foreground reflecting a luminous sky and set off by dark trees, was something which everyone agreed was beautiful' (Clark, 1976, p. 147).

Despite the use of photography as a record of landscape and the rise of modern, non-representational art, landscape art retains an eternal appeal. The Komar and Melamid survey described in the previous chapter found that landscapes were easily the most preferred artistic genre for non-specialists. The universality and persistence of landscape as a preferred genre suggests that it may tap into a fundamental human need. The 'savannah' hypothesis (Orians and Heerwagen, 1992) proposes that we have an innate preference for landscapes similar to the African savannah environment in which our Pleistocene ancestors lived, a relatively open countryside sparsely populated with trees. According to the theory, a preference for this kind of landscape evolved because it affords the best habitat: plentiful plants and animals, with sufficient tree coverage for shelter, while avoiding the large predators that could hide in more densely wooded terrain. Pleistocene hunter–gatherers needed to move on to new habitats frequently, so their survival depended crucially on appropriate habitat choices. These pressures, the theory argues, led to an evolved preference for landscapes similar to the ancient savannah, the optimal environment. This preference finds expression today in our attraction to landscape art.

Several empirical studies appear to support the savannah hypothesis. One study (Lohr & Pearson-Mims, 2006) found that people typically have a high aesthetic preference for trees with a spreading canopy, similar to those found on the African savannah, rather than for trees with a rounded or conical form. Other studies used coloured slides of savannah, forest and desert environments, and found that people expressed a preference for the savannah slides over the others (Balling & Falk, 1982; Falk & Balling, 2010).

Unfortunately, there are a number of significant weaknesses in the studies that claim to support the savannah hypothesis and in the hypothesis itself, at least as an explanation for visual aesthetic preferences. Firstly, studies of landscape preference often do not enquire directly about visual beauty. In the two studies just mentioned, participants were asked: 'How much would you like to live permanently in an area that looked like the slide?' (Balling & Falk, 1982; Falk & Balling, 2010). This kind of judgement clearly is not just about visual aesthetic appeal. Preferences may partly reflect judgements about factors such as climate, safety and health, although one could argue that these affordances should legitimately form part of aesthetic appeal. More seriously, there is no universally agreed definition of precisely what a savannah landscape is like in a physical sense, leading to inconsistencies in materials used in different studies. Nor can one claim convincingly that the preferences revealed in the Komar and Melamid survey support the savannah hypothesis specifically, because the questions used in the survey were too general. A recent study (Han, 2007) on landscape preference did ask subjects to rate landscape photographs for their scenic beauty and used all six widely recognised ecological environments: desert, tundra, grassland, coniferous forest, deciduous forest and tropical forest.

The study found that tundra and coniferous forests were the most preferred landscapes and that grassland and desert were the least preferred (Figure 9.1). These preferences are inconsistent with the savannah hypothesis. Tundra is cold and arid, so is unlikely to be preferred because of the favourable habitat that it offers. The tundra slides used in the study were mostly of alpine tundra rather than Arctic tundra, so the high preference for these images may reflect the presence of mountainous scenery (a possible source for such a preference is described later in the chapter).

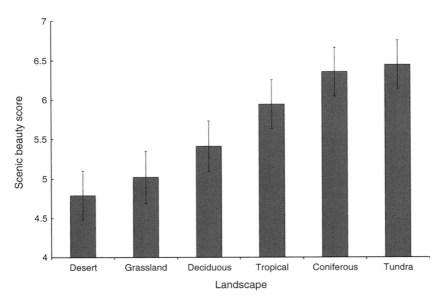

Figure 9.1 Results of a study of preferences for scenic beauty in landscape photographs (data from Han, 2007, Table 3). Tundra and coniferous forest attracted the highest ratings, while desert and grassland attracted the lowest ratings.

The most fundamental problem for the savannah hypothesis is that its basic assumption, namely that Pleistocene hunter–gatherers lived on savannah, is not consistent with archaeological evidence. The archaeological record shows that ancient habitats were not stable but were subject to repeated re-modelling by natural forces during the course of hominid evolution (earthquakes, volcanic eruptions, glaciations; Potts, 1998). Furthermore, early hominids four million years ago did not restrict themselves to a narrow range of habitats. Likely habitats included 'dry, possibly open, wooded or bushland conditions...closed woodland...grassland, scattered trees and nearby woodland' (Leakey et al., 1995, p. 571). Rather than adapting to survive in one particular environment, early humans apparently evolved to cope with environmental variability by becoming more versatile. Flexible anatomy meant that humans could cover open ground easily on two feet while retaining some ability to climb; brain enlargement allowed more flexible cognitive processing; and complex social mechanisms led to coordinated group action and trading (Potts, 1998). This versatility has allowed humans to colonise the whole of the planet. It is implausible that, despite evolutionary adaptations to permit such versatility, humans have retained an enduring aesthetic preference for only one, ancient, ecological niche.

Despite the limitations of the savannah hypothesis, landscape aesthetics may nevertheless offer a useful perspective on the origin of aesthetic preferences in art. One characteristic of landscapes that seems to evoke pleasure and interest is 'mystery'. Occluded or invisible areas such as hidden spaces behind trees or hills, or paths that wind out of sight, excite curiosity and invite exploration. Curiosity is a basic behavioural characteristic exhibited by many animals that rely on foraging for food. Exploratory behaviour is part of the reward market discussed in the previous chapter and seems to be a rewarding activity in itself. Indeed, animal studies of the reward system have found that dopamine levels influence an animal's inclination to explore its environment (Hooks & Kalivas, 1995). Evolution should also have equipped human hunter–gatherers with a motivation to explore their immediate environment, to seek out affordances and so find resources and establish whether predators or competitors were nearby. The pleasure evoked by mystery in landscape art may relate to this ancient biological drive to explore our surroundings.

Humans may also have evolved a motivation to seek out landscape features that offer a good view or prospect of the surrounding area, as well as a place of refuge (Appleton, 1996), because individuals who take best advantage of these features have a greater chance of survival. The inclination to seek locations offering both prospect and refuge still exerts a subtle influence on human behaviour in the modern environment. Studies of seating preference in public spaces such as restaurants find that the most highly preferred locations are those that place the individual in a more private position in a corner or against a wall, with a good view out into the surrounding area (Hwang & Yoon, 2009). Hence, part of the pleasure we gain from viewing landscape art may originate in an unconscious predisposition to explore terrain and to identify viewpoints and refuges. Artists may be inclined to include these features in their landscapes for the same reason.

Many landscape paintings contain people or animals, and studies of landscape preference find that the presence of humans and animals generates interest in the viewer. Other animals and humans are, of course, crucially important for survival because they are a source of food, competition, danger or sex. The visual cortex possesses populations of neurones that are specialised to detect animate forms in images (discussed in the chapter on motion), which may form part of an evolved motivational system for seeking out animate forms in visual scenes. The biophilia hypothesis proposes that humans have a 'love of life or living systems', which attracts them to images containing human and animal forms (Kellert & Wilson, 1993).

In general, our preference for landscape art and for certain recurring features in landscape art, such as mystery, viewpoints, places of shelter and animate forms, may reflect genetic predispositions to search for such features because they signify affordances that are so important for survival. Certainly, the renowned landscape paintings illustrated earlier almost always contain these features.

Energy demand in the brain

There is another plausible reason why evolutionary adaptations may drive us to prefer certain images, which can be applied to a wide spectrum of paintings from landscapes to abstract art. As mentioned in the previous chapter, it is based on the idea that aesthetic experiences are generated by a reward system that steers the individual towards activities that afford the lowest levels of energy expenditure in the brain. The brain is a small but very expensive organ for the body to support. It accounts for only 2% of total body weight in a normal, young human adult, yet consumes 20% of a resting body's overall energy requirement (Attwell & Laughlin, 2001). The brain mostly uses this energy as the power source for the electrical signals generated by its many millions of neurones. However, energy is a limited resource due to restrictions in the brain's blood supply; an expansion in vasculature would allow more blood to be pumped into the brain but would occupy so much space that it would compromise both the shape and the size of the cortex. As a result, the brain makes do by taking in a constant supply of energy regardless of variations in mental activity, apart from lower consumption during sleep or in pathological conditions, and distributing this energy flexibly to different parts of the brain according to need (hence, you cannot think yourself thin). Furthermore, neural activity is very costly in metabolic terms. Metabolic demand increases dramatically as neural activity increases. Coupled with limitations in energy supply, this means that only a tiny fraction, perhaps 3%, of all the neurones in the brain can be highly active at any one time (Lennie, 2003). Therefore, the brain cannot do very many things at once because it cannot deliver sufficient energy to many different specialised areas at the same time. This places a fundamental limit on its capacity to process information; only a few cognitive tasks can be undertaken concurrently. At a functional or psychological level, this often is described in terms of limitations on attention.

Visual processing has a large impact on the brain's energy budget. The cortex accounts for 44% of the brain's energy consumption, and the visual cortex occupies about half of the cortex, so vision alone accounts for nearly 5% of the whole body's energy consumption at rest. Just opening one's eyes eats up a surprising amount of energy: glucose consumption in the visual cortex increases by 50% when the eyes open onto a complex, dynamic visual scene (Lennie, 2003; this explains why closing one's eyes while thinking may really help). Any change in brain function that improves the efficiency of visual processing should confer an advantage during natural selection, because it can deliver a significant saving in overall energy consumption. Selection pressure during evolution will have favoured individuals who possessed a visual system that could process natural images in the most energy-efficient manner possible. If natural images tend to contain recurring features, then the visual system could evolve specialisations for processing those features. At first sight, one might think that there is little scope for such specialisations because natural images are so complex and diverse. Different landscape scenes show dramatic variations in many important image properties, such as the distribution and density of contours, variations of light, dark and colour, and patterns of visual texture. However, despite this diversity, natural images are far from random but are highly structured because the natural surfaces and objects they contain are themselves highly structured and, therefore, possess certain consistent statistical properties. Evolution should have driven the visual system to take advantage of these consistencies in order to maximise processing efficiency. Perhaps the images created by visual artists are so special because of the artist's skill in making them supremely well adapted to the visual system. Visual art may possess statistical properties that are very well matched to those most prevalent in natural scenes and so make art amenable to highly efficient processing by the brain. Is there any evidence to support the provocative idea that artists are intuitively good at natural visual statistics?

Regularities in natural images

The visual system is not truly general-purpose in the sense that it can handle any arbitrary image it receives equally well, although sometimes it is described as such. It evolved to handle a constrained set of images, namely images drawn from the visual environment that made up our ancestral habitat. Any natural surface or object, whether a cloud, a body of water, a rock, a face or an animal, tends to be extended over space and is cohesive in its visual properties. A large cloud tends to be grey or white; a body of water is blue-green in colour and flecked with the regular visual texture created by ripples; animal hide or skin tends to have a characteristic colour and visual texture, and so on. Therefore, natural images tend to contain regions with consistent colour, lightness, or textural properties that correspond to the visible surfaces of the objects in the scene. Now and again there are abrupt changes in these properties that coincide with the bounding contours of the objects present in the scene but, by and large, nearby points in the image will tend to be more similar in terms of lightness, colour, texture and so on than more distant points. In a completely random image, on the other hand, there is no consistent relationship at all between the intensity or colour at any one image point and the intensity or colour at any other point, no matter how near or far apart the two points are in the image. The top-left image in Figure 9.2 displays this property. It contains a random pattern of dark and light pixels (an abbreviation of 'picture elements': the individual dots that make up the image). The graph at the top-right of the figure summarises the similarity (or correlation in mathematical terminology) between pairs of points in the random pattern as a function of their spatial separation. High values denote points that match in the sense that both are bright or both dark, while low values correspond to points that do not match (one bright and the other dark). Notice that the line is flat; there is no greater similarity between nearby points than between far-distant points, and there is, on average, a 50% chance of a match. The image contains a random arrangement of black and white pixels.

In a natural image, on the other hand, there is a consistent relationship between different points in the image. Points near to each other tend to be quite similar, but the similarity declines as the points move further apart. The bottom-left image in Figure 9.2 shows a natural scene, and the graph at the bottom-right plots the similarity in pixel intensity as a function of distance. Notice that the line is sloped, indicating that nearby pixels are more similar than far-distant pixels (Burton & Moorhead, 1987; Ruderman, 1997).

Systematic mathematical analyses of natural images have revealed that the variation in similarity between pairs of points in such images does not depend on whether the viewer zooms into a small region of the image or zooms out to a wide perspective. This remarkable property of natural images, called scale-invariance, is an important source of statistical consistency between them, which the visual system is thought to exploit in the interests of processing efficiency. Scale-invariance stems from two properties of natural objects and their images. Firstly, objects in the environment have a large range of sizes and we view them at a range of distances; hence natural images tend to contain repeating patterns at different sizes.

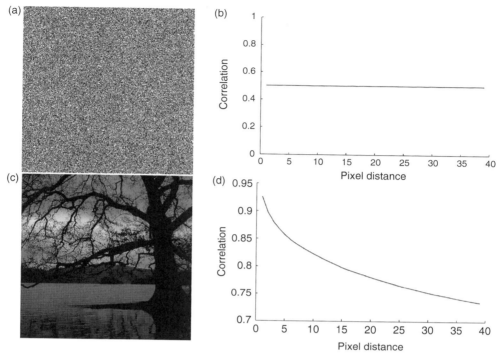

Figure 9.2 (a) A random black-white pattern; the intensity at each point or 'pixel' is randomly selected from two alternatives, black or white, independently of all other points. (b) The similarity or correlation between picture elements (pixels) in the pattern as a function of the distance between them. (c) A natural scene. (d) The similarity or correlation between picture elements (pixels) in the scene as a function of the distance between them.

In the top image of Figure 9.3, for example, a sheep figure appears at different sizes or scales in many different parts of the image; thus, similar variations in pixel correlations will occur at many different scales. Secondly, many natural objects exhibit a property known as self-similarity, which means that they have a similar structure at different scales. A tree, for instance, has a similar branching structure whether one views the whole tree, or just a very small part of it (bottom image in Figure 9.3). The same applies to clouds, rocks, water and many other natural forms. Correspondingly, the visual system analyses images using the same neural structures at many spatial scales in parallel. You read in Chapters 3 and 4 that each neurone in the visual cortex receives information from a circumscribed area of the retina known as its receptive field. Each location on the retina is served by many different cortical

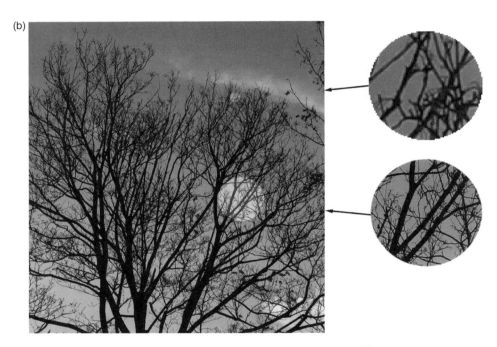

Figure 9.3 Two sources of scale-invariance in natural images. (a) Elements in natural images such as sheep vary in size and in viewing distance, producing similar patterns at different scales or magnifications. (b) Trees have a similar visual structure at different magnifications or spatial scales.

neurones, whose receptive fields overlap substantially (Hubel & Wiesel, 1974). These receptive fields vary substantially in retinal size from one neurone to another but retain a similar spatial structure in terms of their subdivision into excitatory and inhibitory zones. Therefore, the visual system encodes the same information about the image at many different spatial scales in terms of the pattern of response across neurones with receptive fields of different sizes.

Natural objects are never identical to each other and never contain exact copies of themselves at different scales, but vary to some apparently random degree (different sheep and tree branches in the images of Figure 9.3 are not exact copies of each other). As a result, scale-invariance is never exact but is a statistical property that varies to some degree from one image to another. Nevertheless, there is a sufficient degree of regularity and predictability for the visual system to have developed a method of processing natural images that expects to find scale-invariance and exploits it to maximise coding efficiency. Because visual art is created by humans, perhaps it reflects and exploits the scale-invariant properties of human visual processing. In order to evaluate the plausibility of this idea, we need a precise, reproducible method of measuring the scale-invariant properties of natural images, for comparison against corresponding measures from artistic images. Several different measures of image statistics are available (Graham & Field, 2007, 2008a), but two particular mathematical measures of scale-invariance have been used most often in the context of art, one known as 'spectral slope' and the other known as 'fractal dimension'.

Spectral slope

Spectral slope (abbreviated to S) is a direct mathematical measure of the similarity or correlation between the intensities of pixels at different distances across the image. When nearby pixels are generally quite similar in intensity, image intensity fluctuates very slowly over space (each pixel has a similar intensity to all the pixels nearby) or, in more technical terms, at a low spatial frequency. On the other hand, when there is relatively little similarity between the intensities of nearby pixels, intensity fluctuates more rapidly over space, or at a high spatial frequency. As indicated earlier, natural images contain a mixture of low and high spatial frequency fluctuations. Locally, rapid fluctuations of intensity may be superimposed on slower, more gradual changes, like small ripples on large ocean waves. Indeed, the balance between rapid and slow changes (or high and low spatial frequency content) is highly consistent across many natural images. A standard mathematical procedure called Fourier analysis is used to measure the intensity fluctuations at different spatial frequencies in an image. Results are plotted in a graph known as a frequency spectrum,

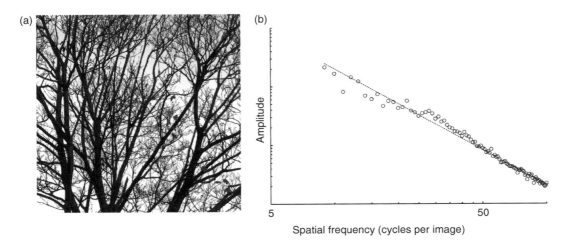

(a)   (b)

Amplitude

5   50

Spatial frequency (cycles per image)

Figure 9.4 (a) A photograph of a tree. (b) The spatial frequency spectrum of the tree image. Intensity variation or amplitude is plotted on the vertical axis, and spatial frequency is plotted on the horizontal axis (the rate of variation in intensity as a function of distance). Amplitude is greater at lower spatial frequencies (slower rates of change over space), reflecting the high degree of similarity between nearby image points.

which shows the amplitude of intensity variation as a function of spatial frequency. Figure 9.4 shows the frequency spectrum of a tree image, which is typical of natural scenes. Intensity variation (amplitude) is greatest at low spatial frequencies, due to the high correlations between adjacent pixels discussed earlier, and declines progressively as frequency increases. In fact, if one plots spatial frequency on a ratio scale as is done in Figure 9.4, then each doubling of spatial frequency produces an approximate halving of amplitude. The amplitudes plotted in Figure 9.4 lie along a straight line, which has a slope near −1.0, reflecting the halving rule. The spectral slope measure of scale-invariance, S, corresponds to the estimated slope of the line in the amplitude plot. The straightness of the line is a mark of scale-invariance, although the actual slope can vary from image to image. When this measure is applied to a large set of natural images, S tends to vary between −0.5 and −1.5, with an average of around −1.2 (Field, 1987; Tolhurst et al., 1992), depending on the particular set of images analysed.

The solid line in Figure 9.5 plots the frequency of different values of S in a set of 106 photographic landscape images (Olmos & Kingdom, 2004). Notice that this sample of natural images clusters around a typical or average value of S of −1.23, with very few images at the extreme values beyond −1.5 and −1.0. The small inset images give examples of images with values near the extremes of the

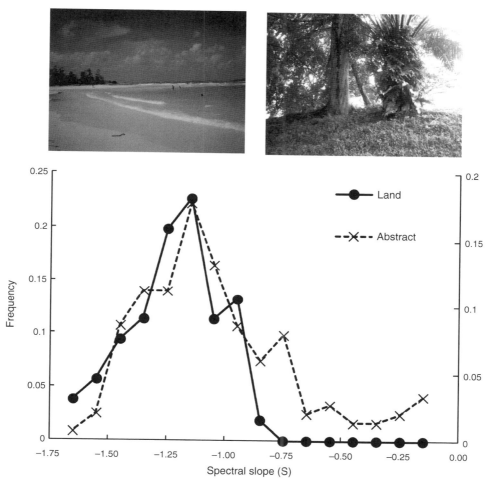

Figure 9.5 Frequency plot of spectral slope values in a large sample of images. Solid line: landscapes (Olmos & Kingdom, 2004); dashed line: abstract paintings. Inset images show examples of landscapes lying at the extremes of the distribution of slope values.

distributions. Images with a very steep slope of around −1.5 tend to contain large areas of gentle change in image brightness, as exemplified by beach and sunset scenes, which results in a preponderance of lower spatial frequencies. Images with a shallow slope of around −1.0 tend to include large areas of fine texture containing rocks, water ripples or vegetation, as exemplified by the woodland scene. These latter images contain relatively more information at higher spatial frequencies. Most images fall in between the two extremes, showing a balance between uniform and textured regions, which results in a moderate spectral slope value in the region of −1.2.

Fractal dimension

Benoit Mandelbrot, a mathematician working at IBM and Harvard University in the USA in the 1970s, was intrigued and fascinated by the irregular, complex structure of natural objects. He noticed that the same patterns seem to repeat at many different scales (self-similarity as mentioned earlier). The main trunk and largest branches of a tree, for instance, create a characteristic branching pattern, but when one zooms in to inspect a specific large branch, the smaller branches attached to it create a similar branching pattern. Zooming in again to inspect even smaller branches reveals a branching pattern at yet another level of detail. Self-similarity can be observed in objects as diverse as clouds, rock formations, water ripples, lightning forks, waterfalls and so on. Mandelbrot developed a measure of self-similarity called fractal dimension, abbreviated to D (Mandelbrot, 1977, 1998). The most commonly used method to estimate D involves 'box-counting'. An application of the technique to visual images is illustrated in Figure 9.6.

The two landscape images from Figure 9.5 are rendered as three-dimensional plots. The two axes running horizontally in each plot represent the horizontal and vertical position of each pixel in the image (512 pixels along each axis). The vertical axis represents the intensity of each pixel (again with 512 possible values). Two-dimensional images create three-dimensional landscapes in these spaces; areas of relatively uniform high luminance, such as the beach, appear as high plateaux, while darker areas carve out deep valleys. The dense texture of vegetation creates a bristling array of sharp luminance spikes. Fractal dimension measures the extent to which the landscape defining the image fills

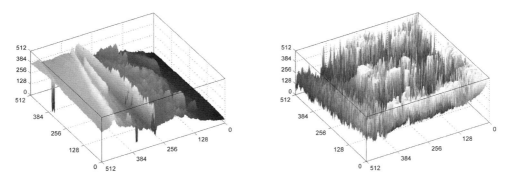

Figure 9.6 Illustration of the image representation used in the three-dimensional box-counting algorithm for estimating D, based on the two images displayed in Figure 9.5. The near corner of the three-dimensional surface plot corresponds to the bottom-right corner of the image.

the three-dimensional volume of the space. The beach scene fills only a small proportion of the space while the woodland scene fills quite a lot of the space. The box-counting technique measures space occupation as follows. Imagine that the three-dimensional space is a container that can be filled with small boxes. The plots in Figure 9.6 each have a volume of 512 x 512 x 512 individual cells, so each plot could be filled with about 64 x 64 x 64 or 262,000 small boxes each measuring 8 x 8 x 8 cells, or over 32,000 boxes each measuring 16 x 16 x 16, or 512 boxes each measuring 64 x 64 x 64. The box-counting technique involves filling the entire volume with boxes of a particular size and counting how many of those boxes intersect the surface defining the image. The count is repeated at a range of box sizes. Let us assume that the image actually contains nothing, a blank grey canvas. The corresponding landscape in the three-dimensional surface plot would be a flat plane measuring 512 x 512 cells horizontally but occupying only one cell vertically. When the full three-dimensional space is filled with boxes measuring 8 x 8 x 8 cells (64 boxes along each side of the 512 x 512 x 512 space), only 64 x 64 = 4,096 boxes would be occupied by the plane; with a box size of 16 x 16 x 16 pixels, 32 x 32 = 1,024 boxes would be filled; and with a box size of 64 x 64 x 64, 8 x 8 = 64 boxes would be filled. Notice that the number of boxes filled corresponds to (b^2) where b is the number of boxes on each side of the space. At the other extreme, imagine a highly intricate pattern that fills just about the entire three-dimensional volume of the space. Now all the boxes, of whatever size, are filled by the pattern, which relates to an occupation rate of (b^3). The box-counting measure of fractal dimension D measures the proportion of boxes filled by the pattern and corresponds to the exponent, b^D. D therefore varies between 2.0 (the simplest pattern, a flat plane) and 3.0 (the most intricate, space-filling pattern). For the beach scene in Figure 9.5, D = 2.3, while for the woodland scene D = 2.62.

Although three-dimensional box-counting is a well-defined technique for estimating fractal dimension in images (Sarkar & Chaudhuri, 1994; Li et al., 2009), it has not been applied to visual art. Researchers interested in the fractal properties of art have tended to use a two-dimensional form of box-counting in which the image is first 'thresholded' to produce a black-and-white pattern; all pixels above a certain grey-level value are changed to white pixels and all those below that value are changed to black pixels (Taylor et al., 1999; Forsythe et al., 2011). Box-counting is then performed on the thresholded pattern. The particular choice of threshold value necessarily determines the detailed structure of the resulting black-and-white image. At the extremes, if a value near to black

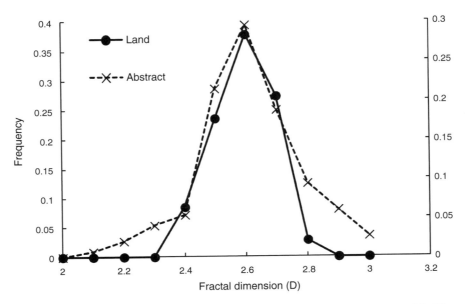

Figure 9.7 Frequency plot of D values for the same set of images as used in Figure 9.5. Notice that D values near 2.6 are much more common than values below 2.3 or above 2.8, although extreme values are more common in abstract paintings than in landscapes.

(or near to white) is selected as the threshold, then the resulting image will be almost entirely white (or black). Threshold values near the middle of the range produce less radical effects but still influence the final black-and-white pattern. Thus, estimates of D vary with the choice of threshold, making replication of two-dimensional measures very difficult if the threshold is not specified. For this reason the three-dimensional measure of D should be regarded as a more stable estimate of D.

To assess the fractal properties of the same set of landscape images as used for the slope estimates in Figure 9.5, a three-dimensional box-count measure of D was applied to each image. The solid line in Figure 9.7 plots the frequency of different values of D in the image set. Notice that images of natural scenes cluster tightly around a value of D in the region of 2.6. The average value of D for these images is 2.52, with very few images scoring D values below 2.3 or above 2.8. Low values of D are associated with sparse images that contain relatively little detail, while high values are associated with complex images containing a high degree of spatial detail.

How closely related are the S and D measures of the same image? If they were perfectly related, then one could use either measure completely interchangeably.

Analysis of the results shown in Figures 9.5 and 9.7 reveals a moderate level of agreement between the two measures. The seaside image in Figure 9.5 has extreme S and D scores at one end of their range (-1.42 and 2.33); the woodland scene has S and D scores at the other end (-1.02 and 2.65, respectively). For the landscape image set used in Figures 9.5 and 9.7, S and D have a correlation of 0.77 (a perfect relationship between the two would correspond to a correlation of 1.0, while a lack of any relationship would correspond to a correlation of zero). Hence, S and D measure similar but not identical aspects of image complexity and scale-invariance. A given value of S cannot predict a precise value of D, at least for natural images (although for a very restricted set of artificial images, the relationship between the two measures may be much closer). An interesting but as yet unresolved issue concerns the relative merits of the two measures in the context of artistic appreciation.

Scale-invariance and visual processing

Natural images show a high degree of regularity in their statistical properties, whether one uses S or D as a measure (it should be borne in mind that particular values of S or D do not guarantee the presence of fractal-like scaling or self-similarity; see Graham & Field, 2008a). The most typical value of S is around -1.2, while the most common value of D is around 2.5, dependent on the sample of images analysed. The earlier discussion argued that coding strategies in the human visual system should have evolved to take advantage of this statistical regularity in order to maximise coding efficiency. A clear prediction of this theory is that our ability to perform fine visual discriminations between similar patterns should be most efficient when those patterns have statistical properties that fall near the ideal values. A number of researchers have tested this prediction. Tolhurst and Tadmor (2000) created hybrid images that blended together two very different natural scenes, such as scenes containing a street and a tree, and asked experimental participants to discriminate between images with slightly different degrees of blending (e.g. biased more towards a street or more towards a tree). They varied the spectral slope, S, of the scene to test whether discrimination performance depended on the value of S and found that discrimination performance was best, in the sense that it required the smallest change in blend for the shift to be visible, when the images had a spectral slope near -1.2. Other research has also found that observers can make fine discriminations between images more efficiently for values of S near the most prevalent values found in natural images (Knill et al., 1990; Parraga et al., 1999; Hansen & Hess, 2006). There have been no perceptual discrimination studies based on measures of D rather than S. Laboratory research, therefore, supports the idea that the human visual system is tuned to process images that have visual statistics that coincide with the values that are most prevalent in natural scenes.

Scale-invariance and art

As a product of a visual system (belonging to the artist), which is designed to be viewed by other visual systems (belonging to patrons and gallery visitors), visual art should reflect its adaptations, including any that maximise coding efficiency. Hence, it has been proposed that artists re-create the regular visual statistics of the natural world in their work. Graham and Field (2007, 2008a) and Redies et al. (2007) analysed the spectral slope of a large sample of artworks and found that S varied over the same range as is found in natural images. The mean value of S for the thirty artworks reproduced in this book is −1.26, quite close to the mean value for the landscapes (−1.22). Interestingly Graham and Field (2007) also found slightly steeper slopes for paintings than for photographs. The mean value of D in the artworks is also very close to that in the natural images, at 2.49. Three paintings by Monet are clustered towards one end of each distribution, with shallow spectral slope values near −1.0 and correspondingly high fractal dimension values around 2.6, perhaps reflecting the high degree of textural detail characteristic of his work. On the other hand, earlier artworks such as those by Raphael, Pontormo and Beccafumi, which contain smooth gradations of tone and colour, tend to be clustered at the opposite end of the distribution, with steep spectral slopes and low fractal dimension scores. (A separate list of illustrations includes the calculated S and D values for all the artworks used.)

One might argue that some statistical similarity between representational art and natural images is only to be expected. If representational art is based on real natural images such as landscapes, then, inevitably, it will tend to possess the same statistical properties as natural images. Moreover, photographs such as those used for the analyses in Figures 9.5 and 9.7 are not completely random samples of natural images. They have been selected and composed by the photographer. Perhaps photographs and representational art share similar statistics because both are driven by a preference for certain landscapes; statistical similarity may emerge as a by-product of landscape preference.

One way to assess the force of these criticisms is to analyse the statistical properties of non-representational artworks. By definition, abstract art avoids any straightforward representational meaning. The artist has a completely free choice about what marks to make and where to place them. If abstract art is also found to conform to expectations based on the statistics of real-world images, then the argument that statistics play a role in aesthetic response becomes more convincing (Graham et al., 2009).

Although abstract art does not attempt to portray recognisable objects, it is generally far from random. Indeed, it is quite difficult (and rare) for an artist to create a truly random work of art. One of the few examples of true randomness in art was created by the French artist Francois Morellet (1960) in 'Random Distribution of 40,000 Squares Using the Odd and Even Numbers of a Telephone Directory'. In a Herculean task, he enlisted his wife and son to read him numbers from the telephone directory for the town of Cholet in France. They read nearly 7,000 numbers (40,000 digits) to Morellet over several evenings. Working systematically across a grid of squares on his canvas, Morellet painted a blue square for every even digit and a red square for every odd digit (Temkin, 2008). Morellet's 'Random Distribution...' would be a familiar image to any vision scientist. Similar patterns of random elements are standard visual stimuli in vision research, precisely because they contain no meaningful information that could confound simple judgements of basic sensory qualities such as depth or motion direction. Figure 9.2 is an example of such a 'random dot' image. If the elements were coloured red and blue, it would be indistinguishable from Morellet's painting. Of course, vision scientists do not have to resort to telephone directories when creating their stimuli; modern computers can create dense arrays of random elements in a fraction of a second.

Apart from such attempts to impose true randomness on an abstract artwork, artists necessarily exercise some judgement when deciding where to place their marks. In the case of Jackson Pollock's drip paintings, for instance, Pollock poured paint from tins or dripped it from brushes, moving rapidly across vast canvases, swinging the stick with dance-like flourishes and flicks. In the act of exercising such judgements, abstract artists, therefore, may unconsciously generate a scale-invariant design that reflects natural visual statistics. Jackson Pollock's drip paintings have no obvious similarity to real scenes, but their restless energy and whirling visual rhythms suggest choreographed dance or music. An analysis of the statistical properties of these paintings claimed that Pollock may have refined his technique so that the paintings migrated towards a consistent value of D that is close to that of natural scenes. Taylor et al. (1999,

2002) used two-dimensional box-counting to estimate D in Jackson Pollock's abstract drip paintings (using the thresholding technique described earlier). For his earliest work in the 1940s, D was 1.12, while later 'classic' paintings had D values near 1.89 (Taylor et al., 2002; note that two-dimensional box-counting produces D values ranging between 1.0 and 2.0). This development, Taylor et al. argue, was driven by aesthetic preference. It is even claimed that one can use such image statistics to assess the authenticity of drip paintings that are attributed to Pollock. However, Taylor et al. (1999, 2002) did not present an analysis of natural visual scenes using their algorithm for computing D to support their claim that a D value of 1.7 is most prevalent. To address this point, the dotted lines in Figures 9.5 and 9.7 present frequency distributions of S and D in a large sample of 150 abstract artworks by professional artists obtained from the internet, calculated using the same procedure as used for the landscape image sets also plotted in the graphs. There is clearly quite good agreement between the distributions of natural images and those of abstract artworks, supporting the idea that even abstracts reflect the statistical properties of natural images. The mean slope for abstract artworks is −1.05, somewhat below that for natural images (−1.23), while the mean fractal dimension is 2.56, slightly higher than that for natural images (2.51). Graham and Field (2008a) also found that the mean spectral slope was slightly lower for abstract art. Figures 9.5 and 9.7 reveal that a significant minority of abstract artworks have a shallow spectral slope, or a fractal dimension close to the maximum value of 3.00. These artworks seem to violate expectations based on natural images deliberately and contain very high levels of textural detail. Morellet's 'Random Distribution...', not surprisingly, is among these unnatural images, as is Bridget Riley's 'Cataract 3' and works by Gerhard Richter and Sol LeWitt. The aesthetic of these artworks seems to be detached from natural images.

Why would most artists reproduce the statistics of natural images in their work? One idea is that they are intuitively aware of the most efficient means of visual communication: artists optimise their work for viewing by the human visual system by re-creating optimal statistics. Such images would be perceived more easily and processed more efficiently (Graham & Field, 2007). Redies (2007) takes this argument one step further and argues that artists aim to achieve a state of 'aesthetic resonance' in the visual system of the viewer. According to this view, images with the most ideal statistics are also the most aesthetically pleasing because they put the visual system in an ideal resonant state (by analogy with musical wind instruments that resonate most strongly at certain pitches). Aesthetic pleasure is part of a general motivational system that regulates an individual's behavioural tendencies, as discussed in the previous chapter. In the case of the aesthetic resonance theory of art, the argument is that aesthetic resonance guides us towards images that can be processed most efficiently and, therefore, with the minimum of energy expenditure. Even a slight preference for images that can be processed more efficiently may have been sufficient for natural selection to favour individuals expressing such a preference.

Redies et al. (2007) reported that S values in artistic monochrome portraits are close to those typical of natural images (around −1.0), even though photographs of faces usually have a much steeper slope nearer to −2.0. They argued that portrait artists adjust the statistics of their work towards the optimal value, driven by aesthetic considerations. However, the argument here is relatively weak for two reasons. Firstly, Redies et al. (2007) did not compare corresponding photographic and artistic versions of the same images directly, so possible differences due to aesthetics were confounded with differences due to image content. Secondly, it is possible that artists adjust visual statistics simply to improve perceptibility rather than to heighten aesthetic appeal.

The first weakness in Redies et al.'s (2007) argument can be remedied by comparing artistic and photographic representations of exactly the same scene. It is relatively rare to find such closely matched image pairs, but some examples do exist. Machotka (1996) juxtaposed a number of Cezanne's landscape paintings with corresponding photographs of the same scenes, and Fuchs et al. (2011) reported briefly that the spectral slopes of Cezanne's paintings and the photographs were quite similar. To look at this issue, a small sample of works by different artists was assembled. Arshile Gorky based his painting 'The Artist and His Mother' (c.1926–1936) closely on a photograph. Coke (1964), Scharf (1968), Kosinski (1999) and Easton (2011) supply other examples. The graphs in Figure 9.8 compare S and D values calculated from fifteen such matched image pairs which, in addition to Gorky, also include work by Cezanne ('Melting Snow, Fontainebleau', 1879), Courbet ('Chateau de Chillon', 1874), Delacroix ('Odalisque', 1857), Hartley ('Great Good Man', 1942), Robinson ('Two in a Boat', 1891; 'The Layette', c.1891), Sickert ('Conversation Group', c.1927) and others. Fractal dimension scores (right-hand graph in Figure 9.8) are quite well correlated between paintings and photographs (r = 0.65), and the mean D score for photographs (2.56) is virtually the same as that for paintings (2.52). The best-fitting line relating D in paintings to D in photographs has a slope of less than unity (0.42), indicating that artists may reduce the D value of high-scoring images. The difference between image and art is more marked for spectral slope

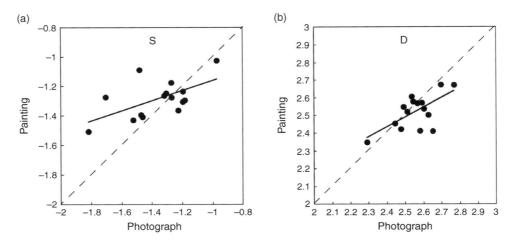

Figure 9.8 Spectral slope (a) and D (b) scores for fifteen matched pairs of paintings and photographs. The dashed lines represent unit slope, and the solid lines are the best-fitting straight lines through the data points. The range of slope or D values is narrower in paintings than in photographs (best-fitting lines have slopes below unity).

values (left-hand graph in Figure 9.8). The correlation in S values between photographs and paintings is not quite so high ($r = 0.59$), and the mean S score for photographs (-1.36) is a little higher than that for paintings (-1.28). However, notice that the slope of the best-fitting line is rather shallow (0.34), indicating that steep spectral slopes above about -1.25 in the photographs are made less steep in the paintings, and shallow spectral slopes below -1.25 are made more steep in the paintings. Thus, on the basis of this analysis, it does seem that artists may adjust image properties towards values that are most typical of natural images. Of course one should not place too much reliance on results from a small sample of fifteen artworks, most simply scanned from books and analysed using just two measures, but results are at least suggestive of an adjustment effect.

Does the adjustment serve to improve perceptibility or aesthetic appeal? Only a few studies have investigated the relationship between statistics and aesthetic preference (Aks & Sprott, 1996; Spehar et al., 2003). Spehar et al. (2003) showed observers pairs of black-white (thresholded) images each containing a natural object, such as a cauliflower, clouds or tree branches, and asked them to select the image that was more aesthetically pleasing. They then compared aesthetic preference against the measured D value for each image. Aesthetic preference peaked shallowly for images with a D value of 1.3. Spehar et al. (2003) also measured aesthetic preference for cropped images of Pollock's paintings and found that preference was highest for images with a D value of 1.5. Another study by Aks and Sprott (1996) found that aesthetic preference for computer-generated fractal patterns peaked at a D value of 1.26. Inconsistencies in preferred D values across studies may reflect variations in the one-dimensional box-counting algorithms used to estimate D or in the properties of the images used. Unfortunately, one-dimensional D values cannot be compared to two-dimensional values or to S measures easily, for reasons discussed earlier.

In combination, the results surveyed in this section provide initial evidence that, other things being equal, artists prefer to create and we prefer to view artworks that display scale-invariant properties similar to those exhibited by natural scenes, and that this preference is based on processing efficiency. A preference for scale-invariant images may also account for some aspects of landscape preference discussed earlier (Hagerhall et al., 2004). We may prefer the appearance of certain landscapes or tree shapes because they have the best scale-invariant properties. The notion of scale-invariance has even been used to explain the visual appeal of Japanese Zen gardens (van Tonder et al., 2002), in which the arrangement of rock 'islands' can be described in terms of a fractal-like branching structure. Fractals have also been invoked to explain preferences for architecture. The Victorian art critic, writer and artist John Ruskin astutely observed a deep correspondence between mountainous scenery and Gothic architecture:

> ...this wildness of thought, and roughness of work; this look of mountain brotherhood between the cathedral and the Alp; ... (Ruskin, 1893, p. 157.)

Views of mountains have scale-invariant, fractal properties. Corresponding jagged shapes can be seen at many scales, from the smallest (rocks and boulders) to the largest (rocky outcrops and mountainous silhouettes). Some architectural styles, particularly the Gothic style employed in many Northern European religious buildings, are also characterised by repeating shapes and patterns at multiple scales, and it may be this similar scale-invariant property that Ruskin had detected. Even more remarkably, Ruskin's insight led him to create a fractal pattern long before fractal geometry was discovered. In volume five of *Modern Painters* (1902), he illustrated how a tree-like shape can be created by repeating the same bifurcating pattern at successively finer scales (Figure 9.9):

> Assume, for example's sake, the stem to separate always into two branches, at an equal angle, and that each branch is three-quarters of the length of the preceding one.

Figure 9.9 Ruskin's example of how to construct a tree-like shape by following simple iterative rules, which actually specify a fractal pattern. (Taken from Ruskin, 1902, Figure 56, p. 67.)

Diminish their thicknesses in proportion, and carry out the figure any extent you like. (Ruskin, 1902, p. 67.)

In Gothic design, a certain shape such as an arch or spire may describe a whole façade but may be repeated in the shape of window openings and then in window panels. Hindu architecture also exhibits a tendency for repeating patterns (see the photograph of Rouen cathedral in Plate 8). Not all architecture is fractal, of course. Modernist architecture rejects ornament and employs Euclidean geometry (straight lines, simple geometric shapes) rather than fractal geometry. Modernist architecture, like modern art, deliberately avoids traditional aesthetic design principles based on ornamentation and beauty, although it is not universally popular by any means. Perhaps the appeal of fractal design in art and architecture reflects a preference for such patterns that has been conditioned during evolution by our exposure to natural images (Crompton, 2002; Joye, 2007).

Fractal geometry and scale-invariance seem to capture some fundamental properties of our aesthetic response to patterns and shapes. It may play a role in our response to landscapes, paintings and buildings. Given its statistical nature, this approach is best viewed as capturing a general tendency for observers to prefer certain kinds of image over others.

Organisation in natural images

It is important to bear in mind that the statistical features discussed in the previous section are global features of an image that do not depend on specific details such as the exact identity or placement of an object in the scene. Both measures discussed, S and D, integrate information across the whole image to produce a single numerical quantity that summarises the statistical properties of the entire image, independently of its meaning. While it is fascinating to discover how much explanatory power these global statistical quantities possess, image details are also bound to have a bearing on aesthetic judgement. The previous chapter described several aspects of image content that influence visual pleasure, including the presence of biological forms and an element of mystery. Another piece of the jigsaw that makes up image aesthetics is organisation: the arrangement of objects and features.

You may recall from Chapter 3 that visual analysis in the brain is known to involve a successive series of neural processing stages. During the earliest stages of processing in the occipital lobe, neurones encode local simple features of the image such as line or edge position, orientation, size, contrast, colour and motion. At higher levels of processing in the temporal lobe, this local information is combined so that neural activity encodes the properties of larger image regions or entire objects. Therefore, when the image of an object is cast onto the retina of the eye, it triggers a cascade of neural processing that courses through successive areas of the visual cortex, initially encoding simple local features and culminating in activation of a stored representation of that object: visual recognition. Remarkably, this entire process is completed in less than one-fifth of a second (Schmolesky et al., 1998). The artist with agnosia described in Chapter 3 (Figure 3.3) had suffered damage to neural processes that integrate across local visual attributes, so he was unable to organise disparate image features into coherent shapes and surfaces.

A picture of a feather could be described exhaustively in a long list of words that describe its detailed structural features, including the quill, the shaft and all the smaller barbs running off it at various angles. Alternatively, it could be much more succinctly described by a single word, 'feather'. When you look at a feather, the brain creates an internal description of it in a cascade of neural activity that flows through the visual cortex. During the initial stages of analysis, this neural representation captures all the feather's local features, analogous to the exhaustive verbal description above, and is likely to involve activity that is distributed among a correspondingly large ensemble of neurones. At the highest levels of neural analysis where recognition occurs, the neural representation is likely to be much more sparsely distributed among only relatively few neurones, akin to the simple verbal description 'feather'. Given the energy demands of neural activity outlined earlier in the chapter, the high-level description is much more desirable on the grounds of energy conservation; it requires far fewer active neurones. Furthermore, it would be inefficient to maintain a high level of activity in lower-level visual processing areas once a sparse high-level representation has been created. Thus, it would be plausible to assume that the brain strives to find organisation and meaning in images and, once it has succeeded, it reduces low-level activity to a minimum. Activity reduction could be achieved by neurones in high-level processing areas sending signals down to those in lower-level areas to suppress their activity. Indeed, recent research in neuroscience argues that the brain continuously generates predictions about what to expect next in the way of sensory inputs and propagates these predictions down to the lowest levels of sensory analysis in the cortex, where they are checked against current input. Prediction errors then flow up through the processing stream and allow the brain to modify its predictions based on the most up-to-date evidence. As a result, visual processing involves a continuous back-and-forth flow of information through the hier-archy of areas in the visual cortex, which maximises efficiency and allows us to anticipate events rather than react to them passively as they occur (Lee & Mumford, 2003; Van de Cruys & Wagemans, 2011). This two-way traffic is probably responsible for the phenomenon of pareidolia illustrated in Figure 5.8.

A number of recent brain imaging studies has found evidence to support the idea that visual processing involves a continuous seesaw-like modulation of activity in different cortical areas (Murray et al., 2004; Fang et al., 2008; Summerfield et al., 2008; Alink et al., 2010). One study employed a perceptually bistable motion display, which alternates in its appearance, sometimes appearing as a set of individual lines moving in different directions and, at other times, appearing as a single, coherent diamond shape (Fang et al., 2008). fMRI signals were used to monitor changes in cortical activity while perception switched between these two states. They found that when a coherent shape was perceived, activity increased in the secondary cortex and decreased in the primary cortex compared to when the percept was disorganised. Similarly, Alink et al. (2010) found smaller responses to motion stimuli in the primary visual cortex when the onset or direction of the stimulus could be predicted from the surrounding stimuli. Further evidence comes from an fMRI study of a phenomenon called repetition suppression (Summerfield et al., 2008), in which neural responses to stimuli are suppressed when those stimuli are repeatedly presented (i.e. are predictable). Summerfield et al. (2008) systematically varied the likelihood of repetition (and hence predictability) and found that the degree of suppression was reduced for repetitions that were less predictable. An evolutionary adaptation to prefer images that are well composed, meaningful and predictable thus can be explained by the need to conserve neural energy during visual processing. It also accounts for three of Ramachandran and Hirstein's (1999) laws of artistic experience: namely, grouping to segment figure from ground, problem-solving in 'peekaboo' experiences and aesthetic abhorrence of peculiar vantage points. The search for meaning in an image, the transition from uncertainty to predictability, should be pleasurable in itself.

This account of preference predicts that images which are familiar and, therefore, have left a trace of their previous processing to facilitate future processing, should be preferred over novel images. Humans do indeed have a preference for familiar images, a phenomenon known as the mere exposure effect (Zajonc, 2001). Simply repeating exposure to a stimulus leads to the formation of a preference in favour of that image, with no cognitive mediation. The phenomenon must contribute to the effectiveness of advertising, but it also influences artistic judgements. Research shows that preferences for individual artworks are influenced by the degree of previous exposure to them, regardless of content (Cutting, 2003). The mere exposure effect could amplify artistic preferences: a slight preference for a certain kind of painting may lead to more such paintings being commissioned and displayed in galleries, which in turn increases preferences for those paintings. As far as the brain is concerned, the old saying 'I know what I like' should be changed to 'I like what I know'.

Summary

Humans have depended on landscapes for survival over millions of years. Hence, a fascination for landscape features is deeply embedded in the human psyche. This fascination finds expression in landscape art. Recurring artistic features such as places of refuge, look-outs, mystery, water and biological forms all reflect the vital need to appreciate these aspects of our environment. Natural scenes also possess consistent statistical properties, which can be summarised as a tendency for the same patterns to occur at many different spatial scales: scale-invariance. Evidence indicates that the visual system evolved to exploit scale-invariance during neural processing as a means of minimising energy consumption. Even visual art with no overt similarity to landscape tends to have the same scale-invariant properties as natural scenes, and initial evidence indicates that scale-invariance may be aesthetically appealing in itself. However, statistical scale-invariance reflects the global properties of images and disregards specific details, so it cannot offer an account of why any specific image might be preferred over another when they have very similar fractal properties. Content and meaning clearly play a part in preference as well as statistics. Organisation, structure and familiarity in visual art also seem to be appealing because they promote more energy-efficient processing in the brain.

Aesthetic judgements of art are clearly multi-faceted. The pleasure we experience when viewing visual art depends on a complex interaction between many visual qualities, which include biophilic landscape features, meaning, statistical properties, organisation and familiarity. Of course cultural and historical factors (genre, provenance and so on) have an important role to play as well.

10 Evolution and art

Introduction

Charles Darwin's theory of evolution came to the fore in the previous two chapters during discussions of aesthetic preference. Humans may have evolved a preference for certain landscape features in art such as mystery and vantage points because these features are important for survival in a natural environment. Similarly, humans may have evolved a preference for certain images because their statistical and organisational properties afford the most efficient neural processing. This final chapter discusses the relevance of evolutionary theory to two general but important questions about visual art, namely the perennial artistic fascination with certain aspects of the human form and the enduring human compulsion to create works of art. Beforehand, it will be useful to reiterate some salient features of evolutionary theory and to introduce the concept of a 'fitness indicator' because it is an essential component of the evolutionary theory of art.

The theory of evolution underpins modern biological science. It proposes that all persistent, universal human traits, including those which relate to art, should be considered as evolved adaptations. According to Darwin's theory, new traits arise initially by chance due to genetic mutations during reproduction. If a specific trait confers an advantage on a particular individual by enhancing his or her chances of survival and reproduction, then it is passed on to that individual's offspring who, in turn, passes it on to his or her own offspring. Conversely, traits that do not confer an advantage do not become established in the gene pool. Over generations, adaptive traits can become established across an entire population, even if they enhance survival rates by only a tiny amount.

The eye itself is a good example. Primitive sensitivity to light should confer an advantage on any organism that depends on sunlight for energy, leading to more successful transmission of the genes coding for light sensitivity. Sensitivity to ambient illumination, therefore, is a universal adaptation found in even the simplest organisms. Complex mobile organisms have evolved sophisticated light-sensing organs, which typically take the form of a pit or enclosed chamber that forms an image of the outside world on a sheet of light-sensitive cells. Images are extremely useful for performing complex tasks such as visual navigation and recognition, provided that the organism possesses a brain with sufficient processing capacity. The span of time required for light sensitivity to evolve from the most primitive sense organ to a human-like eye may be as short as 400,000 years (Nilsson & Pelger, 1994).

Fitness indicators

Darwin developed the theory of sexual selection to explain how animals select mates and he argued that aesthetic judgement of beauty plays a central role. The core idea of the theory is that certain adaptations act as 'fitness indicators': they advertise an individual's fitness to other individuals. These advertisements serve to deter predators or sexual rivals and to attract mates. It is crucial that fitness indicators offer honest signals of fitness. Indicators that are costly for the individual to develop and maintain are thought to offer the most honest signals of fitness, because only the fittest individuals can meet those costs. As a species, birds seem to appear more frequently than any other species in studies of fitness indicators.

When female barn swallows search for prospective mates, they prefer males with long symmetrical feathers bearing large white spots. To test the theory that these spots really do influence mating success, researchers experimentally reduced the size of the spots in a group of males by painting on the feathers. They found that this group produced fewer offspring compared to other groups, the spots of which were left intact (Kose et al., 1999). Why should females prefer bigger spots when spots seem purely decorative, with no obvious connection to health and fitness? Bigger spots are actually a handicap, because they are associated with an increased risk of feather breakage and are also the preferred breeding site for feather-eating lice. As a result, they are costly for a male to produce and to maintain. It is thought that long, spotted feathers actually signal the high genetic quality of their owner, because only the fittest birds can survive the handicap that the feathers impose. In general, the more costly such signals are to produce, the more reliable they are as a fitness indicator, because only the fittest individuals can produce them and survive. The more reliable a signal is, the stronger is the selection pressure in its favour. Female mate selection over countless generations leads to the evolution of ever more costly displays of plumage. This is the Darwinian explanation for the extravagant plumage seen in many male birds such as peacocks during mating displays. These displays do seem to reflect their owner's health status honestly. Experimental studies have found that when peacocks were experimentally injected with bacteria, their rate of display declined, but males with a higher number of eye-spots on their feathers were better able to cope with the immune challenge and maintained higher levels of feather displays (Loyau et al., 2005; Dakin & Montgomerie, 2011).

The attractiveness of extravagant male plumage to female birds thus appears to originate in its role as a fitness indicator. The feathers of the male Argus pheasant have eye-spot or ocelli markings, which have a remarkable *trompe l'oeil* quality. Each spot even has a specular highlight to enhance its three-dimensional appearance (Figure 10.1). These markings drew Darwin to comment on their artistic perfection as examples of natural aesthetics, 'more like a work of art than of nature'. As evidence of an aesthetic sensibility in the female pheasant, Darwin noted that the ocelli are not visible to the female until the male assumes the bodily attitude of courtship:

He who thinks that he can safely gauge the discrimination and taste of the lower animals may deny that the female Argus pheasant can appreciate such beauty; but he would then be compelled to admit that the extraordinary attitudes assumed by the male during the act of courtship, by which the wonderful beauty of his plumage is fully displayed, are purposeless; and this is a conclusion which I for one will never admit. (1901, p. 609.)

Darwin's evolutionary theory of aesthetics challenged the prevailing religious view that beauty was a gift from God. Darwin argued that the source of beauty was in natural laws, not in divine creation; beauty served a purpose in signalling fitness. According to Darwin, sexual selection explained the fascinating and otherwise mysterious varieties of colour, ornament, song, music and dance found in the animal world, as well as the presence of secondary sexual characteristics found in males.

Darwin's theory did, of course, provoke outrage at the time it was first published. Part of the Victorian resistance to Darwin's theory of sexual selection derived from the importance it placed on female aesthetic judgement. Women at

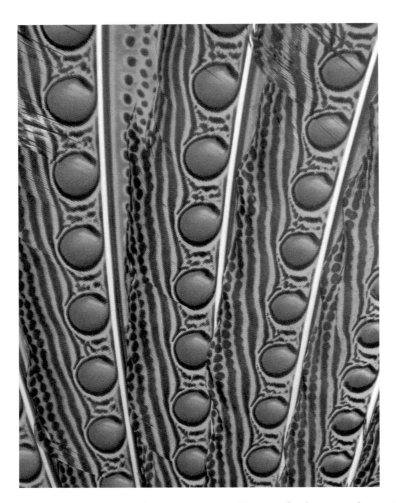

Figure 10.1 Ocelli markings on Argus pheasant feathers, as observed by Darwin. (Taken from a photograph of one of Darwin's specimens in the Museum of Zoology, University of Cambridge.)

the time were widely considered to be fickle and less capable of sound, rational judgement than men. Women were regarded as too chaste and demure for such base sexual urges to influence their behaviour. For Darwin's objectors, ornamentation such as the peacock's tail was an example of the Creator's love of beauty for its own sake. According to Ruskin, Darwin's aesthetic theory reflected his ignorance and lack of artistic ability and failed to consider what, for Ruskin, were the most fundamental aspects of aesthetics, namely its moral and spiritual dimensions (Smith, 2009). Only towards the end of the twentieth century did Darwin's notion of aesthetic fitness begin to make some headway as part of a serious scientific theory of aesthetics. Modern scientific views on human attractiveness (and on the human motivation to create art, discussed later) acknowledge the role of Darwinian fitness indicators in sexual selection.

The human body in art

The human body has been a preoccupation of artists throughout the history of art. Indeed, prior to the twentieth century, one could argue that one of the primary functions of art was figurative, to depict the human form. In the Middle Ages, these depictions were devoid of individuality, personality or expression. Faces and bodies were rendered as prototypes, all with the same basic features and rigid pose. During the Renaissance, artists became interested in depicting real people with individual features and recognisable emotions. Giotto, for example, is famed for the emotion and personality he was able to convey in the faces and gestures of the protagonists in his religious scenes. Nudes, especially female nudes, became a popular subject for (male) artists and their patrons in the Italian Renaissance. Great value was placed on anatomical accuracy and artists spent a great deal of time studying human anatomy. Ancient Greek statuary discovered in the sixteenth to eighteenth centuries was celebrated for the purity and beauty of its subjects: naked athletes, gods and goddesses. These ancient Greek bodies were considered more beautiful than the modern human form because they expressed the greater purity and health attributed to ancient civilisations. Greek and Roman statues became the epitome of human beauty. 'The Laocoön', in particular (Figure 10.2), has been much copied. It shows a Trojan priest, Laocoön, and his two sons wrestling with a serpent. Laocoön has a toned, powerful male physique with bulging, well-developed musculature. The influence of this idealised representation of male physical beauty can be seen in Italian Renaissance art, as in many of Michelangelo's paintings and sculptures. In his 'Last Judgement', for instance, even elderly male characters are depicted with well-toned, muscular bodies. Many later depictions of the male form took their lead in turn from Michelangelo's work. Leonardo studied human anatomy in order to render more realistic representations of the body, but he and other artists tended to portray idealised forms.

The ancient Greek statue of 'Venus de Milo' and its Roman copies became the inspiration for the artistic ideal of female beauty. Female nudes in Italian Renaissance art are soft and sensual, displaying graceful beauty with soft curves, delicate features and languid poses. Famous works such as Botticelli's

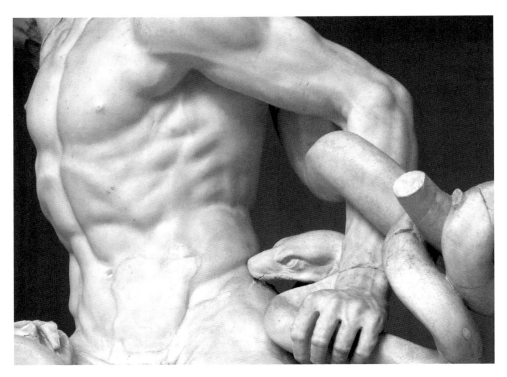

Figure 10.2 Detail from 'Laocoön and his Sons'. The powerful male physique inspired many later depictions of the male form. (Taken from a photograph of the statue in the Vatican Museums, Rome.)

'Venus' and Titian's 'Venus of Urbino' have inspired many later depictions of the female form and were themselves inspired by ancient statuary. Modern art largely rejects traditional aesthetic considerations, but the work of many contemporary artists such as Lucian Freud, Chuck Close and Ron Mueck demonstrates a continuing fascination with the human body. Conceptions of human beauty seem to be timeless and universal and they have found expression in visual art throughout history. Why do we find certain physical characteristics so attractive that they are ubiquitous in art?

Human fitness indicators

Research has revealed that many human physical traits appear to function as fitness indicators. In men, the list includes stature, upper body musculature, beard growth and jaw size. In women, the list of sexually attractive fitness indicators includes breasts, buttocks and waist size, as well as skin condition. Facial attractiveness is important for both sexes (Hoenekopp et al., 2007). Artistic depictions of attractive human figures generally focus on the most attractive traits, as we saw earlier. If attractive traits and preferences for attractive traits are sexually selected, then one would expect those traits to be associated with mating success. Studies of human sexual behaviour do indeed find a link between attractiveness and sex. Large-scale surveys find that both men and women judged as more attractive to the opposite gender have more sexual partners (Rhodes et al., 2005). Hoenekopp et al. (2007) measured the physical fitness of 80 young men and found that it correlated positively with their rated attractiveness by 27 women and with their self-reported mating success.

Some physical traits clearly signal fitness in a fairly obvious way. A large, muscular man is more likely to offer protection and plentiful resources to a mate. Female breast and hip development, on the other hand, signal child-bearing potential. But what is it about facial attractiveness that makes it a fitness indicator? Three facial traits were highlighted in Chapter 8 as characteristics of attractive faces: sexual dimorphism, symmetry and averageness. These characteristics do offer useful signals to prospective mates about mate quality. Sexual dimorphism in facial appearance reflects the action of sex hormones, so it is not surprising that it influences attractiveness during sexual selection (Perrett et al., 1998; Penton-Voak & Chen, 2004). In males, testosterone promotes muscle growth and aggression, both desirable in a potential mate with a future role in protection and resource acquisition, while female oestrogen indicates high fertility. Facial symmetry and averageness offer signals about health. Animal studies have found that asymmetrical, idiosyncratic features may reflect problems during development such as poor nutrition, pollution and parasite load. In humans they are linked with premature birth, psychosis and mental retardation (Rhodes, 2006). In modern human societies with higher standards of healthcare, attractiveness is no longer such a reliable indicator of mate quality, although there is still a moderate association. Lower than average attractiveness ratings have an association with poor health, but higher than average ratings are not associated with good health. Nevertheless, selection pressure over many generations may have led to a persisting preference for certain facial features as indicators of mate quality, and the subjective correlate of this preference is attractiveness. Recent research also finds a surprising possible link between humans and animals in the use of cosmetics. Pigments ingested in their food cause the pink colouration of flamingo plumage, and Amat et al. (2011) found that flamingos use a pink-coloured oil to preen their feathers and enhance the pink colouration, especially during the mating season.

Colouration, either natural or artificial, also affects the rated attractiveness of human faces, which presumably fuels the cosmetics industry (Jones et al., 2004; Stephen et al., 2010).

From an evolutionary perspective, the enduring artistic fascination with well-proportioned, toned, healthy-looking human bodies and faces is due to the fact that these physical attributes act as fitness indicators and so help to satisfy a fundamental human need, namely sexual reproduction. Ramachandran and Hirstein's (1999) first law of artistic experience, namely 'peak-shift', is based on the exaggeration of visual characteristics that are aesthetically appealing. They mostly cited examples of exaggerated human sexual characteristics, and acknowledged their debt to Darwin, so their law largely relates to fitness indicators.

The role of fitness indicators is not restricted to purely physical attributes such as facial symmetry but also extends to behavioural tendencies. A controversial theory argues that the human urge to create art springs from the evolutionary role of art itself as a fitness indicator. The story begins with another bird species, the bowerbird.

Bowerbird aesthetics

Male bowerbirds, which are native to New Guinea and Australia, build bowers or boudoirs with the sole purpose of attracting female bowerbirds for copulation. Fourteen different species build distinctively different bowers. Some species build an avenue from two vertical walls of sticks, which opens out onto a broad display area where decorations are carefully arranged. Others build a maypole up to two metres high. Decoration varies between species and includes colourful snail shells, pebbles, feathers, insects or insect parts and bone fragments. Ornaments are chosen primarily on the basis of their colour, which must contrast against the natural background and the bird's plumage (Endler & Day, 2006). Bowerbirds building bowers near to human settlements help themselves to man-made objects that fit into their colour scheme, such as coins, glass, jewellery and nails. Avenue builders fine-tune their composition by viewing it from the perspective of a female visitor and then adjusting the arrangement accordingly. Human interference with the composition is swiftly corrected.

Juvenile bowerbirds learn their building skills from adults outside the mating season. But during the breeding season, male bowerbirds are known to destroy other bowers or steal their decorations, so competition to produce the most impressive bower is intense. Female bowerbirds inspect a number of bowers before selecting a male with which to mate. The most successful bowers earn their owners copulation with at least thirty females during the mating season, while the owners of less successful bowers do not mate at all (Borgia, 1986). Mating success seems to depend on the neatness and symmetry of the display; when researchers interfere with decorations, mating success suffers. Thus, bowerbirds seem to have evolved a fitness indicator based on the aesthetic quality of a constructed ornament, namely the bower. Female bowerbirds appear to use their aesthetic judgement to select a mate that is most likely to pass on the best genes to their offspring. Aesthetic quality indicates genetic quality.

The function of the bower is to demonstrate its creator's superior judgement and discrimination, as well as their ability to assemble and preserve their chosen design. Some species of bowerbird create much more complex bowers than others, and Madden (2001) found that the species capable of producing more complex bowers have larger brains than those able to build only rudimentary bowers. The judgements required to build complex bowers clearly require the more sophisticated cognitive processes that are possible with a larger brain. The relationship between brain size and bower complexity was found for both male and female birds, although it was stronger in male birds. A large brain is clearly an advantage when judging more complex bowers, as well as when building them. These results have been interpreted as support for the idea that sexual selection may have driven the evolution of a large human brain as a response to female mate choice that favours complexity and novelty in male behaviour.

Art as a fitness indicator

It is not surprising from the foregoing account of bowerbird behaviour that these birds have become the prime example in the animal kingdom of how aesthetic artefacts can play a role in sexual selection. In humans, it has been argued that artistic activities including visual art, music and dance act as aesthetic ornamentation, which signals fitness in humans in the same way that bowers signal fitness in bowerbirds (Miller, 2001). According to this theory, our motivation to create art springs from an instinct to advertise genetic fitness. Art, undoubtedly, is a form of display; most artists like to see their work viewed by as many people as possible, as one would expect of an advertisement. Several other characteristic features of art are consistent with the idea that it is a fitness indicator. Art is ubiquitous across societies, cultures and history, as it should be if it arises from a universal human trait. It also triggers the same reward circuits in the brain as other biological motivators such as food, as it should if it is an evolved motivational trait. Furthermore, art is almost always costly to produce in terms of time, energy and effort and so conforms to the handicap principle outlined earlier in the examples of barn swallows and peacocks. Fitness indicators must entail cost if they are to act as honest signals of quality. Painters and sculptors can spend many months working with exotic, expensive materials such as rare pigments and precious metals. Lastly, individuals differ in terms of their ability to create art, another essential aspect of art as a driver for sexual selection.

A clear prediction of the aesthetic fitness theory, borne out in the case of barn swallows and bowerbirds, is that high-quality individuals who create the most aesthetically pleasing artefacts should have more mating success. Human mate selection is certainly much more complex than it is in birds and depends on a whole range of factors. But nevertheless, research does indicate that it is subject to the influence of physical fitness indicators such as facial attractiveness and stature. For instance, a study of US military personnel found that tall men had more reproductive opportunities (more marriages, younger second wives) and used them to have more children than shorter colleagues (Mueller & Manzur, 2001). The effect was not mediated by status (rank) or health. If the propensity to create great art is itself a fitness indicator, then one should expect to find that human artistic achievement is associated with greater mating success. One questionnaire-based study gathered information from 425 British adults on their (self-rated) creative activity and sexual history. It found that 'serious and professional producers [of art] have larger numbers of sexual partners than non-producers and hobby producers' (Nettle & Clegg, 2006, p. 613). The study found no gender differences; when either gender invests in creative output, it has a similar effect on mating success. An obvious biological difference between the genders is that female fertility fluctuates over the menstrual cycle while male fertility remains relatively stable throughout adult life. Another study looked at the effect of male artistic talent on rated attractiveness in females (Haselton & Miller, 2006). It found that women rated artistic men as more sexually desirable during the fertile phase of their menstrual cycle. Women especially valued artistic men over wealthy men when they were ovulating and were rating men as short-term mates.

Miller (1999) argued that visual art is but one of a whole range of human courtship displays:

A strong version of my cultural courtship model would make the following prediction: this universal profile will be found for every quantifiable human behaviour that is public (i.e. perceivable by many potential mates) and costly (i.e. not affordable by all sexual competitors). (p. 87.)

Miller (1999) considered that other forms of art such as music and writing are also courtship displays. His data on the production of all these art forms as a function of age indicated that output increases rapidly after puberty, peaks in early adulthood and declines thereafter. This profile is consistent with the proposal that the impulse to create art is driven, at least partly, by a primeval desire to procreate. Kanazawa (2000) tested whether publications by well-known scientists (another aspect of cultural behaviour) also conforms to the age profile expected in a courtship display. Scientific output is well documented and easily quantified. Kanazawa (2000) found that the peak achievement of male scientists occurred, on average, at the age of 35 years and declined sharply both before and after this age. Moreover, there was a consistent relationship between the age profile of scientific output and marriage. The mean delay between marriage and peak output was two and a half years. The output of married scientists also declined more sharply after marriage than the output of age-matched unmarried scientists. A whole multitude of factors must affect the creative output of an artist or scientist, and Miller's (1999) and Kanazawa's (2000) data cannot reveal causal relationships, but the pattern is at least consistent with the fitness theory.

Hence, the picture emerging from research to date supports the view that the human urge to engage in art and other cultural activities may have originated, at least partly, because these activities served as fitness indicators. The high status and desirability of artists, actors and musicians in modern society is consistent with this view. However, even if true, the fitness theory of art does not preclude the possibility that visual art currently serves other functions as well, which also help to explain its universal presence in human culture (Berlyne, 1971). One possibility is that art evolved as a form of mental exercise that ensures that certain cognitive functions and neural structures operate at peak efficiency. Perhaps the old adage 'use it or lose it' applies as much to subtle aesthetic visual judgements of beauty and landscape as it does to finely honed physical skills. Art, like sport, can also be viewed as a form of play that helps to keep us in peak condition, both mentally and physically. Another possible function for art draws on its expressive nature. It is a form of communication, particularly regarding the emotional state of the artist. Expressive communication is widespread among animals because it promotes social cohesion and group survival: alarm cries warn of danger; submissive gestures maintain social hierarchies and avoid potentially dangerous intra-species violence. The benefits of emotional expression were recognised by Charles Darwin in the context of natural selection. Indeed, he devoted an entire book to the evolution of emotional expression, entitled *The Expression of the Emotions in Man and Animals*.

There are many ways to express emotion, and humans are capable of far more flexible forms of communication than animals. Perhaps art should be numbered among them. Finally, one could view art as a form of exploratory behaviour. Humans find exploration and novelty rewarding in its own right, as you read earlier, because such behaviour aids survival. Humans may seek out and enjoy the challenge of creating (or experiencing) new artworks because it satisfies our primal drive to explore the world and to satisfy our curiosity. After all, a defining quality of art is its uniqueness and novelty. Such a drive can, of course, also explain many other human activities such as scientific endeavour and voyages of exploration.

Summary

If one accepts Charles Darwin's general thesis regarding evolution by natural selection, then the human capacities for aesthetic appreciation and artistic creation must have earned their keep as biological adaptations in order to have persisted as genetically transmitted traits in the human species. The theory of sexual selection offers a credible explanation for the evolutionary origin of art as a fitness indicator. Numerous animal studies are consistent with the idea, including aesthetic artefacts created by bowerbirds and cosmetics applied by flamingos. Physical beauty is an external, visible sign of genetic quality, and the artistic preoccupation with the human body can be traced to our need to find the best genes with which to mix our own. An ability to create aesthetically pleasing objects, works of art, may in turn be an advertisement of our own genetic fitness. Visual art may well serve other basic evolved needs as well, including the need for self-expression, the urge to explore and the desire for healthy mental exertion.

Epilogue

The central thesis of this book has been to argue that a full appreciation of visual art requires a detailed consideration of the visual system's structure, function and evolution. Even before light reaches the retina, the changes brought about by its passage through the cornea and lens can have visible effects on visual art. Once light energy is converted into neural activity in the visual system, the huge complexity of the central nervous system is brought to bear on the problem of making sense of the retinal image. Visual art is intimately linked with the human capacity to sense light and inextricably bounded by its predispositions and limitations, many of which have firm evolutionary origins. There are manifold ways in which the characteristics of neural processes find expression in the spatial, chromatic and dynamic properties of visual art.

Evolution provides an over-arching theoretical framework for understanding all of human behaviour and offers a reasoned account of the capacity to create and appreciate art. Selection pressure has ensured that the visual system is supremely well adapted to the task of extracting meaning from natural visual images. The demands of optimal tuning and energy conservation have profound consequences for our ability to perceive, retain and appreciate certain spatial details, chromatic variations and dynamic changes in all visual images, including artistic images. Evolution has also equipped humans with a deep interest in nature, in landscape and in biological forms, and this interest finds expression in the enduring preoccupations of visual artists. The impulse to create art may be driven, at least in part, by a desire to advertise genetic quality to potential mates.

However, it is worth emphasising again that the insights gained from science in no way diminish the contributions of scholars in other disciplines including art history, art theory and philosophy. But science should occupy a legitimate place in the spectrum of disciplines that can be applied fruitfully to deepen our understanding of art.

It is to be hoped that when you next visit an art gallery or browse through a book on art and take some time to ponder the qualities of a particular work, new considerations will spring to mind that had not previously occurred to you. For example:

- Where are your eyes drawn to, and why?
- How has the artist exploited or catered for limitations in the visual system's spatial resolution or memory?

- How does the use of colour relate to the chromatic axes of perceptual colour space?
- How do the dynamic qualities of the image relate to cortical motion processing?
- Is your visual pleasure driven partly by the work's biophilic features?
- Does the balance between simplicity and complexity in the image relate to natural scale-invariance?

I am sure that you can think of others too. If thoughts about any of these questions help you to understand better and appreciate the effects achieved by the artist, then the book will have achieved its aim.

References

Aharon, I., Etcoff, N., Ariely, D., Chabris, C. F., O'Connor, E., et al. (2001). Beautiful faces have variable reward value: fMRI and behavioral evidence. *Neuron*, 32(3), 537–551.

Aks, D. J. & Sprott, J. C. (1996). Quantifying aesthetic preference for chaotic patterns. *Empirical Studies of the Arts*, 14(1), 1–16.

Alink, A., Schwiedrzik, C. M., Kohler, A., Singer, W. & Muckli, L. (2010). Stimulus predictability reduces responses in primary visual cortex. *Journal of Neuroscience*, 30(8), 2960–2966.

Allport, G. W. & Pettigrew, T. F. (1957). Cultural influence on the perception of movement: the trapezoidal illusion among Zulus. *Journal of Abnormal and Social Psychology*, 55, 104–113.

Amat, J. A., Rendón, M. A., Garrido-Fernández, J., Garrido, A., Rendón-Martos, M., et al. (2011). Greater flamingos Phoenicopterus roseus use uropygial secretions as make-up. *Behavioral Ecology and Sociobiology*, 65(4), 665–673.

Anstis, S. (2002). Was El Greco astigmatic? *Leonardo*, 35(2), 208.

Appleton, J. (1996). *The Experience of Landscape*. New York, NY: Wiley.

Attwell, D. & Laughlin, S. B. (2001). An energy budget for signaling in the grey matter of the brain. *Journal of Cerebral Blood Flow and Metabolism*, 21(10), 1133–1145.

Avant, L. L. (1965). Vision in the Ganzfeld. *Psychological Bulletin*, 64, 246–258.

Ballard, D. H., Hayhoe, M. M. & Pelz, J. B. (1995). Memory representations in natural tasks. *Journal of Cognitive Neuroscience*, 7(1), 66–80.

Balling, J. D. & Falk, J. H. (1982). Development of visual preference for natural environments. *Environment and Behavior*, 14, 5–28.

Banks, W. P. & Kane, D. A. (1972). Discontinuity of seen motion reduces the visual motion aftereffect. *Perception and Psychophysics*, 12, 69–72.

Barnett, J., Miller, S. & Pearce, E. (2006). Colour and art: a brief history of pigments. *Optics & Laser Technology*, 38(4–6), 445–453.

Barrera, M. E. & Maurer, D. (1981). Recognition of mother's photographed face by the three-month-old infant. *Child Development*, 52, 714–716.

Bateson, M., Nettle, D. & Roberts, G. (2006). Cues of being watched enhance cooperation in a real-world setting. *Biology Letters*, 2(3), 412–414.

Bearleant, A. (1993). The aesthetics of art and nature. In S. Kemal & I. Gaskell, eds. *Landscape, Natural Beauty, and the Arts*. Cambridge: Cambridge University Press, pp. 228–243.

Berlyne, D. E. (1971). *Aesthetics and Psychobiology*. New York, NY: Appleton Century Crofts.

Bertamini, M., Latto, R. & Spooner, A. (2003). The Venus effect: people's understanding of mirror reflections in paintings. *Perception*, 32(5), 593–599.

Birmingham, E., Bischof, W. F. & Kingstone, A. (2009). Saliency does not account for fixations to eyes within social scenes. *Vision Research*, 49(24), 2992–3000.

Blakemore, S.-J., Boyer, P., Pachot-Clouard, M., Meltzoff, A., Segebarth, C., et al. (2003). The detection of contingency and animacy from simple animations in the human brain. *Cerebral Cortex*, 13(8), 837–844.

Bomford, D. & Finaldi, G. (1998). *Venice through Canaletto's Eyes*. London: National Gallery Publications.

Borgia, G. (1986). Sexual selection in bowerbirds. *Scientific American*, 254, 92–100.

Brown, S., Gao, X., Tisdelle, L., Eickhoff, S. B. & Liotti, M. (2011). Naturalizing aesthetics: brain areas for aesthetic appraisal across sensory modalities. *NeuroImage*, 58, 250–258.

Brownlow, K. (1980). Silent films: what was the right speed? *Sight and Sound*, summer 1980, 164–167.

Burr, D. C. & Ross, J. (2002). Direct evidence that 'speedlines' influence motion mechanisms. *Journal of Neuroscience*, 22(19), 8661–8664.

Burton, G. J. & Moorhead, I. R. (1987). Color and spatial structure in natural scenes. *Applied Optics*, 26(1), 157–170.

Butter, C. M. (2004). Anton Raederscheidt's distorted self-portraits and their significance for understanding balance in art. *Journal of the History of the Neurosciences*, 13, 66–78.

Callaway, E. M. (2005). Structure and function of parallel pathways in the primate early visual system. *Journal of Physiology*, 566, 13–19.

Campbell, F. W. & Robson, J. G. (1958). Moving visual images produced by regular stationary patterns. *Nature*, 181, 362.

Castiglione, B. (1528). *The Book of the Courtier*. C. S. Singleton, trans., 1959. New York, NY: Doubleday.

Cavanagh, P. (2005). The artist as neuroscientist. *Nature*, 434(7031), 301–307.

Cavanagh, P., Chao, J. & Wang, D. (2008). Reflections in art. *Spatial Vision*, 21(3–5), 261–270.

Cerf, M., Harel, J., Einhauser, W. & Koch, C. (2008). Predicting human gaze using low-level saliency combined with face detection. *Advances in Neural Information Processing Systems*, 20, 241–248.

Changizi, M. A., Zhang, Q. & Shimojo, S. (2006). Bare skin, blood and the evolution of primate colour vision. *Biology Letters*, 2, 217–221.

Chatterjee, A. (2011). Neuroaesthetics: a coming of age story. *Journal of Cognitive Neuroscience*, 23, 53–62.

Clark, K. (1976). *Landscape into Art*. 2nd edn. London: John Murray.

Clottes, J. (2001). *La Grotte Chauvet: l'art des Origines*. Paris: Seuil.

Cohen, D. J. (2005). Look little, look often: the influence of gaze frequency on drawing accuracy. *Perception & Psychophysics*, 67(6), 997–1009.

Cohen, D. J. & Jones, H. J. (2008). How shape constancy relates to drawing accuracy. *Psychology of Aesthetics, Creativity, and the Arts*, 2(1), 8–19.

Cohen, L., Gray, F., Meyrignac, C., Dehaene, S. & Degos, J.-D. (1994). Selective deficit of visual size perception: two cases of hemimicropsia. *Journal of Neurology, Neurosurgery, and Psychiatry*, 57, 73–78.

Coke, V. D. (1964). *The Painter and the Photograph*. Albuquerque, NM: University of New Mexico Press.

Cole, B. L. & Nathan, J. (2002). An artist with extreme deuteranomaly. *Clinical and Experimental Optometry*, 85(5), 300–305.

Conard, N. J. (2009). A female figurine from the basal Aurignacian of Hohle Fels Cave in south-western Germany. *Nature*, 459, 248–252.

Conway, B. R., Hubel, D. H. & Livingstone, M. S. (2002). Color contrast in macaque V1. *Cerebral Cortex*, 12(9), 915–925.

Crompton, A. (2002). Fractals and picturesque composition. *Environment and Planning B: Planning and Design*, 29, 451–459.

Croucher, C. J., Bertamini, M. & Hecht, H. (2002). Naive optics: understanding the geometry of mirror reflections. *Journal of Experimental Psychology: Human Perception and Performance*, 28(3), 546–562.

Crutch, S. J., Isaacs, R. & Rossor, M. N. (2001). Some workmen blame their tools: artistic change in an individual with Alzheimer's disease. *Lancet*, **357**, 2129–2133.

Cunningham, M. R., Roberts, A. R., Barbee, A. P., Druen, P. B. & Wu, C.-H. (1995). 'Their ideas of beauty are, on the whole, the same as ours': consistency and variability in the cross-cultural perception of female physical attractiveness. *Journal of Personality and Social Psychology*, **68**, 261–279.

Cutting, J. E. (2002). Representing motion in a static image: constraints and parallels in art, science, and popular culture. *Perception*, **31**(10), 1165–1193.

    (2003). Gustave Caillebotte, French impressionism, and mere exposure. *Psychonomic Bulletin and Review*, **10**(2), 319–343.

Dagognet, F. (1992). *Etienne-Jules Marey: A Passion for the Trace*. New York, NY: Zone Books.

Dakin, R. & Montgomerie, R. (2011). Peahens prefer peacocks displaying more eyespots, but rarely. *Animal Behaviour*, **82**, 21–28.

Darwin, C. (1901). *The Descent of Man and Selection in Relation to Sex*. London: John Murray.

Davenport, R. K. & Rogers, C. M. (1971). Perception of photographs by apes. *Behaviour*, **39**(3), 318–320.

DeLoache, J. S., Pierroutsakos, S. L., Uttal, D. H., Rosengren, K. S. & Gottlieb, A. (1998). Grasping the nature of pictures. *Psychological Science*, **9**(3), 205–210.

Denis, M. (1890). Definition of Neo-Traditionism. *Art and Criticism*, August 1890.

Deregowski, J. B. (1989). Real space and represented space: cross-cultural perspectives. *Behavioral and Brain Sciences*, **12**, 51–119.

Dutton, D. (2009). *The Art Instinct: Beauty, Pleasure, & Human Evolution*. Oxford: Oxford University Press.

Easton, E. W. (2011). *Snapshot: Painters and Photography, Bonnard to Vuillard*. New Haven, CT: Yale University Press.

Einhauser, W., Spain, M. & Perona, P. (2008). Objects predict fixations better than early saliency. *Journal of Vision*, **8**(14): **18**, 1–16.

Elliott, D. B. & Skaff, A. (1993). Vision of the famous: the artist's eye. *Ophthalmic and Physiological Optics*, **13**, 82–90.

Endler, J. A. & Day, L. B. (2006). Ornament color selection, visual contrast and the shape of color preference functions in great bowerbirds Chlamydera nuchalis. *Animal Behavior*, **72**, 1405–1416.

Espinel, C. H. (1996). de Kooning's late colours and forms: dementia, creativity, and the healing power of art. *Lancet*, **347**, 1096–1098.

Falk, J. H. & Balling, J. D. (2010). Evolutionary influence on human landscape preference. *Environment and Behavior*, **42**(4), 479–493.

Fang, F., Kersten, D. & Murray, S. O. (2008). Perceptual grouping and inverse fMRI activity patterns in human visual cortex. *Journal of Vision*, **8**, 2–9.

Farah, M. J. (2004). *Visual Agnosia*. Cambridge, MA: MIT Press.

Fermueller, C., Ji, H. & Kitaoka, A. (2010). Illusory motion due to causal time filtering. *Vision Research*, **50**, 315–329.

Field, D. J. (1987). Relations between the statistics of natural images and the response profiles of cortical cells. *Journal of the Optical Society of America*, A4, 2379–2394.

Flaherty, A. W. (2005). Frontotemporal and dopaminergic control of idea generation and creative drive. *Journal of Comparative Neurology*, **493**(1), 147–153.

Fornazzari, L. R. (2005). Preserved painting creativity in an artist with Alzheimer's disease. *European Journal of Neurology*, **12**(6), 419–424.

Forsythe, A., Nadal, M., Sheehy, N., Cela-Conde, C. J. & Sawey, M. (2011). Predicting beauty: fractal dimension and visual complexity in art. *British Journal of Psychology*, **102**, 49–70.

Fryer, M. (2006). Complementarity. *Optics & Laser Technology*, 38(4–6), 417–430.

Fuchs, I., Ansorge, U., Redies, C. & Leder, H. (2011). Salience in paintings: bottom-up influences on eye fixations. *Cognitive Computation*, 3(1), 25–36.

Gage, J. (2006). *Colour in Art*. London: Thames & Hudson.

Gegenfurtner, K. R. (2003). Cortical mechanisms of colour vision. *Nature Reviews Neuroscience*, **4**, 563–572.

Gibson, J. J. (1977). The theory of affordances. In R. Shaw & J. Bransford, eds. *Perceiving, Acting, and Knowing*. Hillsdale, NJ: Lawrence Erlbaum Associates.

Gooding, M. (1998). *Painter as Critic. Patrick Heron: Selected Writings*. London: Tate Gallery Publishing.

Gordon, N. (2005). Unexpected development of artistic talents. *Postgraduate Medical Journal*, **8**, 753–755.

Graham, D. J. & Field, D. J. (2007). Statistical regularities of art images and natural scenes: spectra, sparseness and nonlinearities. *Spatial Vision*, 21(1–2), 149–164.

(2008a). Variations in intensity statistics for representational and abstract art, and for art from the Eastern and Western hemispheres. *Perception*, **37**(9), 1341–1352.

(2008b). Global nonlinear compression of natural luminances in painted art. *Proceedings of SPIE*, **6810**, 68100K.

Graham, D. J., Friedenberg, J. D. & Rockmore, D. N. (2009). Efficient visual system processing of spatial and luminance statistics in representational and non-representational art. *Proceedings of SPIE: Human Vision and Electronic Imaging*, **7240**, 1N1–1N10.

Grossman, E. D. & Blake, R. (2002). Brain areas active during visual perception of biological motion. *Neuron*, **35**, 1167–1175.

Hagen, M. & Jones, R. (1978). Cultural effects on pictorial perception: how many words is one picture really worth? In R. Walk & H. Pick, eds. *Perception and Experience*. New York, NY: Plenum.

Hagerhall, C. (2004). Fractal dimension of landscape silhouette outlines as a predictor of landscape preference. *Journal of Environmental Psychology*, **24**(2), 247–255.

Han, K. (2007). Responses to six major terrestrial biomes in terms of scenic beauty, preference, and restorativeness. *Environment and Behavior*, **39**, 529–556.

Hansen, B. C. & Hess, R. F. (2006). Discrimination of amplitude spectrum slope in the fovea and parafovea and the local amplitude distributions of natural scene imagery. *Journal of Vision*, 6(7), 3.

Harkness, N. (2006). The colour wheels of art, perception, science and physiology. *Optics & Laser Technology*, 38(4–6), 219–229.

Harrison, C. (2009). *An Introduction to Art*. New Haven, CT: Yale University Press.

Haselton, M. G. & Miller, G. F. (2006). Women's fertility across the cycle increases the short-term attractiveness of creative intelligence. *Human Nature*, **17**, 50–73.

Hayhoe, M. M., Bensinger, D. G. & Ballard, D. H. (1998). Task constraints in visual working memory. *Vision Research*, 38(1), 125–137.

Heider, F. & Simmel, M. (1944). An experimental study of apparent behavior. *American Journal of Psychology*, 57(2), 243–259.

Henderson, J. M. (2003). Human gaze control during real-world scene perception. *Trends in Cognitive Sciences*, 7(11), 498–504.

Henshilwood, C. S., d'Errico, F., Yates, R., Jacobs, Z., Tribolo, C., et al. (2002). Emergence of modern human behavior: Middle Stone Age engravings from South Africa. *Science*, **295**, 1278–1280.

Hochberg, J. & Brooks, V. (1961). Pictorial recognition as an unlearned ability: a study of one child's performance. *American Journal of Psychology*, **75**, 624–628.

Hockney, D. (2001). *Secret Knowledge*. London: Thames & Hudson.

Hoenekopp, J., Rudolph, U., Beier, L., Liebert, A. & Muller, C. (2007). Physical attractiveness of face and body as indicators of physical fitness in men. *Evolution and Human Behavior*, **28**, 106–111.

Hofer, H., Carroll, J., Neitz, J., Neitz, M. & Williams, D. R. (2005). Organization of the human trichromatic cone mosaic. *Journal of Neuroscience*, **25**, 9669–9679.

Hooks, M. S. & Kalivas, P. W. (1995). The role of mesoaccumbens-pallidal circuitry in novelty-induced behavioural activation. *Neuroscience*, **64**(3), 587–597.

Hubel, D. & Wiesel, T. (1962). Receptive fields, binocular interaction and functional architecture in the cat's visual cortex. *Journal of Physiology*, **160**, 106–154.

Hubel, D. H. & Wiesel, T. N. (1974). Uniformity of monkey striate cortex: a parallel relationship between field size, scatter, and magnification factor. *Journal of Comparative Neurology*, **158**(3), 295–305.

Hudson, W. (1960). Pictorial depth perception in sub-cultural groups in Africa. *Journal of Social Psychology*, **52**, 183–208.

Hwang, J. & Yoon, S. (2009). Where would you like to sit? Understanding customers' privacy-seeking tendencies and seating behaviours to create effective restaurant environments. *Journal of Foodservice Business Research*, **12**, 219–233.

Ikemoto, S. & Panksepp, J. (1999). The role of nucleus accumbens dopamine in motivated behavior: a unifying interpretation with special reference to reward-seeking. *Brain Research Reviews*, **31**(1), 6–41.

Itti, L. & Koch, C. (2000). A saliency-based search mechanism for overt and covert shifts of visual attention. *Vision Research*, **40**, 1489–1506.

Jacobsen, T., Schubotz, R. I., Höfel, L. & Cramon, D. Y. V. (2006). Brain correlates of aesthetic judgment of beauty. *Neuroimage*, **29**(1), 276–285.

Jahoda, G. & McGurk, H. (1974). Pictorial depth perception in Scottish and Ghanaian children. *International Journal of Psychology*, **9**, 255–267.

Johansson, G. (1973). Visual perception of biological motion and a model for its analysis. *Perception and Psychophysics*, **14**, 201–211.

(1976). Spatio-temporal differentiation and integration in visual motion perception. *Psychological Research*, **38**, 379–393.

Johnson, K. L. & Shiffrar, M., eds. (2012). *People Watching: Social, Perceptual and Neurophysiological Studies of Body Perception*. Oxford: Oxford University Press.

Jolicoeur, P. (1985). The time to name disoriented natural objects. *Memory and Cognition*, **13**(4), 289–303.

Jones, B. C., Little, A. C., Burt, D. M. & Perrett, D. I. (2004). When facial attractiveness is only skin deep. *Perception*, **33**, 569–576.

Joye, Y. (2007). Architectural lessons from environmental psychology: the case of biophilic architecture. *Review of General Psychology*, **11**(4), 305–328.

Kanazawa, S. (2000). Scientific discoveries as cultural displays: a further test of Miller's courtship model. *Evolution and Human Behavior*, **21**(5), 317–321.

Kanwisher, N. & Yovel, G. (2006). The fusiform face area: a cortical region specialized for the perception of faces. *Philosophical Transactions of the Royal Society of London, Series B*, **361** (1476), 2109–2128.

Kawabata, H. & Zeki, S. (2004). Neural correlates of beauty. *Journal of Neurophysiology*, **91**, 1699–1705.

Kellert, S. R. & Wilson, E. O., eds. (1993). *The Biophilia Hypothesis*. Washington DC: Island Press.

Kemp, M. (1990). *The Science of Art*. New Haven, CT: Yale University Press.

Kim, C.-Y. & Blake, R. (2007). Brain activity accompanying perception of implied motion in abstract paintings. *Spatial Vision*, 20(6), 545–560.

Knill, D. C., Field, D. J. & Kersten, D. (1990). Human discrimination of fractal images. *Journal of the Optical Society of America, A*, 7(6), 1113–1123.

Kose, M., Mand, R. & Moller, A. P. (1999). Sexual selection for white tail spots in the barn swallow in relation to habitat choice by feather lice. *Animal Behaviour*, 58(6), 1201–1205.

Kosinski, D. (1999). *The Artist and the Camera*. New Haven, CT: Yale University Press.

Kourtzi, Z. & Kanwisher, N. (2000). Activation in human MT/MST by static images with implied motion. *Journal of Cognitive Neuroscience*, 12(1), 48–55.

Kudielka, R., ed. (1999). *The Eye's Mind: Bridget Riley, Collected Writings 1965–1999*. London: Thames & Hudson.

Land, M., Mennie, N. & Rusted, J. (1999). The roles of vision and eye movements in the control of activities of daily living. *Perception*, 28(11), 1311–1328.

Land, M. F. & Nilsson, D.-E. (2002). *Animal Eyes*. Oxford: Oxford University Press.

Langmuir, E. (2003). *Narrative*. London: National Gallery Company.

Leakey, M. G., Feibel, C. S., McDougall, I. & Walker, A. (1995). New four million-year-old hominid species from Kanapoi and Allia Bay, Kenya. *Nature*, 376(6541), 565–571.

Leder, H., Belke, B., Oeberst, A. & Augustin, D. (2004). A model of aesthetic appreciation and aesthetic judgments. *British Journal of Psychology*, 95, 489–508.

Lee, T. S. & Mumford, D. (2003). Hierarchical Bayesian inference in the visual cortex. *Journal of the Optical Society of America, A*, 20(7), 1434–1448.

Lee, T.-won, Wachtler, T. & Sejnowski, T. J. (2002). Color opponency is an efficient representation of spectral properties in natural scenes. *Vision Research*, 42, 2095–2103.

Leibowitz, H. & Bourne, L. E. (1956). Time and intensity as determiners of perceived shape. *Journal of Experimental Psychology*, 51(4), 277–281.

Lennie, P. (2003). The cost of cortical computation. *Current Biology*, 13, 493–497.

Lennie, P. & D'Zmura, M. (1988). Mechanisms of color vision. *Critical Reviews in Neurobiology*, 3(4), 333–400.

Leslie, A. M. & Keeble, S. (1987). Do six-month-old infants perceive causality? *Cognition*, 25(3), 265–288.

LeWitt, S. (1967). Paragraphs on conceptual art. *Artforum*, June.

Li, J., Du, Q. & Sun, C. (2009). An improved box-counting method for image fractal dimension estimation. *Pattern Recognition*, 42, 2460–2469.

Livingstone, M. (2002). *Vision and Art: The Biology of Seeing*. New York, NY: Abrams.

Locher, P. J., Krupinski, E. A., Mello-Thoms, C. & Nodine, C. F. (2007). Visual interest in pictorial art during an aesthetic experience. *Spatial Vision*, 21(1–2), 55–77.

Lohr, V. I. & Pearson-Mims, C. H. (2006). Responses to scenes with spreading, rounded, and conical tree forms. *Environment and Behavior*, 38(5), 667–688.

Lorteije, J. A., Kenemans, J. L., Jellema, T., van der Lubbe, R. H., de Heer, F., et al. (2006). Delayed response to animate implied motion in human motion processing areas. *Journal of Cognitive Neuroscience*, 18(2), 158–168.

Loyau, A., Petrie, M., Saint Jalme, M. & Sorci, G. (2008). Do peahens not prefer peacocks with more elaborate trains? *Animal Behaviour*, 76, e6–e9.

Machotka, P. (1996). *Cézanne: Landscape into Art*. Cumberland, RI: Yale University Press.

MacKay, D. M. (1957). Moving visual images produced by regular stationary patterns. *Nature*, 180, 849–850.

Madden, J. (2001). Sex, bowers and brains. *Proceedings of the Royal Society, B,* **268**(1469), 833–838.

Mamassian, P. (2008). Ambiguities and conventions in the perception of visual art. *Vision Research,* **48**(20), 2143–2153.

Mandelbrot, B. B. (1977). *Fractals: Form, Chance and Dimension.* San Francisco, CA: Freeman. (1998). Is nature fractal? *Science,* **279**, 783.

Mannan, S. K., Ruddock, K. H. & Wooding, D. S. (1997). Fixation patterns made during brief examination of two-dimensional images. *Perception,* **26**, 1059–1072.

Marmor, M. F. (2006). Ophthalmology and art: simulation of Monet's cataracts and Degas' retinal disease. *Archives of Ophthalmology,* **124**(12), 1764–1769.

Marmor, M. F. & Lanthony, P. (2001). The dilemma of color deficiency and art. *Survey of Ophthalmology,* **45**(5), 407–415.

Marmor, M. F. & Ravin, J. G. (1997). *The Eye of the Artist.* Orlando, FL: Mosby.

Marmor, M. F. & Ravin, J. G. (2009). *The Artist's Eyes.* New York, NY: Abrams.

Mather, G. (2000). Integration biases in the Ouchi and other visual illusions. *Perception,* **29**, 721–727.

(2009). *Foundations of Sensation and Perception.* Hove: Psychology Press.

(2010). Head–body ratio as a visual cue for stature in people and sculptural art. *Perception,* **39**(10), 1390–1395.

Mather, G., Pavan, A., Campana, G. & Casco, C. (2008). The motion aftereffect reloaded. *Trends in Cognitive Sciences,* **12**(12), 481–487.

Matthews, W. J. & Adams, A. (2008). Another reason why adults find it hard to draw accurately. *Perception,* **37**(4), 628–630.

McClure, S. M., York, M. K. & Montague, P. R. (2004). The neural substrates of reward processing in humans: the modern role of fMRI. *The Neuroscientist,* **10**(3), 260–268.

McManus, I. C., Zhou, F. A., l'Anson, S., Waterfield, L., Stöver, K., et al. (2011). The psychometrics of photographic cropping: the influence of colour, meaning, and expertise. *Perception,* **40**, 332–357.

Mell, J. C., Howard, S. M. & Miller, B. L. (2003). Art and the brain: the influence of frontotemporal dementia on an accomplished artist. *Neurology,* **60**, 1707–1710.

Mendez, M. F. (2004). Dementia as a window to the neurology of art. *Medical Hypotheses,* **63**(1), 1–7.

Michotte, A. (1963). *The Perception of Causality.* London: Methuen.

Miller, B. L., Ponton, M., Benson, D. F., Cummings, J. L. & Mena, I. (1996). Enhanced artistic creativity with temporal lobe degeneration. *Lancet,* **348**, 1744–1745.

Miller, G. F. (1999). Sexual selection for cultural displays. In R. Dunbar, C. Knight & C. Power, eds. *The Evolution of Culture: An Interdisciplinary Review.* New Brunswick, NJ: Rutgers University Press, pp. 71–91.

(2001). Aesthetic fitness: how sexual selection shaped artistic virtuosity as a fitness indicator and aesthetic preferences as mate choice criteria. *Bulletin of Psychology and the Arts,* **2**(1), 20–25.

Miller, J. (1998). *On Reflection.* London: National Gallery.

(2010). *On the Move: Visualising Action.* London: Estorick Foundation.

Mitchell, P., Ropar, D., Ackroyd, K. & Rajendran, G. (2005). How perception impacts on drawings. *Journal of Experimental Psychology: Human Perception and Performance,* **31**(5), 996–1003.

Mollon, J. (2006). Monge: The Verriest Lecture, Lyon, July 2005. *Visual Neuroscience,* **23**, 297–309.

Monaco, J. (2009). *How to Read a Film*. Oxford: Oxford University Press.

Montague, P. R. & Berns, G. S. (2002). Neural economics and the biological substrates of valuation. *Neuron*, 36(2), 265–284.

Morgan, M. J. & Aiba, T. S. (1985). Positional acuity with chromatic stimuli. *Vision Research*, 25, 689–695.

Morgan, M. J., Dillenburger, B., Raphael, S. & Solomon, J. A. (2012). Observers can voluntarily shift their psychometric functions without losing sensitivity. *Attention, Perception and Psychophysics*, 74(1), 185–193.

Mottron, L. & Belleville, S. (1995). Perspective production in a savant autistic draughtsman. *Psychological Medicine*, 25, 639–648.

Mueller, U. & Mazur, A. (2001). Evidence of unconstrained directional selection for male tallness. *Behavioral Ecology and Sociobiology*, 50, 302–311.

Murray, S. O., Schrater, P. & Kersten, D. (2004). Perceptual grouping and the interactions between visual cortical areas. *Neural Networks*, 17(5–6), 695–705.

Nettle, D. & Clegg, H. (2006). Schizotypy, creativity and mating success in humans. *Proceedings of the Royal Society, B*, 273, 611–615.

Newton, I. (1952). *Optiks or a Treatise of the Reflections, Refractions, Inflections and Colours of Light*. Based on the 4th edn. London, 1730; New York, NY: Dover.

Nilsson, D.-E. & Pelger, S. (1994). A pessimistic estimate of the time required for an eye to evolve. *Proceedings of the Royal Society, B*, 256, 53–58.

Norman, D. (1998). *The Design of Everyday Things*. London: MIT Press.

Olmos, A. & Kingdom, F. A. A. (2004). A biologically inspired algorithm for the recovery of shading and reflectance images. *Perception*, 33, 1463–1473.

Orians, G. H. & Heerwagen, J. H. (1992). Evolved responses to landscapes. In J. H. Barkow, L. Cosmides & J. Tooby, eds. *The Adapted Mind: Evolutionary Psychology and the Generation of Culture*. New York, NY: Oxford University Press, pp. 555–579.

Osorio, D. & Vorobyev, M. (1996). Colour vision as an adaptation to frugivory in primates. *Proceedings of the Royal Society, B*, 263(1370), 593–599.

Ostrovsky, Y., Cavanagh, P. & Sinha, P. (2005). Perceiving illumination inconsistencies in scenes. *Perception*, 34(11), 1301–1314.

Ouchi, H. (1977). *Japanese Optical and Geometrical Art*. New York, NY: Dover.

Palmer, S. E., Rosch, E. & Chase, P. (1981). Canonical perspective and the perception of objects. In J. Long & A. D. Baddeley, eds. *Attention and Performance IX*. Hillsdale, NJ: Lawrence Erlbaum Associates, Inc.

Panofsky, E. (1955). *Meaning in the Visual Arts*. New York, NY: Doubleday.

Parraga, C. A., Troscianko, T. & Tolhurst, D. J. (1999). The human visual system is optimised for processing the spatial information in natural images. *Current Biology*, 10, 35–38.

Pavan, A., Cuturi, L. F., Maniglia, M., Casco, C. & Campana, G. (2011). Implied motion from static photographs influences the perceived position of stationary objects. *Vision Research*, 51, 187–194.

Penton-Voak, I. S. & Chen, J. Y. (2004). High salivary testosterone is linked to masculine male facial appearance in humans. *Evolution and Human Behavior*, 25, 229–241.

Perrett, D., Harries, M., Mistlin, A. J. & Chitty, A. J. (1990). Three stages in the classification of body movements by visual neurons. In H. B. Barlow, C. Blakemore & M. Weston-Smith, eds. *Images and Understanding*. Cambridge: Cambridge University Press, pp. 94–107.

Perrett, D. I., Lee, K. J., Penton-Voak, I. S., Rowland, D. R., Yoshikawa, S., et al. (1998). Effects of sexual dimorphism on facial attractiveness. *Nature*, 394, 884–887.

Petersen, S. E., Baker, J. F. & Allman, J. M. (1985). Direction-specific adaptation in area MT of the owl monkey. *Brain Research*, **346**(1), 146–150.

Picard, D. & Durand, K. (2005). Are young children's drawings canonically biased? *Journal of Experimental Child Psychology*, **90**, 48–64.

Pickford, R. W. (1969). The frequency of colour vision defective students in a school of art and the influence of their defects. *Journal of Biosocial Science*, **1**(1), 3–13.

Pinna, B., Brelstaff, G. & Spillmann, L. (2001). Surface color from boundaries: a new 'watercolor' illusion. *Vision Research*, **41**(20), 2669–2676.

Pirenne, M. H. (1970). *Optics, Painting and Photography*. Cambridge: Cambridge University Press.

Pluhar, W. S. (1987). *Translation of Immanuel Kant, 'Critique of Judgment'*. Indianapolis, IN: Hackett Publishing Company.

Polland, W. (2004). Myopic artists. *Acta Ophthalmologica Scandinavica*, **82**, 325–326.

Pook, G. & Newall, D. (2008) *Art History: The Basics*. London: Routledge.

Potts, R. (1998). Variability selection in hominid evolution. *Evolutionary Anthropology*, **7**(3), 81–96.

Pring, L. (2005). Savant talent. *Developmental Medicine and Child Neurology*, **47**(7), 500–503.

Ramachandran, V. S. & Hirstein, W. (1999). The science of art: a neurological theory of art. *Journal of Consciousness Studies*, **6**, 15–51.

Rankin, K. P., Liu, A. A., Howard, S., Slama, H., Hou, C. E., et al. (2007). A case-controlled study of altered visual art production in Alzheimer's and FTLD. *Cognitive and Behavioral Neurology*, **20**(1), 48–61.

Ratliff, F. (1972). Contour and contrast. *Scientific American*, **226**(6), 90–101.

Ravin, J. G., Anderson, N. & Lanthony, P. (1995). An artist with a color vision defect: Charles Meryon. *Survey of Ophthalmology*, **39**(5), 403–408.

Reber, R., Schwarz, N. & Winkielman, P. (2004). Processing fluency and aesthetic pleasure: is beauty in the perceiver's processing experience? *Personality and Social Psychology Review*, **8**(4), 364–382.

Redies, C. (2007). A universal model of esthetic perception based on the sensory coding of natural stimuli. *Spatial Vision*, **21**(1–2), 97–117.

Redies, C., Hänisch, J., Blickhan, M. & Denzler, J. (2007). Artists portray human faces with the Fourier statistics of complex natural scenes. *Network*, **18**(3), 235–248.

Rensink, R. A., O'Regan, J. K. & Clark, J. J. (1997). To see or not to see: the need for attention to perceive changes in scenes. *Psychological Science*, **8**(5), 368–373.

Rhodes, G. (2006). The evolutionary psychology of facial beauty. *Annual Review of Psychology*, **57**, 199–226.

Rhodes, G., Simmons, L. W. & Peters, M. (2005). Attractiveness and sexual behaviour: does attractiveness enhance mating success? *Evolution and Human Behavior*, **26**, 186–201.

Robman, L. & Taylor, H. (2005). External factors in the development of cataract. *Eye*, **19**, 1074–1082.

Rodin, A. (1984). *Art: Conversations with Paul Gsell*. Berkeley, CA: University of California Press.

Ruderman, D. L. (1997). Origins of scaling in natural images. *Vision Research*, **37**(23), 3385–3398.

Ruskin, J. (1893). *The Stones of Venice*. London: George Allen.

(1902). *Modern Painters: Volume V*. London: George Allen.

Sacks, O. & Wasserman, R. (1987). The case of the colorblind painter. *The New York Review*, November, 25–33.

Sarkar, N. & Chaudhuri, B. B. (1994). An efficient differential box-counting approach to compute fractal dimensions of image. *IEEE Transactions on Systems, Man, and Cybernetics*, **24**, 115–120.

Saygin, A. P., McCullough, S., Alac, M., & Emmorey, K. (2010). Modulation of BOLD response in motion-sensitive lateral temporal cortex by real and fictive motion sentences. *Journal of Cognitive Neuroscience*, **22**(11), 2480–2490.

Scharf, A. (1968). *Art and Photography*. London: Allen Lane.

Schmolesky, M. T., Wang, Y., Hanes, D. P., Thompson, K. G., Leutgeb, S., et al. (1998). Signal timing across the macaque visual system. *Journal of Neurophysiology*, **79**, 3272–3278.

Schnapf, J. & Baylor, D. (1987). How photoreceptor cells respond to light. *Scientific American*, **256**(4), 32–39.

Scholl, B. J. & Tremoulet, P. (2000). Perceptual causality and animacy. *Trends in Cognitive Sciences*, **4**(8), 299–309.

Schultz, J., Imamizu, H., Kawato, M. & Frith, C. D. (2004). Activation of the human superior temporal gyrus during observation of goal attribution by intentional objects. *Journal of Cognitive Neuroscience*, **16**(10), 1695–1705.

Segall, M., Campbell, D. & Herskovits, M. (1963). Cultural differences in the perception of geometrical illusions. *Science*, **139**, 769–771.

Selfe, L. (1977). *Nadia: A Case of Extraordinary Drawing Ability in an Autistic Child*. London: Academic Press.

Senior, C., Barnes, J., Giampietro, V., Simmons, A., Bullmore, E. T., et al. (2000). The functional neuroanatomy of implicit-motion perception or representational momentum. *Current Biology*, **10**(1), 16–22.

Simion, F., Regolin, L. & Bulf, H. (2008). A predisposition for biological motion in the newborn baby. *Proceedings of the National Academy of Sciences of the United States of America*, **105**(2), 809–813.

Slater, A., Von der Schulenburg, C., Brown, E., Badenoch, M., Butterworth, G., et al. (1998). Newborn infants prefer attractive faces. *Infant Behavior and Development*, **21**, 345–354.

Smith, J. (2009). Evolutionary aesthetics and Victorian visual culture. In D. Donald & J. Munro, eds. *Endless Forms: Charles Darwin, Natural Science and the Visual Arts*. New Haven, CT: Yale University Press.

Solnit, R. (2003). *Motion Studies: Time, Space and Eadweard Muybridge*. London: Bloomsbury.

Spehar, B., Clifford, C. W. G., Newell, B. R. & Taylor, R. P. (2003). Universal aesthetic of fractals. *Computers & Graphics*, **27**(5), 813–820.

Steadman, P. (2001). *Vermeer's Camera*. Oxford: Oxford University Press.

Stephen, I. D., Coetzee, V. & Perrett, D. I. (2010). Carotenoid and melanin pigment coloration affect perceived human health. *Evolution and Human Behavior*, **32**(3), 216–227.

Stewart, A. F. (1990). *Greek Sculpture: An Exploration*. New Haven, CT: Yale University Press.

Summerfield, C., Trittschuh, E. H., Monti, J. M., Mesulam, M. M. & Egner, T. (2008). Neural repetition suppression reflects fulfilled perceptual expectations. *Nature Neuroscience*, **11**(9), 1004–1006.

Takeuchi, H., Taki, Y., Sassa, Y., Hashizume, H., Sekiguchi, A., et al. (2010). White matter structures associated with creativity: evidence from diffusion tensor imaging. *NeuroImage*, **51**(1), 11–18.

Taylor, R., Micolich, A. & Jonas, D. (1999). Fractal analysis of Pollock's drip paintings. *Nature*, **399**, 422.

Taylor, R. P., Micolich, A. P. & Jonas, D. (2002). The construction of Jackson Pollock's fractal drip paintings. *Leonardo*, **35**(2), 203–207.

Teghtsoonian, R. (1971). On the exponents in Stevens' law and the constant in Ekman's law. *Psychological Review*, **78**(1), 71–80.

Temkin, A. (2008). *Color Chart: Reinventing Color, 1950 to Today*. New York, NY: Museum of Modern Art.

Thouless, R. H. (1932). Individual differences in phenomenal regression. *British Journal of Psychology: General*, 22(3), 216–241.

Tolhurst, D. J. & Tadmor, Y. (2000). Discrimination of spectrally blended natural images: optimisation of the human visual system for encoding natural images. *Perception*, 29(9), 1087–1100.

Tolhurst, D. J., Tadmor, Y. & Chao, T. (1992). The amplitude spectra of natural images. *Ophthalmic and Physiological Optics*, 12, 229–232.

Tremoulet, P. D. & Feldman, J. (2000). Perception of animacy from the motion of a single object. *Perception*, 29, 943–951.

Trevor-Roper, P. (1988). *The World Through Blunted Sight*. London: Penguin.

Ulrich, R. S. (1984). View through a window may influence recovery from surgery. *Science*, 224, 420–421.

Van de Cruys, S. & Wagemans, J. (2011). Putting reward in art: a tentative prediction error account of visual art. *i-Perception*, 2(9), 1035–1062.

Van Tonder, G. J., Lyons, M. J. & Ejima, Y. (2002). Visual structure of a Japanese Zen garden. *Nature*, 419(6905), 359–360.

Vandenheede, M. & Bouissou, M. F. (1994). Fear reactions of ewes to photographic images. *Behavioural Processes*, 32(1), 17–28.

Vartanian, O. & Goel, V. (2004). Neuroanatomical correlates of aesthetic preference for paintings. *NeuroReport*, 15, 893–897.

Vishwanath, D., Girshick, A. R. & Banks, M. S. (2005). Why pictures look right when viewed from the wrong place. *Nature Neuroscience*, 8(10), 1401–1410.

Wade, N. J. & Verstraten, A. J. (1998). Introduction and historical overview. In G. Mather, F. J. Verstraten & S. Anstis, eds. *The Motion Aftereffect: A Modern Perspective*. Cambridge, MA: MIT Press.

Wang, Q., Klein, E. K., Klein, R. & Moss, S. E. (1994). Refractive status in the Beaver Dam eye study. *Investigative Ophthalmology and Visual Science*, 35, 4344–4347.

Wapner, W., Judd, T. & Gardner, H. (1978). Visual agnosia in an artist. *Cortex*, 14, 343–364.

Watt, S. J., Akeley, K., Ernst, M. O. & Banks, M. S. (2005). Focus cues affect perceived depth. *Journal of Vision*, 5(10), 7.

Winawer, J., Huk, A. C. & Boroditsky, L. (2008). A motion aftereffect from still photographs depicting motion. *Psychological Science*, 19(3), 276–283.

Winckelmann, J. J. (1764). *History of the Art of Antiquity*. H. F. Mallgrave, trans., 2006. Los Angeles, CA: Getty Research Institute.

Windhager, S., Slice, D. E., Schaefer, K., Oberzaucher, E., Thorstensen, T., et al. (2008). Face to face. *Human Nature*, 19(4), 331–346.

Wolfflin, H. (1915). *Principles of Art History*. M. D. Hottinger, trans., 1950. New York, NY: Dover.

Wypijewski, J., ed. (1997). *Painting by Numbers: Komar and Melamid's Scientific Guide to Art*. Berkeley, CA: University of California Press.

Yarbus, A. (1967). *Eye Movements and Vision*. New York, NY: Plenum.

Yue, X., Vessel, E. A. & Biederman, I. (2007). The neural basis of scene preferences. *NeuroReport*, 18, 525–529.

Zajonc, R. B. (2001). Mere exposure: a gateway to the subliminal. *Current Directions in Psychological Science*, 10(6), 224–228.

Zanker, J. M., Doyle, M. & Walker, R. (2003). Gaze stability of observers watching Op Art pictures. *Perception*, 32, 1037–1049.

Zanker, J. M., Hermens, F. & Walker, R. (2010). Quantifying and modeling the strength of motion illusions perceived in static patterns. *Journal of Vision*, 10, 1–14.

Zeki, S. (1999). *Inner Vision: An Exploration of Art and the Brain.* New York, NY: Oxford University Press.

Zeki, S. & Marini, L. (1998). Three cortical stages of colour processing in the human brain. *Brain,* 121(9), 1669–1685.

Zihl, J., von Cramon, D., Mai, N. & Schmid, C. (1991). Disturbance of movement vision after bilateral posterior brain damage: further evidence and follow up observations. *Brain,* 114(5), 2235–2252.

Artworks

Figure	Artist	Title	Date	Spectral slope	Fractal dimension
1.2	Cimabue	The Virgin and Child Enthroned with Two Angels	1280–1285	−1.24	2.49
1.3	Rembrandt Harmenszoon van Rijn	Self-Portrait at the Age of 34	1640	−1.55	2.32
2.3	Georges-Pierre Seurat	Bathers at Asnieres	1884	−1.47	2.42
2.5	Hilaire-Germain-Edgar Degas	Young Spartans Exercising	c.1860	−1.44	2.47
	Hilaire-Germain-Edgar Degas	Russian Dancers	c.1899	−1.12	2.59
4.2	Jan Gossaert	The Adoration of the Kings	1510–1515	−1.36	2.51
4.4	Canaletto	Venice: Piazza San Marco	c.1758	−0.99	2.57
5.6	Bartolome Bermejo	Saint Michael Triumphant over the Devil	1468	−1.33	2.48
5.7	Hans Holbein the Younger	Erasmus	1523	−1.13	2.45
6.1	John Wootton	A Race on the Round Course at Newmarket	c.1750	−1.36	2.48
6.5	Tim Layzell	1960 Goodwood TT		−1.37	2.48
6.7	Bridget Riley	Fall	1963	0.41	3.0

Plate	Artist	Title	Date	Spectral slope	Fractal dimension
1	Giovanni Bellini	The Blood of the Redeemer	1460–1465	−1.44	2.48
	Raphael	Saint Catherine of Alexandria	1507	−1.59	2.37
2	Claude	Landscape with the Marriage of Isaac and Rebekah	1648	−1.44	2.36
3	Claude-Oscar Monet	The Water-Lily Pond	1899	−1.07	2.61
4	Andre Derain	Barges on the Thames	1906	−1.48	2.47
	Mark Rothko	Untitled	1950	−1.19	2.28
5	Diego Velasquez	The Toilet of Venus	1647–1651	−1.64	2.31
	Pieter Brueghel the Elder	Hunters in the Snow	1565	−1.08	2.61
9	Claude-Oscar Monet	Rouen Cathedral at the End of the Day, Sunlight Effect	1892	−1.02	2.60
10	Claude-Oscar Monet	The Japanese Bridge	1919–1924	−1.03	2.62
11	Jan Gossaert	The Adoration of the Kings	1510–1515	−1.36	2.51
13	Johannes Vermeer	Young Woman Standing at a Virginal	1670–1672	−1.44	2.38
14	Antonello Da Messina	Saint Jerome in his Study	1475	−1.25	2.48
15	Domenico Beccafumi	The Story of Papirius	c.1520	−1.47	2.41
16	Rogier van der Weyden	The Exhumation of Saint Hubert	c.1430	−1.29	2.53
	Joachim Beuckelaer	The Four Elements: Fire	1570	−1.33	2.50
17	Jacopo Pontormo	Joseph with Jacob in Egypt	1518	−1.52	2.45
18	Titian	Bacchus and Ariadne	1520–1523	−1.37	2.45
20	Vincent Van Gogh	The Bedroom	1888–1889	−1.23	2.43

Index

SAMPLE

Made in the USA
Charleston, SC
31 December 2014